THE HISTORICAL DEVELOPMENT OF CODE PLEADING IN AMERICA AND ENGLAND

WITH SPECIAL REFERENCE TO THE CODES OF

NEW YORK, MISSOURI, CALIFORNIA, KENTUCKY, IOWA, MINNESOTA, INDIANA, OHIO, OREGON, WASHINGTON, NEBRASKA, WISCONSIN, KANSAS, NEVADA, NORTH DAKOTA, SOUTH DAKOTA, IDAHO, MONTANA, ARIZONA, NORTH CAROLINA, SOUTH CAROLINA, ARKANSAS, WYOMING, UTAH, COLORADO, CONNECTICUT, AND OKLAHOMA.

BY

CHARLES M. HEPBURN
OF THE CINCINNATI BAR

THE LAWBOOK EXCHANGE, LTD.
Union, New Jersey
2002

ISBN 1-58477-220-4

Second printing 2004

Printed in the United States of America on acid-free paper

THE LAWBOOK EXCHANGE, LTD.
33 Terminal Avenue
Clark, New Jersey 07066-1321

Please see our website for a selection of our other publications and fine facsimile reprints of classic works of legal history:
www.lawbookexchange.com

Library of Congress Cataloging-in-Publication Data

Hepburn, Charles M. (Charles McGuffey), 1858-1929.
The historical development of code pleading in America and England with special reference to the codes of New York, Missouri, California, Kentucky, Iowa, Minnesota, Indiana, Ohio, Oregon, Washington, Nebraska, Wisconsin, Kansas, Nevada, North Dakota, South Dakota, Idaho, Montana, Arizona, North Carolina, South Carolina, Arkansas, Wyoming, Utah, Colorado, Connecticut, and Oklahoma / by Charles M. Hepburn.
p. cm.
Originally published: Cincinnati: W.H. Anderson & Co., 1897.
Includes bibliographical references and index.
ISBN 1-58477-220-4 (cloth: alk. paper)
1. Code pleading—United States—States. 2. 1. Code pleading—Great Britain. I. Title.

KF8870.Z95 H47 2002
347.73'72—dc21

2001050458

THE HISTORICAL DEVELOPMENT OF CODE PLEADING IN AMERICA AND ENGLAND

WITH SPECIAL REFERENCE TO THE CODES OF

NEW YORK, MISSOURI, CALIFORNIA, KENTUCKY, IOWA, MINNESOTA, INDIANA, OHIO, OREGON, WASHINGTON, NEBRASKA, WISCONSIN, KANSAS, NEVADA, NORTH DAKOTA, SOUTH DAKOTA, IDAHO, MONTANA, ARIZONA, NORTH CAROLINA, SOUTH CAROLINA, ARKANSAS, WYOMING, UTAH, COLORADO, CONNECTICUT, AND OKLAHOMA.

BY

CHARLES M. HEPBURN

OF THE CINCINNATI BAR

CINCINNATI:
W. H. ANDERSON & CO.
1897.

TO

ARPHAXED LOOMIS,
DAVID GRAHAM,
DAVID DUDLEY FIELD,

COMMISSIONERS WHO FRAMED THE

NEW YORK CODE OF PROCEDURE OF 1848,

AND THE PROPOSED

NEW YORK CODE OF CIVIL PROCEDURE OF 1850.

THEIR WORK,

THE WORK OF PIONEERS, STILL ENDURES, AND THROUGH ITS WIDE INFLUENCE AT HOME AND ABROAD HAS STAMPED ITS CHARACTER UPON THE FIRST STAGE OF OUR PROGRESS TOWARDS THE MORE SIMPLE, UNIFORM, AND DURABLE

AMERICAN CODE.

CONTENTS.

CHAPTER V.

CHAPTER VI.

INTRODUCTION.

The history of what the law has been is necessary to the knowledge of what the law is.—*Holmes.*

Unless the history and philosophy of law were well understood no good code could possibly be constructed; and unless those branches of knowledge continued to be studied a good code, even when constructed, would infallibly deteriorate.—*Austin.*

INTRODUCTION.

Practical importance of the subject.

My aim in the following pages has been to define and illustrate the essentials of code pleading from the side of its historical development in America and England. The field is a wide one and for the most part still unoccupied. In these days of multitudinous law books it is strange that so little attention has been given to the historical side of the codes. The light which it affords is not merely of curious interest to students of jurisprudence; it concerns practitioners as well. Excepting only the careful study of the very words of the codes themselves, hardly anything throws a clearer light upon the path which practitioners in code states are daily called upon to follow. For code pleading is essentially a science of historical development. Of every one of our codes of civil procedure it is eminently true that "to comprehend clearly what it is, we must see how it came to be so". After fifty years, it is still from the historical side of his code that the practitioner can obtain the readiest access to the true nature and successful application of those principles and rules with which he has to do in the actual business of pleading.

Tendencies which it opposes.

That we need a clearer view of the historical bearings and the *locus in quo* of code pleading, and of each of the codes, is abundantly evident. It appears in a very common tendency to ignore the nature of the new pleading as a distinct science, springing from, yet independent of, the common law system. It appears also in the tendency to look to the mere letter of code pleading and no further, ignoring the causes which gave it form and substance. It appears again in the tendency to ignore the wider relationship of our codes as members of a great statutory system of pleading, still in its formative stages, but already more widely established among English-speaking peoples, on both sides of the Atlantic, than was common law pleading in its palmiest days.

(*a*) *Tendency to ignore the nature of code pleading as a distinct science.*

The first of these tendencies is especially prominent in the introduction which many law students receive to the general subject of code pleading. No true friend of the codes is likely to disparage the study of common law pleading. For many years to come it will be essential to their comprehension. The habit of exact and logical discrimination which its rules impose still goes into the making of the masters of code pleading. But just here, as it seems to me, the law schools and the law offices, even in code states, often commit the young practitioner to the wrong road. He is required, first of all, to study the admirable system of rules which Stephen, some seventy years ago, laid down for the law students of his own day, and then is hurried through the rules of code pleading, as if they were but modifications of his hastily digested common law rules.

It is, of course, going a little too far to say, as an early writer on the codes once said, that "the Chinese system of pleading is just as operative in a code state as the common law system". But it is entirely true (1) that code pleading, although built out of materials derived from the common law, is, as a system, wholly distinct from it—as distinct, in this sense, as "the Chinese system of pleading"; and (2) that code pleading is deserving of study in itself as a systematic whole, standing upon its own principles, subject only to its own laws. But this fact, of fundamental importance, especially to the beginner, is often concealed from him by his way of approach to the codes. The general characteristic which he would ascribe to the new procedure, if his view accords it the dignity of some individuality as a whole, is too often that of a mere offshoot from the common law. Nor is the mischief only theoretical. The natural inclination after such a beginning is to force the rules of the codes into the intricate mold of the older procedure. In the effort, the simplicity of code pleading is quite lost sight of; its principles are distorted; its uses confused. In many code states, if not in all, the new pleading has often run into strange, uncouth forms—a plentiful crop of hybrid precedents, neither common law nor code, and equally unworthy of both. It is as if a goodly number of practitioners had never escaped from the mists which veiled their entrance into code pleading. With no clear view of its cardinal principles, unable to say where the old pleading ends and the new begins, the younger practitioner appears to be ready to lay hold of whatever offers itself as a precedent. Not without assistance from some of the form books, he envelops his petition or complaint, his answer, even his reply, in useless words and phrases inherited from the days, not yet remote, when the fashion was to involve common law pleading "in all that perplexity could suggest or prolixity supply". He is fearful of simplicity. He loads his pleading down with details which are worse than useless. He fortifies himself behind broad but empty averments of legal conclusions. And yet, following precedents derived from the general pleading permitted at common law, he often quite omits the material facts required for the validity of his claim under the reformed procedure. "Our code," says a judge in a state where code pleading strikes a fair average of directness and simplicity, "requires the pleading to be in *ordinary and concise language*, but no one would suspect from an examination of the files of any of our courts that such provision existed."[1] And the same writer is careful to point out that in the course of more than forty years, we have not only not gone forward in the simplification of civil pleadings, but "have been constantly refining upon and encumbering them with useless phrases and innumerable repetitions, until our pleadings, instead of being simple statements of fact in ordinary and concise language, have become intricate and complex systems of special pleading".

(*b*) *Tendency to look only to the letter of the codes.*

The second tendency referred to above ignores a no less important fact, that the true spirit of code pleading is best seen in the light of the causes which gave it birth. However unwilling the lawyer, hurried with the details of business, anxious for present results, may be to look to the past, the fact stands that the procedure with which he has had to do, the very enactment, it may be, on which he relies for the sufficiency of his pleading, has arisen out of the older systems, because of their faults and defects; that the framers of his code wrought with these faults and defects in mind, and directly with a view to remedying them; that today, in case of doubt, the construction of a provision in the code often requires that the old law and the mischief which it failed to prevent, and the code aims to remedy, shall be considered along with the words of the code itself. Innocent enough in some cases, a blind following of the letter of a code will yet, in the long run, re-establish one of the chief causes of the fossilization

[1] Hon. Charles Pratt, address as President before Ohio State Bar Association, 1895. Reports, Vol. XIV, p. 103.

which kept common law pleading so far behind the needs of its later days. The instinct working here is that of archaic law, which ever sacrifices the spirit to the letter, and whose strength in a judicial system is inversely with the learning of the bench.

The evident danger under this tendency is that the essentially liberal spirit of the reformed procedure will be lost sight of; that its provisions will be applied according to the dictates of a narrow and arbitrary judgment; that the system as a whole will degenerate into a jargon of formal rules. Perhaps the mischief has run further in New York than in other code states, but there is a far-reaching significance in the recent declaration of a New York lawyer that "the reformed procedure, instead of simplifying practice, has in the long run made it more technical".[1] Civil procedure in Ohio has kept closer to the intended simplicity of the codes—apparently it is no more involved than the procedure of most code states, perhaps it is less involved than that of many; yet an Ohio judge addressing the Bar Association of that state in 1895, thought it apparent to the most casual observer that the courts of Ohio were spending too much time and labor "upon mere forms and technicalities. They are hearing and determining intricate questions of pleading and practice which have no relations whatever, in many if not in most cases, to the merits of the controversies which come before them."[2] Whatever the progress in modern days, the old maxim still holds, *qui haeret in litera, haeret in cortice.* If our courts, applying the provisions of code pleading, ignore its fundamental purpose and are content "to stick in the bark," we have only escaped the narrowness and technicality of common law pleading to encounter hardly less narrow and technical formalities under the codes.

[1] Cf. 53 Alb. Law Journ., 151 (1896).

[2] Ohio State Bar Ass'n, 1895, Address of Judge Pratt, Reports, Vol. XVI, p. 105.

(*c*) *Tendency to ignore the wider relationship of the codes.*

Very close akin to this narrow spirit is the third tendency mentioned above, that, namely, to ignore the wider relationship of the codes. Its present extent was suggestively shown at the meeting of the American Bar Association in August, 1896, by the report of its committee on a uniform system of legal procedure. Replies obtained by this committee from many different sources throughout the Union indicate, says the report, that little or no attention has been given in any state to the workings of the systems of pleading adopted in other American states or in England, but rather that there is "a blind, unreasoning, and unreasonable adherence to or adoption of certain theories without investigation or inquiry". Certainly this is to shut out the healthful influence of one of the most remarkable and useful results in the whole history of American and English law. With the breaking up of common law pleading, there was danger that every state would go a different way, and establish, under the impetuosity of legislation, a system of pleading which was not only independent of, but radically different from, the code pleading of every other state. As it turned out, however, the statutory pleading which has arisen not only in most of our states, but in England also, and in many of the British colonies—wherever, for the most part, the substantive common law of England prevails—is essentially of one and the same kind. Our different codes make one system. They have followed a common example, and followed it often with painstaking exactness, yet with suggestive differences. Some of these codes, notably the code established in England in 1873 and 1875, the kindred code of Ontario, as revised in 1895, are characteristically later developments of the original principle, after years of experiments. Like most such developments they show marked improvements towards the end of simplicity and directness, improvements which are still lacking in those codes, a great majority of the whole, which were framed originally upon the old model. The study of these later designs would afford much of practical value in every state of the Union, in every code state especially. They go far toward enabling students of code pleading to distinguish the essential from the non-essential in the workings of the new systems. They tend to prevent our tithing of the mint, anise, and cummin, and neglecting the weightier matters of the law.

Scope and divisions of the book.

What I have said may, however, imply rather more as to the purpose of this book than I intend; a craft so lightly built can not hope to stem the full current of these wide-spreading tendencies in our law. But keeping these tendencies in mind, I have endeavored to set forth briefly, clearly, and with their true bearings, all the cardinal facts in the development of code pleading among peoples dominated by the substantive common law, whether in the new world or the old, and this with a view to the light which these facts, if properly presented, throw upon the essentials of our American codes of civil procedure. It has not been easy to keep the subject within the limits of a small book, so numerous are the ramifications; but, while endeavoring to state all the cardinal facts, I have been at no less pains to avoid all discursive theories and excessive elaboration. A prime aim has been to make an inexpensive book which will go hand in hand with the immediate study of each of our codes of civil procedure, and serve as a practical introduction to the true nature of each. If its design has been achieved, the book will be of some real assistance to the practitioner in any one of the code states, and in each of the following respects—it will indicate how his code came to be what it is; it will define the *locus in quo* of code pleading in general, and of his own code in particular; it will put him into touch with his code as part of a widespread, modern, and progressive system of pleading; it will reveal the bearings of the more important principles in the new procedure and afford some light as to its essentials.

C. M. H.

15 AND 16 CARLISLE BUILDING,
CINCINNATI, FEBRUARY 5, 1897.

PART I.

ORIGIN OF CODE PLEADING.

HISTORICAL DEVELOPMENT OF CODE PLEADING.

CHAPTER I.

NATURE AND EXTENT OF CODE PLEADING IN GENERAL.

1. THE TERMS "CODE," "CODE STATE," "CODE PLEADING."
   1. THE WORD "CODE" AS A TERM OF LAW.
   2. THE CONVENTIONAL USE OF "CODE STATE" AND "CODE PLEADING."
2. LEADING CHARACTERISTICS OF CODE PLEADING IN THE USUAL ACCEPTATION OF THE TERM.
   1. CODE PLEADING AS A STATUTORY SYSTEM COMMON TO MANY STATES.
   2. IN WHAT THE FAMILY LIKENESS OF THE CODES CONSISTS.
   3. WHERE CODE PLEADING OF THIS TYPE PREVAILS.
      1. ITS EXTENT AND THAT OF COMMON LAW PLEADING IN ITS PALMIEST DAYS.
      2. PRESENT EXTENT OF CODE PLEADING AND COMMON LAW PLEADING.
      3. CODE PLEADING AND THE "AMERICAN SYSTEM."

The word "code" as a term of law.

Sec. 1. The word "code" is of comparatively recent use by American and English lawyers. As late as 1850 its appearance among our terms of law was apt to excite remark, so rarely was it then found in such company;[1]

[1] Cf. Burrill's Law Dictionary, 2d ed., "Code."

and its derivations "codify" and "codification" had scarcely escaped from the ridicule and abuse which had been heaped upon them as barbarous innovations in a bad cause. Apart from its derivations, however, "code" is an old word in English. It had appeared there, coming out of the Latin through the French, as early as the days of Chaucer; apparently it was on a secure footing in the language at the beginning of the fifteenth century. But at the beginning of the nineteenth century "code" was still without standing in the vocabulary of our law, on either side of the Atlantic.

Early use of "code" in English as a lay word.

Sec. 2. Its general use in English meanwhile had been that of a lay term, and of vague import. Because of the etymological meaning and use of its Latin original—*codex*, or *caudex*, the trunk of a tree, and hence the wax-smeared tablet of wood originally used by the ancients in writing, and so the writing itself—"code" in English might convey, and to some extent did convey, the general notion of anything reduced to *writing*. It is synonymous in most of the early dictionaries with our native word "book," whose etymology, curiously enough, it parallels. More particularly it denoted a collection of writings. At the close of the eighteenth century Paley refers, as a matter of course, to the Bible as consisting of two "codes," the "code, or collection, of Christian sacred writings" and the "code, or collection, of Jewish sacred writings." More often, the word, while still a lay term, had a flavor of the law. Whether or not our older dictionaries define it merely as a "book," "a volume," they steadily define it as "a book of the civil law"; for the best-known collections of Roman law bore each the name of *codex*.

These two meanings are the only meanings which "code," when used by itself in English, was popularly supposed to bear, until about the year 1800. It had no definite reference to any aspect of English law. When qualified, the word might indeed denote several distinct things in the field of law, widely separated in time and in their natures. It could refer to the code of Theodosius, published in the fifth century, or to the more famous code of Justinian, published a century later. The Ordonnances of Louis the Fourteenth might be called a code. The collection of Prussian laws which was published in French and in German under the auspices of Frederick the Great bore the name of "Code Frederic."

Its long absence from our legal nomenclature, and the significance thereof.

Sec. 3. But all these applications of the word, both general and specific, lay outside of English and American law. "Code" found no place in Jacob's Dictionary "explaining the rise, progress, and present state of the English law"; even ten editions and the added researches of Tomlins had failed to note it as a term of our jurisprudence as late as the year 1797.

The real significance of this should not be overlooked. It does not lie in the absence of the word from our legal nomenclature, but in the absence of the thing from our legal system. The word was at hand, ready for use, but at this time, the beginnings of the nineteenth century, there was no one thing, actual or clearly designed, in the legal system of either England or the United States, to which "code" was naturally and specifically applicable.

Appearance of "code" as a term of modern law.

Sec. 4. A little after the year 1800 the word began to come into use among English and American lawyers as denoting something new in the scope and purpose of our jurisprudence. The French codes, promulgated at short intervals and with reiterated emphasis between the years 1804 and 1810;[1] the writings of Jeremy Bentham, before and after this period—notably his View of a Complete Code of Laws, his offer to the president of the United States, and afterwards to the governor of every state, to prepare a code for the use of the American States, "or such of them, if any, as may see reason to give their acceptance to it",[2] his Codification Proposal, addressed "to all nations professing liberal opinions"; the codes actually drafted by Edward Livingston for the State of Louisiana,—these and other causes operated in the opening years of the nineteenth century to give the ancient word "code" an effective introduction as an important term of modern law.[3] They gave it also a suggestive embodiment. It presently came to stand for something tangible in our science of law. More than this, it became the watchword of a new and aggressive spirit of law reform on both sides of the Atlantic.[4] And it is significant of the progress which this reform has already made that the legal neologism "code" is now

[1] The Civil Code (Code Napoleon), appeared in 1804; Code de Procédure Civile in 1806; Code de Commerce in 1807; Code d'Instruction Criminelle in 1808; Code Pénal in 1810.

[2] Cf. Bentham's letter to President Madison, 1811; Bentham's letter to the Governor of Pennsylvania, 1814; the latter's message to the Pennsylvania legislature, 1816; Bentham's communications to the governors of the several States, June, 1817; and his address to the citizens of the United States, July, 1817; see papers relative to Codification, 4 Bentham's Works (Bowring ed., 1843), 451 et seq.

[3] With "code" came also "codify," "codification," etc. The latter are of Bentham's extensive coinage.

[4] Then, as now, however, the word was ambiguous (cf. infra, Sec. 5). Austin, for instance, points out that the term *code*, as signifying a body of law, "expressed in general formulae arranged systematically, and complete, and the term *codification*, as meaning the reduction of an existing body of law into such a côde, are not expressive." . . . "We want," said he, in 1832, "a term to denote a complete body of statute law being, or intended to be, the only positive law obtaining in the community." (2 Austin's Juris., 1061, 671.) But to express this idea, he could find no word so well suited as "code."

in the most familiar daily use by both the bench and the bar of all the United States.

Its varied use in American law.

Sec. 5. It is significant of another aspect of this reform movement—its lack, in some respects, of scientific accuracy—that few law terms are applied to so many different things in our jurisprudence as the word "code." It has been applied to mere collections of existing statutes into one book; it has also been applied to proposed revisions of the whole law of the land—both the written and the unwritten law—and its definite, systematic statement as one enactment, or series of enactments, made with such omissions, additions, and modifications as might be deemed proper for the purpose of clear, scientific expression, and promulgated with such completeness and authority as to supersede all prior statutes and the volumes of decisions; and it has denoted nearly every grade between these two extremes.

There is a marked diversity even in the official or semi-official use of the term. Legislatures, here and there, have given the name "code" indifferently to these three different things: (1) a compilation of existing statutes; (2) a consolidation of statute law into a more or less systematic form; (3) a revision of the whole law, written and unwritten, upon a given subject and the reduction of its principles to a clear, compact, and scientific enactment.

Its proper application.

Sec. 6. The latter, it is now safe to say, is codification properly so called. A mere reduction of the unwritten law upon one or more general subjects to a statutory form is not a code; neither is a mere compilation of statutes; nor a revision of statutes; nor a revision and consolidation of all the statute law of the state, if there remains a body of unwritten law upon the principles of the subjects treated. On the other hand, a code does not necessarily comprise all the law of the land; it may relate to one subject and not to another. Nor does it attempt to prescribe specifically for mere details. But, as far as it goes, a *code*, in the proper sense of the term, is a complete statutory declaration of the principles of law governing the subject in hand.

It signifies the substitution, through statutory enactment, of the complete for the incomplete, the simple for the complex, the clear for the obscure, the systematic for the chaotic.[1] Its chief ends are certainty and simplicity—uniformity when uniformity can be had, diversity when diversity must be permitted, but in all cases certainty.[2] Yet it is to be remembered that while this appears to be the meaning into which the word *code* is slowly settling down as a law term, it may still in fact be found doing duty in several of the other senses indicated above.

States which have "codes," yet are not "code states."

Sec. 7. A like process is to be noted with respect to the terms "code state" and "code pleading"; but here the results are already somewhat better defined. In their familiar use for more than a generation these phrases have acquired each a special meaning, which tends to become exclusive in the general usage of our decisions and textbooks.

Curiously enough, this semipopular usage shows a better discrimination than the official applications of the word "code" have sometimes shown. Not every state whose statutes bear the title of "code" is popularly classed as a

[1] Cf. 3 Jurid. Rev. 97 (1891).

[2] The principle was so laid down about the year 1833 by one of the earliest codifiers, Macaulay, in a speech on the question of framing a complete and definite code of laws for British India: "Our principle is simply this—uniformity when you can have it, diversity when you must have it, but in all cases certainty."

code state. For example, the systematic compilations which have been made from time to time of the Virginia statutes are styled the "Code of Virginia," and this has been their official title since 1849;[1] yet Virginia is not a "code state." So in the case of Georgia. In 1860 the legislature of that State passed[2] an elaborate bill whose avowed purpose was "not only to condense and arrange the verbose and somewhat chaotic mass of the statutes of Georgia, but also to interweave therewith those great, leading principles of jurisprudence necessary to fill out and make perfect the body of our laws, of which the statutes constitute disjointed parts"; and to this very comprehensive enactment both the legislature and the people of Georgia gave the name of a "code." Nevertheless, Georgia is not generally classed among the "code states." We have also the "Code of Alabama" and the "Code of Tennessee," and in each case the phrase is an old phrase, established in local and official use for upwards of half a century;[3] yet neither Alabama nor Tennessee is a "code state" as "code states" are now commonly enumerated.[4]

States which have only partial codification, but yet are "code states."

Sec. 8. On the other hand, the term is not confined to states in which the great body of the law, both substantive and adjective, both civil and penal, has been codified. Such are "code states" par excellence; as a class they

[1] They were popularly known as "codes" at a much earlier day; there was a "Code" of Virginia in 1792.

[2] Act of December 19, 1860.

[3] The "Code of Alabama" dates from 1852; the "Code of Tennessee" from 1857.

[4] See infra; cf. Dillon, Laws and Juris., 260; Phillips, Code Pleading, 166*n*; 1 Bates, Code Pleading, xvi; Bryant, Code Pleading, pp. 344–5; 19 Alb. Law Journ. 192, 194 (1879); 25 Am. Law Rev. 515 (1891); 1 Jurid. Rev. 18; Anderson's Law Dict., "Code."

might well bear a distinctive designation. But long-established usage has placed with them as "code states" a full score of states where codification is admittedly partial, but which do possess "code pleading."

Here, again, it is worth noting that the name which has been formally given to the official compilations of statute law in these code states is not decisive. The case is the converse of that just noticed in Alabama, Georgia, Tennessee, and Virginia, whose statute books bear the name of "codes" but are not generally accepted as such. Thus the official revision and consolidation which was made of the Ohio statutes in 1879 does not profess in terms to be or to contain a code; it is officially the "Revised Statutes of Ohio";[1] yet Ohio is recognizeed as a "code state" of long standing. The same thing is true in many other instances.[2] For example, we have the "General Statutes of Connecticut," the "Revised Statutes of Indiana," the "Statutes of Minnesota," the "Compiled Statutes of Nebraska," each a systematic consolidation of the existing statute law of its state; but, while these voluminous statute books are not held forth as "codes," and are not codes in the strictest sense, the states referred to, and other states represented by them, are admitted to be "code states."

Sec. 9. The test lies in the fact mentioned above, that in one form or another, these compilations of statute law contain enactments which establish "code pleading".[3] Nor is this wholly an arbitrary thing. The enactment of what is called "code pleading" was not only a startling, a revolutionary change, it was also the first great achieve-

[1] The revisers suggested that their work might be called the "Ohio Code" (Preface, iii, Ohio Rev. St.); but the phrase has not come into use.

[2] For enumeration of the "code States" see infra.

[3] Generally code pleading has been established by a separate act, entitled a "code of procedure," a "practice act," or otherwise; this act is afterwards merged in a general revision of the statutes.

ment in America of the movement towards codification; and "code pleading," its nature and extent considered, is still the most notable result of this movement. Naturally enough, therefore, the states which so far took part in the revolution as to enact code pleading have come to be ranked as code states even when their codification extends no further than the law of pleading.

What meant by "code pleading."

Sec. 10. What, then, is "code pleading"? In its natural and widest sense it is any system of pleading which has been reduced to the form of a statute.[1] So understood, "code pleading" would apply as well to the statutory pleading of Louisiana as to that of New York, to the statutory pleading of Germany as to that of England. But popular usage in our courts, while not refusing the term its wider meaning, tends to apply it to one kind of statutory pleading as if it were the only kind. For the system to which American decisions and textbooks commonly refer as unqualifiedly "code pleading" is not found in every country or even in every state of the Union which has a reformed statutory pleading. Rather, it is a peculiar system, preeminent in geographical extent. A word or two as to both these things—the peculiar traits and the geographical extent of this system—will be in season here, although the topics will come up again.

[1] Cf. 3 Stephen, Hist. Crim. Law 350: "Codification means merely the reduction of the existing law to an orderly written system, freed from the needless technicalities, obscurities, and other defects which the experience of its administration has disclosed." See also Dillon, Laws and Juris., 256.

Leading characteristics of "code pleading" in the usual acceptation of the term.

Sec. 11. It is apparently an abuse of terms to speak of any system of statutory pleading as if it were common to distinct states. For code pleading, ex vi termini, always rests definitely upon the existing enactments of some particular state—enactments which have no virtue of their own beyond the state line. In any given case, the code pleading of one state can properly enough be regarded as standing by itself, a distinct system independent of the code pleading of every other state. Nevertheless it is customary to speak of the peculiar form of statutory pleading under consideration as if it were one system possessed in common by many states. Standard textbooks have long treated, not of the "code pleading of New York," or the "code pleading of Ohio," or the code pleading of this, that, or the other state or group of states, but simply of "code pleading." The same tone appears time and again in the decisions. And, in fact, there is excellent warrant for this in the remarkable family likeness of all these codes.

In what the family likeness of the codes consists.

Sec. 12. Wherever the "code pleading" of our decisions and textbooks is found, its cardinal characteristics center about two things—a common origin and a common purpose. Characteristically, code pleading with us is that form of statutory pleading which (1) has arisen out of the English common law procedure, and (2) provides for the following: (a) a single judicial instrument—a "single form of action"—for the protection of all primary rights, whether legal or equitable; (b) a limited pleading characterized by plain and concise statements of the substantive facts, and none but the substantive facts, of the cause of action; (c) the bringing in of new parties, and the joinder of different causes of action between the necessary parties, with a view to the complete determination of the whole controversy; (d) the adjustment of the relief according to the substantial rights, pleaded and proven, of all the parties before the court, and of each of them, be they few or many.

With such characteristics "code pleading" is often antagonistic to common law pleading. Yet the causes which gave rise to code pleading lay in the common law itself, and the materials out of which code pleading is constructed are those which had become available through the development of English and American jurisprudence in both legal and equitable causes. Revolutionary as it seemed to be, the direct aim of the codes was not so much to destroy both the root and the branch of the existing systems —the pleading at law and the pleading in equity—and to put an entirely new pleading in their place, as to reduce these venerable and often conflicting modes of pleading to one simple, uniform system, free from the faults and defects which the experience of centuries had revealed in them. The result was, indeed, a new pleading, markedly different from both the older systems. But it is plain at every turn that the new pleading is built out of the old. Much is discarded, but rarely is new material introduced. And not only was code pleading built out of the older systems, it was designed for the same purpose which they had sought to serve—the administration of the substantive common law of England.

So marked is their common origin and common purpose that these different systems of "code pleading," however distinct and independent each of the other, as being statutes of sovereign states, still make up a highly individualized group of codes.[1] They may well be considered together as constituting a system of their own, or as but distinct expressions ot the same system.

[1] Infra, § 14.

This family likeness is heightened, in America at least, by another fact: very many of these codes have been framed with painstaking exactness upon the lines of one or the other of the two or three earliest codes, themselves formed after one model, as will appear presently. The same general topics, the same arrangement of divisions and subdivisions, the same phraseology are steadily repeated through more than a score of American codes. They are one in spirit; to a marked degree they are one in the letter also. And, while the letter of this system has not been so often repeated outside of the United States, the cardinal characteristics mentioned on a previous page are found in many other statutes besides those which establish the American codes.

Where code pleading of this type prevails.

Sec. 13. Apart from any question as to the merits of this type of pleading, its geographical extent gives it an easy preeminence over every other American and English statutory pleading, and over what is left of common law pleading. The latter was not so wide-spread in its palmiest days. For "code pleading" has already supplanted it or usurped its natural place in twenty-seven states of the American Union, and in essentials if not in the very letter has dispossessed common law pleading in its ancestral home, even in England, and found a way into India, into the colonies of Australia, into the Dominion of Canada, and widely elsewhere among the British Possessions. Following the sway of the Anglo-Saxon, it has encircled the earth. It may well claim the respect which is due to widest dominion.

Sec. 14. Within the American Union code pleading now prevails in four of the Atlantic States, in three of the Central States, and almost exclusively in the West—in Connecticut, New York, North Carolina, and South Carolina; in Kentucky, Ohio, and Indiana; and through the vast region occupied by the contiguous commonwealths of Wisconsin, Minnesota, Iowa, Missouri, Arkansas, Oklahoma, Kansas, Nebraska, South Dakota, North Dakota, Montana, Wyoming, Colorado, Arizona, Utah, Nevada, Idaho, Washington, Oregon, and California.

The twenty-seven states named above make up what are commonly called the "code states"; there is a tendency to group all the other members of the Union as "common law states." But here a distinction or two must be kept in mind. In every one of the United States statutory modifications of the older procedure have been so many and so great that the science of common law pleading no longer exists anywhere with us in its entirety. By "common law states," then, is to be understood those states in which the pleading is partly according to common law rules, whether now existing as unwritten law or in the form of statutory enactments, and partly according to new statutory requirements, *with the common law element predominating*. The term may be applied, with more or less appropriateness, to the States of Maine,[1] New Hampshire, Vermont, Rhode Island, New Jersey, Pennsylvania, Delaware, Maryland, Virginia, West Virginia, and Florida, Illinois, and Michigan, the Territory of New Mexico, and the District of Columbia.

But not all the remaining states are "common law states" even in this loose sense. Massachusetts, Maryland, Tennessee, Georgia, Alabama, Mississippi, and Texas have not established "code pleading" in the sense already explained, but they have established fairly complete statutory

[1] Maine, however, is sometimes included among the "code states" (So Dillon, Laws and Jurisprudence, 260*n*, and Phillips, Code Pleading, 166*n*, both quoting from Mr. David Dudley Field's paper for the Columbian Exposition); but the published statutes of Maine fail to bear this out. It is rather a common law state with statutory modifications.

systems, which, like "code pleading," arise out of the common law,[1] and in other respects are very near akin to "code pleading." In a sharply drawn division between "code states" and "common law states," they are to be ranked with the former. For convenience they may be referred to as quasi-code states.

Code pleading and the "American system."

Sec. 15. Another distinction is to be noted here. Predominant in the United States and first established there, "code pleading" has been somewhat formally designated the "American system," as if it were peculiar to the United States. This was true enough for a quarter of a century, and the term is still a convenient term in several ways; but, when used with respect to the essentials of the system to which it refers, it is now apt to mislead. "Code pleading," in the sense already explained, is no longer peculiar to the United States. It holds an even more complete sway in England, in Ontario, in Nova Scotia, in Victoria, and elsewhere in the British Empire. Wherever the substantive common law of England, the common inheritance of English commonwealths, in the New World as in the Old, is now established, whether as lex non scripta or in the form of statute law, there, in its essentials, this type of code pleading is now in force. In all its more important aspects, it is characteristically the form of pleading which the great majority of English-speaking peoples have deliberately adopted in these last days for courts of record.

[1] It will be observed that Louisiana stands by itself in this classification; its system of pleading arises out of the civil law. The rules of civil pleading in Texas also had a different origin from the common law, but their statutory enactment has approximated the form of rules found in the "code states" generally.

CHAPTER II.

Causes which Led to the Overthrow of Common Law Pleading.

1. Their historical aspect.
2. The fundamental cause of the change—an inveterate incongruity between our procedure and our substantive law.
    1. Occasion of this incongruity.
        1. As to the natural distinction between procedure and substantive law.
        2. The exclusiveness of procedure in our earlier legal theory.
        3. The growing inadequacy of procedure.
        4. The failure of parliament, the king, and the courts to furnish effectual relief.
        5. The kinds of relief which were afforded.
    2. Its inveterate nature.
        1. The early period at which our law of procedure ceased to develop.
            1. Rise of our substantive law.
            2. The brief period of progress in English procedure.
            . Our age of stagnation.
        2. The conservatism of the lawyer.
3. Leading special causes of the change.
    1. The wall of separation between legal and equitable procedure.
    2. The many distinct and arbitrary forms of action at law.
    3. The artificial restrictions of the common law as to joinder of causes and joinder of parties.
    4. The verbiage or the vagueness of common law pleading.

The barbarian invasion of the codes.

Sec. 16. The change from common law pleading to code pleading of the type referred to in the preceding chapter came, when it did come, as suddenly as a barbarian invasion; and for many years it was hotly resisted as something barbarous by a host of able practitioners. Conservative lawyers have scarcely yet ceased to ascribe the change to a "love of innovation," to "barbaric empiricism," to the "suggestions of sciolists, who invent new codes and systems of pleading to order".[1]

But such were far from being its real causes. The overthrow of common law pleading was not due to a mere whim of legislative vandalism. Its causes had grown out of an urgent, practical, long-felt need, out of an oft-repeated failure of justice, out of a public sense of substantial injustice. They had been gathering strength for centuries. Their beginnings lay in the very foundations of our older systems of pleading.

Their true source.

Sec. 17. Considered in their most general aspects, the causes of the change may be said to rest in one—an inveterate incongruity between our law of procedure and our substantive law. The former had early lost the power of developing along with the substantive law. It had petrified while our modern substantive law was still in its budding growth. But the chief grounds of complaint which were urged against common law pleading were more specific. They related to the wall of separation between legal and equitable relief; to the labyrinth of arbitrary forms of action at law; to the artificial restrictions of the common law as

[1] Such were the stock phrases, in use but yesterday. The introduction of Tyler's Stephen on Pleading affords a good illustration. See also McFaul v. Ramsey, 20 How. (U. S.), 523, 525 (1857).

to joining parties and as to joining causes of action; to the concealment of the real facts of a case through the verbiage or the vagueness of common law pleading. It will tend to clearness of view if both these things, this general underlying cause and this group of leading particular causes, are kept in mind and their nature considered as if they were distinct, although in fact they are rather different phases of one and the same thing.

The fundamental cause of the change—an inveterate incongruity between procedure and substantive law.

Sec. 18. Nowadays we divide the whole body of law, both common and statutory, into two parts: (1) the law which defines the primary legal rights subsisting between man and man in general, and (2) the law which specifies the means whereby these rights may be maintained or redressed when they are violated in particular instances. The former has received the name of "substantive" law; the latter, the name of "adjective" law, or the law of procedure. Substantive law is primary, even, in a sense, creative. It defines the rights which courts of justice are established to enforce or protect. It is the law to be administered, as distinguished from the method of administration. Its definitions, in this primary way, cover the whole field of law—the rights of the person, natural or artificial, and of personal relations, the rights as to property, both real and personal, the rights which grow out of contract, the rights which grow out of tort. It operates, proprio vigore, upon all within the state.[1] Adjective law, on the other hand, is secondary in its purpose. As its name, "adjective," imports, it exists for the sake of some-

[1] Convenient collections of substantive law may be found in the "Civil Codes" of California, North Dakota, and Montana. Cf., infra. See also Vol. 1, Anglo-Indian Codes (Stokes). Cf. Austin, Jurisprudence, 611, 788, 791.

thing else—for the sake of "substantive" law. It has three great branches, the law of pleading, of evidence, and of practice.[1] It operates only upon occasion, when invoked to maintain or redress a particular right given by the substantive law. It is the machinery of justice.

Sec. 19. But, while we speak of these two kinds of law as distinct, we should bear in mind another thing. They are distinct only in a sense, somewhat as the bed of a river is distinct from the water which flows within it. Adjective and substantive law together make up one whole. Each presupposes the existence of the other. Until the rights which the substantive law defines are observed by all men voluntarily, the substantive law must exist in vain save for the law of procedure. Yet the two can have a separate development. New substantive rights may be granted, former substantive rights may be withdrawn or modified, but the procedure may remain wholly unchanged. Likewise, the procedure may change without the substantive rights themselves being altered in kind or in any degree.

Historic relation of our procedure and our substantive law.

Sec. 20. Now it is a fact of great consequence in the history of both English and American jurisprudence that substantive law with us continued to grow after adjective law had stopped growing. The existing remedies became inadequate for the proper administration of primary rights while these rights were still in their formative stages. For centuries our law presented this anomaly—a developing

[1] More generally, "it comprises the rules for (1) selecting the jurisdiction which has cognizance of the matter in question; (2) ascertaining the court which is appropriate for the decision of the matter; (3) setting in motion the machinery of the court so as to produce its decision; and (4) setting in motion the physical force by which the judgment of the court is, in the last resort, to be rendered effectual." Holland's Jurisprudence, 305-306 (5th ed.).

body of substantive rights united to a petrified body of remedial rights.

The fact of this abnormal condition was emphasized by the costly experience of generations of suitors. Relief was sought on many occasions, but without effective result. The movement which brought on the codes was, in effect, merely a more determined renewal of these efforts. Its one great purpose was to bring procedure into a simple and natural relation with substantive law by altering the former when its alteration was necessary for the effective and speedy administration of the latter. It is true that this work of alteration went very far, even to displacing the foundation-stones of common law procedure. But it was prompted by no mere caprice of ignorant or wanton legislation. Some centuries of experience had indicated that a less radical course would defeat the object in view, and again fail to give a natural and vigorous vitality to a maxim which the law had long placed before itself as the ideal—wherever a right, there a remedy.

Exclusiveness of procedure in early legal theory.

Sec. 21. In theory, of course, the courts were always able to find a remedy whenever a substantive right was violated; but, in fact, it was often a doubtful question whether the plaintiff had any remedy, and if so, what.

The maxim *ubi jus, ibi remedium* had important qualifications even after it became current; in the beginnings of our jurisprudence it had no proper application at all. The principle which then prevailed was rather *ubi remedium, ibi jus.* For the law of procedure came before and gave form, if not substance, to the substantive law, in English as in Roman jurisprudence. The contorted growth which characterizes many of the doctrines of our substantive law, even as practitioners deal with them today, bears striking testimony to the molding influences of adjective law in earlier times. It was not merely that the existence of a remedy was then a practical test for the existence of the substantive right in question — even yet, administrative justice can go little further than this, since it is impossible in practice to separate a primary legal right from the subordinate rights through which it is enforced; but, at the outset, and for centuries after the beginnings of our law as an established system, there was no clear conception of substantive law as such. The whole legal theory was embodied in forms of remedy. Ceremonies had been embalmed as primary and immutable principles of law. Forms and modes of procedure stood in the place of substantive rights; nor could justice see beyond them or above them.

Growing inadequacy of procedure.

Sec. 22. The horizon widened very slowly; yet it did widen. In the general development of a complex civilization new relations of fact between man and man gave rise to novel claims which were unquestionably grounded in natural justice, although no existing form of remedy exactly suited to their enforcement could be found. The distinction which divides the whole body of law into the two parts noticed above, *substantive* and *adjective* law, belongs to the jurisprudence of today; but the difference on which the distinction is based has been felt for centuries. Its traces are still visible in the preambles of old acts of parliament. "Divers of this realm were disinherited," recites one ancient statute, a representative of a class, "by reason that in many cases where remedy should have been had, there was none provided." Very suggestive in this respect is the great statute of Westminster the Second,[1] declaring that "whensoever it shall happen in the chancery that in one case a writ is found and in a like case, falling under

[1] 13 Edw. I, c. 24 (1285).

the same law, and requiring a like remedy, no writ is found, the clerks of the chancery shall agree in framing a writ, or adjourn the complaint to the next parliament, where a writ shall be framed with the consent of the learned in the law, *lest it happen that the court of our Lord the King be long deficient in doing justice to the suitors.*

Failure of parliament, the king, the courts to give effective relief.

Sec. 23. But, while this growing difference between a law which should be administered and the law, or method, of procedure was thus early forcing itself upon public attention as a matter of general concern, relief was not at hand. Parliament in those days acted slowly and only under extreme pressure. The King, shorn of despotic power, could not act directly in the matter, either for good or evil. Effectual relief, if it was to come at this stage of our law, must come from the courts themselves. And the courts did furnish some relief. At an early period, new writs or actions could be issued out of the chancery as new conditions required. Several worn-out archaisms were dispensed with. But this spontaneous growth of adjective law soon came to an end. For the most part it was over when Edward the First ascended the throne in 1272. The relief, such as it was, still came from the courts. Apparently it could come from no other quarter. Such indeed was the incapacity or the negligence of parliament in all these matters, during the succeeding five centuries, that, if the work of adapting the adjective law to the substantive law had not been performed mainly by the judges, it possibly would not have been performed at all.[1] But through all this time the courts were hardly able to do this work well. They were steeped in their traditions. On bench, and bar,

[1] Cf. Austin, Jurisprudence, 4th ed., p. 632.

and the clerks of the chancery lay the paralysis of inviolable custom. They could not find a way to frame new forms of writs as needed to fit new cases. So inveterate was the illiberality of the profession that the leading statute of Westminster the Second failed of its proper effect, and afforded only partial relief.[1] There was no conception as yet of a simple, single judicial instrument through which any substantive right might be redressed upon the facts of its violation. Such a conception was, indeed, to arise; but its dawn was five hundred years and more after Edward the First's day.

Kinds of relief afforded.

Sec. 24. Meanwhile the ancient machinery of justice was continually required to meet new and strange conditions of fact, and under this strain was continually breaking down. It was often repaired; but the relief was, in effect, mere temporary expedient—patchwork which added to the intricacies of the machine.

Speaking generally, and apart from the occasional, halting legislation on the subject, the attempts at reform in English and American procedure from the year 1300 until after the year 1800 were of two kinds: (1) old formulae of action were adapted to new uses by means of *fictions*; (2) the rigidity of the law was further moderated by a resort to *equity*. Both kinds of relief came, of course, from the courts. Both are worthy of further attention here as illustrating one of the causes which prepared the way for the statutory reform of our own age, and gave to these reforms many of their present characteristics.

[1] For one instance, see 3 Bl. Com. 51; and Blackstone, it will be remembered, was not disposed to note defects in the common law.

(1) *Relief sought through legal fictions.*

Sec. 25. In its most general sense a legal fiction is "any assumption which conceals, or affects to conceal, the fact that a rule of law has undergone alteration, its letter remaining unchanged, its operation being modified".[1] New conditions of fact are to be met—the demands of convenience, the requirements of necessity are to be satisfied, without departing from the ancient letter. The old rule retains its outward shape and seeming. In theory it is the same as ever; but in fact it has become a shell, beneath which a new and different principle is working.

Instances of legal fiction are not far to seek in English and American law. We are as yet scarcely out of sight of the loss and finding in trover and conversion, of the "implied" promise in assumpsit, of John Doe and Richard Roe and their train in the action of ejectment.

By the first of these fictions, it will be remembered, the convenient formula which went under the name of the action of trespass in the case in trover and conversion, and originally was designed for the recovery of damages from one who had *found* another's goods and *converted* them to his own use, acquired a very much wider scope. The loss and finding being feigned, but alleged in the pleading as real, the action was "permitted to be brought against anyone who had in his possession, by any means whatsoever, the personal goods of another, and sold them or used them without the consent of the owner, or refused to deliver them when demanded." Bringing this action, a plaintiff was expected to allege the casual loss and finding of, say, a thousand tons of pig-iron.[2]

Still bolder was the use of fictions in the action of ejectment, where the entry, the lease, the ouster, the nominal

[1] Maine, Ancient Law, 25. Cf. ib. xvii, 24.

[2] 3 Bl. Com. 153.

plaintiff, and the nominal defendant were all feigned. The purpose was the same as before—to preserve the letter of an ancient rule when convenience dictated a substantial departure from its spirit. For, by means of these fictions, a very convenient personal action of trespass vi et armis, the original action of ejectment, designed to recover damages for breaking the plaintiff's close and ejecting him, was enabled to dispossess various cumbersome "real actions," and become the almost universal method of trying title to freehold estate.

John Doe and Richard Roe and these other fictions of ejectment, although in actual use within the memory of men still living, are now to be classed among the curiosities of our law; but the feigned promise in the action of assumpsit made its way into our substantive law and has fared better. It has established itself in the definitions of legal right. Lawyers still think in the terms of this old fiction. Its design was substantially the same as the design of the other fictions which I have just mentioned, and no less laudable. It arose out of a desire to bring certain substantive rights for which no convenient formula had been set apart, within the scope of an existing form of remedy, in this instance, the advantageous action of trespass on the case in assumpsit. Now, the cardinal fact in the action of assumpsit was a promise not under seal, and in the case of these substantive rights there was no actual promise of any kind. Accordingly, the law feigned a promise, and asserted it in pleading as real. It was essentially a fiction of procedure, like the fictions in ejectment or in trover and conversion, but, unlike these fictions, the feigned promise in assumpsit has been woven into the texture of the substantive law of England and America.

Their effect in a contorted growth.

Sec. 26. This curious result is worth noticing here, even at the expense of a slight digression. It illustrates as well as any other one thing, not only the general lack of harmony which so long prevailed between adjective and substantive law, but also the contorted growth which this cause imposed upon the latter branch of our jurisprudence, and the complexities of both. English lawyers early grouped civil wrongs into two classes: the wrongs which arise from breach of contract and those which arise out of tort. No intermediate class was known to the law of procedure. But gradually the substantive law attained to the rcognition of legal rights and duties in a class of cases where there was no true contract, either expressed or inferred, but the dealings between the parties had been such as to make it "just and expedient that an obligation analogous to contract should be imposed upon the person receiving the benefit".[1] Such a condition, for example, arose when D wrongfully took and sold the goods of L and received their price;[2] or when W wrongfully usurped the office of H and received the fees annexed to it;[3] or when, pretending to be unmarried, a man took a woman to wife in the lifetime of a first wife, and under color of this pretended marriage, obtained the rents coming to such second wife;[4] or, more generally, whenever one obtained money from another by means of deceit, imposition, oppression, or extortion, or by the commission of a trespass.[5] Here, of course, there was no actual promise to return the money. The real intent of the act was indeed just the opposite.

[1] Wald's Pollock's Contracts, §29; 1 Addison, Contracts, §23.

[2] Lamine v. Dorrell, 2 Ld. Raym. 1216 (1702).

[3] Howard v. Wood, 2 Lev. 245 (1679); Arris v. Stuckley, 2 Mod. 260, 263 (1678).

[4] Hasser v. Wallis, 1 Salk. 28 (1708).

[5] 1 Addison, Contracts, §24.

Nor, in most cases, had there been any representation by the wrong-doer that he held the money for another. But he was clearly under a legal obligation to repay a sum so obtained; and this obligation resembled in a way the obligation which would have arisen if he had promised the true owner, for a valuable consideration, to return him the money. Accordingly, the common law, holding to old and narrow forms while seeking to carry out a wider view of legal duty, itself created such a promise and imposed it upon the wrong-doer. The avowed principle was "that every man hath engaged to perform what his duty or justice requires".[1] The fictitious promise which thus arose was commonly known as "implied,"[2] or "constructive";[3] but in pleading it was always treated as if it were express. The general result, apart from the pleading, was to give an artificial, untrue form to a substantive obligation.[4]

The amending act of early civilization.

Sec. 27. The fictions which I have recited are among the later and more particular fictions which characterized both English and American law. There were many others, some of a limited application, some so vague and general

[1] 3 Bl. Com. 162.

[2] The student will distinguish between an "implied" promise in this sense and an "implied" promise in the sense of a promise *inferred* in fact. See 1 Addison, Contracts, §23; Pollock, Contracts, §28; Maine Ancient Law, 333.

[3] "Constructive contracts are fictions of law adopted for the purpose of enforcing legal duties by actions ex contractu where no proper contract exists." Hertzog vs. Hertzog, 29 Pa. S. 465, 467 (1857), criticising the use of the term "implied." Some later writers designate the obligation by the phrase "quasi contract." See Anson, Contracts, 354. Cf. Keener, Quasi-Contract, 3, 5, 12, 15, 16; Maine, Ancient Law, 332.

[4] It need hardly be said that the abolition of fictions in pleading left the rights of the parties here entirely unchanged. "The obligation to which the action of *assumpsit* conveyed a false air of agreement continues to furnish a cause of action, though that cause of action is now to be stated as it really exists." Anson's Contracts, 357.

as to be felt rather than clearly defined.[1] Nor was the legal fiction confined to English law. Rude as it was, the device was common in most ancient systems of jurisprudence. It was the amending act of early civilization. By it the Jewish doctors of law, the interpreters of the Koran, the Roman praetors, as well as English and American judges, sought to moderate strict legal severity, and harmonize the letter of an ancient rule with the spirit of their own day. And their efforts, it should be remembered, were not altogether in vain. The legal fiction served a useful function.[2] But the price paid for it was very high.

[1] Cf. Maine, Ancient Law, 25.

[2] Blackstone, of course, found more to admire than to blame in the fiction; Bentham treats it with scorn. "A fiction of law," says he, "may be defined—a willful falsehood, having for its object the stealing legislative power by and for hands which could not or durst not openly claim it—and but for the delusion thus produced could not exercise it. Thus it was that, by means of mendacity, usurpation was, on each occasion, set up, exercised, and established." 1 *Bentham, Complete Works*, 243, *Fragment on Government.*

As to the true office of fictions (taking the term in its wider sense), see Maine's Ancient Law, Chap. II, and Dwight's introductory remarks: "Law is stable, society is progressive. How shall this gulf be narrowed which has a perpetual tendency to reopen? There are three agencies with which law is brought into harmony with society—Legal Fiction, Equity, and Legislation. Their historic order follows this arrangement" (p. xvii). "It is not difficult," says Maine, "to understand why fictions in all their forms are particularly congenial to the infancy of society. They satisfy the desire for improvement, which is not quite wanting, at the same time that they do not offend the superstitious disrelish for change, which is always present. At a particular stage of social progress they are invaluable expedients for overcoming the rigidity of law. We must, therefore, not suffer ourselves to be effected by the ridicule which Bentham pours on legal fictions wherever he meets them. To revile them as merely fraudulent is to betray ignorance of their peculiar office in the historical development of the law. But at the same time it would be equally foolish to agree with those theorists who, discerning that fictions have had their uses, argue that they ought to be stereotyped in our system. There are several fictions still exercising powerful influence on English jurisprudence which could not be discarded without a severe shock to the ideas, and considerable change in the language, of

The ancient procedure, unwieldy at the best, became still more unwieldy, and the real needs of justice were often forgotten in the effort to keep the complicated machinery in running order.

(2) *Relief sought through equity.*

Sec. 28. The same thing was true, in a measure, of the other instrumentality mentioned above — the resort to *equity*. By it is meant an appeal to a body of principles which are assumed to exist by the side of the original common law, but to be distinct from it and superior to it in some respects, because of a higher sanctity. Its mode of action differed from that of the fictions in that its interference with the original common law was open and avowed.[1] In one respect, however, the result was the same as in the case of the fictions—an added complexity in the administration of justice. For in English procedure equity, although founded on principles to which, it is claimed, all law should conform, failed for centuries to change the rules of law to its own nature, but, under the forming hands of the chancellors, slowly grew into a separate and often antagonistic jurisdiction. In the end, it is true, the principles of equity were to prevail over those of common law, and the two systems of procedure were to become one. But this was not to occur in America until after the year 1848, nor in England until after the year 1873.

English practitioners; but there can be no doubt of the general truth that it is unworthy of us to effect an admittedly beneficial object by so rude a device as a legal fiction" (p. 26).

[1] Cf. Maine, Ancient Law, 27.

The inveterate nature of the incongruity between procedure and substantive law—(1) The former petrifies while the latter is in its budding growth.

Sec. 29. This incongruity between our law of procedure and our substantive law lay, as I have said, at the root of the movement which brought on code pleading. One of its aspects already alluded to is especially to be kept in mind through all this connection, as dominating the whole subject: common law procedure did not merely cease to grow while our substantive rights were developing, it ceased to grow almost before the development of our modern substantive rights began. The spirit of blind devotion to set form and arbitrary distinction, whose power the rationalism of the thirteenth century had shaken, regained its hold upon our procedure about the close of that century, and retained it thenceforth until after the beginning of the nineteenth century. Whatever development took place in substantive rights meanwhile—and this development was great—their enforcement or protection was through the procedure of a bygone age, itself marked with many of the characteristics of archaic times.

Legal technicality as a characteristic of archaic law.

Sec. 30. "Legal technicality," it has been said, "is a disease, not of old age, but of the infancy of societies"; and common law pleading, while no more afflicted in this way at first than some other ancient systems, never quite recovered from the disease. Its peculiarity was not that it subordinated substance to form at the outset, but that it continued to subordinate substance to form until but the other day.

The early procedure among the Romans, for instance, was marked by an arbitrary and intense formalism. Its characteristic was symbol. Symbolical acts were to be performed with painstaking accuracy—a gesture, a simulated act of violence, a fictitious combat. Material objects were to be produced with elaborate ceremonial—a lance, a tile, a tuft of grass—as symbolizing certain ideas or processes. Sacerdotal words and formulae were to be uttered with punctilious accuracy. He who was so unfortunate as to say "vine" (*vites*) in an action concerning vines, instead of using the term "*arbores*," which was the religious term peculiar to the law of the case, lost his action.[1]

A similar iron rigorism of form characterized the earliest English procedure. Even while pleading was still by word of mouth at the bar of the court, the plaintiff's statement of his case was markedly formal, "bristling with sacramental terms" which were insisted upon as vital to the case. Essentially formal also were the older modes of trial, or rather modes of proof, which followed the plaintiff's statement, as proof by ordeal, by party-witnesses, by wager of law, by wager of battel. They were marked at each step by a punctilious regard for outward observances, which sometimes had an apparent relation to the true nature of the case and sometimes were more like the rigmaroles of children in a game.[2] Elaborate forms of asseveration were required, in which, if there was a mistake of a word, the oath "burst" and the adversary won.[3] A century this side of the conquest the business of the popular courts was still not so much to try a case through the patient sifting of testimony as to determine what formula a party should follow in order to prove his case. Formalism was the characteristic, the vital spirit of procedure. Little

[1] Ortolan, Hist. Rom. Law, 144 (P. & N. trans.); Gai. Inst. 4, 11, 30.

[2] Cf. Thayer, 5 Harv. Law Rev. 47.

[3] "In the twelfth century such elaborate forms of asseveration had been devised that rather than attempt them, men would take their chance at the hot iron." 2 Pollock & Maitland, Hist. Eng. Law, 599.

or nothing was left to judicial discretion; the judges were responsible only for the application of iron rules.[1]

The brief period of progress in English law.

Sec. 31. Much of this formalism was, indeed, outgrown by our law at a comparatively early date. From about 1154 to about 1272 English procedure developed rapidly. Various archaic forms were dispensed with.[2] Chancery, as the *officina justitiae*, was giving out new formulae of writs, or actions, one by one as occasion required. "It was an empirical process, for the supply came in response to a demand; it was not dictated by an abstract jurisprudence; it was conditioned and perturbed by fiscal and political motives; it advanced along the old Roman road which leads from experiment to experiment."[3] The system which thus arose was largely, it is true, a system of rigid formalism; as in the older days, strict adherence to the very letter was a vital matter. To this extent the archaic spirit was still all-powerful. But, however rigid each formula was in itself, the system as a whole possessed a capability of spontaneous growth. New formulae might be had to meet new cases. At least, there were instances in which, for a time, a plaintiff could have a new writ

[1] 2 Pollock & Maitland, Hist. Eng. Law, 561; Thayer, Older Modes of Trial, 5 Harv. Law Rev. 47; see also, for an earlier period, Laughlin, in "Anglo-Saxon Law," 185.

[2] "If we could look at western Europe in the year 1272, perhaps the characteristic of English law which would seem the most prominent would be its precocity. Its substance was, to say the least, as modern and enlightened as was that of the systems with which it could be profitably compared. It had suppressed some archaisms which might still be found in France or at any rate in Germany. It knew nothing of the wergild save as a trait of Welsh barbarism; at the pope's bidding it had abolished the ordeal; it was rapidly confining the judicial combat and the oath with oath-helpers within very narrow limits." 1 Pollock & Maitland, Hist. Eng. Law, 202.

[3] 2 Pollock & Maitland, Hist. Eng. Law, 557.

framed for his particular case if none suited to it appeared in the register of writs, and this without the intervention of any legislation. Thus Bracton, writing about the year 1255, mentions certain "magisterial writs" (brevia magistralia) as he calls them, which were "often varied according to the variety of the cases and complaints".[1] And he does not hesitate to declare that there were as many forms of writs as there were kinds of actions, for no one could sue without a writ.[2] "The common law was not yet a struggling captive netted in the meshes of procedure."

Our age of stagnation.

Sec. 32. But gradually our procedure lost this power of adaptation or development. Even in Bracton's day, the *brevia magistralia*, which might be "varied according to the variety of the cases and complaints," were distinguishable from other writs which, while framed to meet the needs of particular cases, had been granted and approved as of the course and by the common council of the whole realm, and could not be changed in any manner without the consent of the power which had framed them.[3] The tendency already was to regard a writ as drawn up "after the similitude of a rule of law".[4]

Naturally enough, therefore, it presently became a question whether any new writ could be framed except by the consent of the council of the whole realm. Perhaps every such writ was so approved in theory, while, in fact, the consent of the council might often be taken for granted. They assented unless they had dissented expressly or unless

[1] De Leg. f. 413 b.—Saepius variantur secundum varietate casuum et querelarum.

[2] "Tot erunt formulae brevium quot sunt genera actionum, quia non potest quis sine brevi agere." Brac. De Leg. f. 413 b.

[3] Brac. De Leg. f. 413 b.

[4] "Formatum ad similitudinem regulae juris;" cf. Brac. De Leg. f. 413 b.

some special reason was shown why the writ should not be valid; for "it appertains to the King," says Bracton,[1] "to apply a suitable remedy to restrain every injury whatsoever." But, however this may have been, the course of events finally decided that the consent of the council must be given to the framing of every new writ, and that this consent must be real and not assumed—in fine, that only an actual statute could add to the catalogue of writs and the forms of action.[2] Legislation of this sort, however, was slow in coming. It had little or no incentive from the judges and practitioners of the age which succeeded Bracton; their natural conservatism appears to be reinforced by ignorance of any system save their own. Nor had legislation as yet acquired anything of its modern readiness to act. The result was that English procedure as a whole slowly settled down, at this early day, into a hard and fast formulary system of actions.[3]

[1] De Leg. f. 414 b.

[2] "During the earlier part of the thirteenth century the King's general power to make new writs seems unquestioned, though protest, armed protest, may be made against a particular use of that power, specially if it interferes with the feudal jurisdictions. And many new writs must have been made. Of some we know the history. This was made by William Raleigh, that by Walter of Merton. But as the struggle for a parliament drew near, as King Henry forced on that struggle by attempting to govern without chancellor, treasurer, or justiciar, complaints of new and illegal writs became loud, and the general principle was drawn into debate. Bracton, writing some few years before the open outbreak, has left us a transitional doctrine." Maitland, in 1 Bracton's Note Book, 6.

[3] This system was probably of native origin, with, however, a number of striking but superficial resemblances to the formulary system of actions which was found in Roman law. For a comparison between the two, see 2 Pollock & Maitland, Hist. Eng. Law, 557.

Relation to the rise of code pleading.

Sec. 33. With vigilant, active, well-informed legislation, introducing new formulae of actions as needed, and abolishing all such as were obsolete, a formulary system might have been kept in harmony with the changing needs of our civilization, itself ever becoming more complex. And, in this case, the history of English and American procedure would have been very different from what it has been and probably from what it will be. The change from common law to code pleading, instead of coming as an angry torrent from a broken reservoir, would have been a gradual change, extending through centuries.

Its intermediate effect.

Sec. 34. But, in the absence of such legislation, English procedure, in order to make its way around obstacles which should have been removed from before it, was early forced into various crooked courses. Its natural channel of development was closed, and for five centuries and a half from this time our procedure made its way slowly through tortuous and narrow channels, as when the progress of some great river is choked with sands which

> "dam his streams,
> And split his currents; that for many a league
> The shorn and parcell'd Oxus strains along
> Through beds of sand and matted rushy isles—
> A foiled circuitous wanderer."

Other sciences developed a wide capability of simple and effective action, but the science of legal procedure grew more and more complex. Its formalism was accentuated by the very means employed to bring it into some accord with substantive rights—the use of fictions, the resort to equity. Moreover, symbolic ceremonies of a half-barbarous age, ceremonies which had almost disappeared before the year 1300, lived on, "moribund but mischievous," until after the year 1800; with them also lived on a multitude of verbal distinctions, intricacies of thought and expression, which had sprung up in the law at a time when all philosophy was a war of words. With its "closed cycle of original writs," its catalogue of forms of action to which no judge could make addition nor even the King, but only parliament, the law of pleading soon became an occult science. For generations it was a labyrinth of which the key was lost.[1]

This result, of course, came gradually; no one year can be fixed as its precise date. But the change from a developing to a fossilized formalism was very nearly complete by the end of the thirteenth century. The formulary system of the year 1300 was in the main the final system of common law procedure in England and America. Its next renascence came in the nineteenth century, in our own day, with the rise of code pleading.

(2) *The conservatism of the lawyer preserves the incongruity.*

Sec. 35. Through more than five centuries, therefore, common law procedure stood as a complete and ancient system, venerable even in the days of the fathers of our law. It was among the oldest institutions with which English lawyers had to do. It was older than any of the kingless commonwealths on this side of the Atlantic, where its authority was no less than in the mother country. This being so, it is plain that another fact must be reckoned with in considering the rise of the codes—the intense conservatism of the lawyer, his "antipathy to reformation." His instinctive position was, as it is and should be, against

[1] Cf. Maitland, 1 Bracton's Note Book, 7; 1 Pollock & Maitland, Hist. Eng. Law, 204.

changes; and his superstitious disrelish for a change was intensified when the change threatened the common law procedure. In his eyes it was a system to be venerated. It had existed from a time whereof his memory ran not to the contrary. His habit of thought for generations had been, not that common law procedure should be changed to meet new conditions of fact, but that new conditions of fact should be so treated that they would appear to meet the formal requirements of the common law system. The end justified, it was believed, a free use of fictions—of falsehood, as the profane termed it—even in the temple of justice. Rather, so perfect was the system, according to the estimate of many, that it could not fail a suitor however novel his case might be. "Every man," so some boasted, "was sure to find in it a method of relief exactly adapted to his case."[1]

Effects of ultra-conservatism in our law.

Sec. 36. Manifestations of this intense conservatism are to be seen at every hand through all the history of our modern law. They are hardly to be regretted, except when carried to the furthest extreme. Very often they are worthy of commendation, as the workings of a spirit without which we could have no system of law, but only collections of jangling, ephemeral rules. But it is to be borne in mind that this very spirit of conservatism, going to the furthest extreme, was largely responsible for so great a delay in the reform of common law pleading that the popular demand became threatening and dangerous, and produced crude changes which might have been avoided.

A few of the earlier manifestations of this same conservatism may be noticed here, not as having any immediate connection with the rise of code pleading, or as being

[1] 3 Bl. Com. 183.

specially important in themselves, but as serving to show the true nature of a cause which indirectly had a large share in determining the time and the manner in which code pleading finally appeared.

Blackstone and the hard and fast formalism of the common law.

Sec. 37. The "closed cycle of original writs," the hard and fast formulary system of common law procedure, was not regarded as a misfortune by some thoughtful lawyers of a comparatively recent day. As late as 1765, Blackstone, whose influence on the views of practitioners then and for two generations thereafter is hardly to be overestimated, could venture to declare that in "that most ancient and highly venerable collection of legal forms of the registrum omnium brevium, or register of such writs as are suable out of the King's Court, . . . every man who is injured will be sure to find a method of relief, exactly adapted to his own case, described in the compass of a few lines, and yet without the omission of any material circumstance. So that the wise and equitable provision of the Statute Westm. 2,[1] for framing new writs when wanted, is almost rendered useless by the very great perfection of the ancient forms. And, indeed, I know not whether it is a greater credit to our laws to have such a provision contained in them, or not to have occasion, or at least very rarely, to use it."[5]

Wager of battel in modern law.

Sec. 38. The conservatism of common law practitioners, however, could not always keep this self-satisfied bearing. Now and then an archaic, a barbarous form of procedure, long disused and forgotten, would start again

[1] 13 Edw. I, c. 24.

[2] 3 Bl. Com. 183, 184.

into activity, and, uncouth as it was, would vindicate its right to be regarded as part of the law of the land.

In the year 1818, for instance, in the case of Ashford vs. Thornton,[1] pending in the King's Bench, the defendant *pleaded* successfully as follows: "'Not guilty, and I am ready to defend the same by my body'; and thereupon taking his glove off, he threw it upon the floor of the Court." It was the old wager of battel, and the startled court was constrained to hold that "the general law of the land is in favor of the wager of battel."[2]

Wager of law in the nineteenth century.

Sec. 39. In 1824, in an action of debt in simple contract, a defendant ventured to assert in the King's Bench the hoary remedy of wager of law. The books left it doubtful whether six or eleven compurgators were necessary, and he therefore applied to the court "to assign the number of compurgators with whom the defendant should come to perfect his law". His right to the remedy could not be denied, but so antiquated was its procedure that the learned chief justice who heard the case was unwilling to say in advance what rules should govern the game. "The court," it was declared from the Bench, "will not give the defendant any assistance in this matter. He must bring such number of compurgators as he shall be advised are sufficient." The case proceeded no further. Curiously enough, the mere threat of producing this ancient and rusty weapon proved sufficient. "The defendant prepared to bring eleven compurgators," say the reporters, "but the plaintiff abandoned the action."[3] Nine years later

[1] 1 B. & Ald. 405, 409 (1818).

[2] Ib. p. 460. The law was altered by statute in the following year. Stat. 59 Geo. III, c. 46. In New York wager of battel remained a lawful mode of trial until 1786.

[3] King v. Williams, 2 B. & C. 538 (1824).

parliament at last enacted that "no wager of law shall be hereafter allowed".[1]

"*Wherefore he brings his suit,*" *and its significance.*

Sec. 40. A different, but no less curious and suggestive, illustration of this conservative spirit may be given from Stephen on Pleading, whose second and standard edition dates from the year 1827. It is there laid down as an unquestioned rule of good pleading that "the declaration should conclude with the production of suit". Stephen applies the rule to all classes of actions, real, personal, and mixed.[2] And for centuries lawyers were accustomed to conclude their declarations with the clause "wherefore he brings his suit". Yet this was the merest form of words, and meaningless in Stephen's day, if not misleading.[3]

Anciently there had been a real production of a suit, a *suite* rather,[4] or *following*, of one or more who came with the plaintiff into court to give credibility to his claim in its preliminary stages. The Latin original of the phrase, *et inde producit sectam*, was no mere form of words. The thing itself, this *secta*, or *following*, was an actual preliminary to the trial of the plaintiff's case, and well supported by reason and convenience. It was a natural, if not a necessary, feature of the ancient mode of trial, or formal, one-sided proof. For when, as in the earlier periods of English law, a case was "tried," not by weighing testimony in the scales of reason, but by requiring a certain thing to be done, a certain formula to be observed by one party or the other, it was a vital question which party had the proof. Nor was the manner of proof any light thing.

[1] Stat. 3 & 4 Wm. IV, c. 42, s. 13.

[2] Stephen, Pleading, Tyler's ed. 371; ib. Andrews' ed. 220.

[3] As when it was paraphrased into, "wherefore he sues."

[4] Somewhat curiously, the word is so printed in the forms with which many lawyers have long been familiar, those given in 4 Minor's Insts., pp. 1366 et seq.

The formula was clogged with technical detail; it often had little or no rational relation to the actual state of fact involved in the plaintiff's claim; it might be very expensive; it might involve disgrace, bodily danger, or death. A mere complaint, therefore, on the part of the plaintiff, however formal, did not suffice to send a defendant to his proof. Something to make the complaint probable was required at the threshold of the trial. And this something was found in the secta, or suit, who followed the plaintiff to the bar of the court when he came to make his viva voce complaint against the defendant, and gave the case the weight of their presence and support before any answer by the defendant had been made. The secta was like the profert of a deed—part of the preliminaries.[1]

But all this passed as trial by jury, and the examination of witnesses slowly made their way into our procedure. Members of the secta were not necessarily examined at all; accordingly it became the custom in later times not to produce a secta in fact.[2] Nevertheless the old phrase "and therefore he brings his suit," which anciently had heralded the appearance of this following was retained in the pleading. So loth, indeed, were lawyers to give it up that, after five centuries of uselessness, it survived even the rules of Hilary Term, in 1834.

[1] Cf. Thayer, 5 Harv. Law Rev. 48, 49. "It was the office of the secta to support the plaintiff's case in advance of any answer from the defendant. This support might be such as to preclude any denial, as where one was taken 'with the "mainour" and the mainour produced in court, or where the defendant's own tally or document was produced, or where a defendant chose to stake his case on the answer of the secta'" [in which event the defendant won if the plaintiff's secta disagreed among themselves]. Ib.

[2] In 1324 a defendant's demand for the examination of the secta revealed that the plaintiff had none in fact, and this defeated his claim (Year Book, Edw. II, 582). Twenty years later (Year Book, 17 Edw. III, 48, 14), however, the judges are strong in the opinion that the secta is a mere form. Cf. Thayer, 5 Harv. Law Rev. 51.

Surface indications of a functional disorder.

Sec. 41. These things, however, were mere surface indications of a chronic functional disagreement between the law of procedure and the substantive law. They were manifest blemishes, admittedly so even at an early day; but they were not specially important, either then or now, except as indicating the dangers into which an ultra-conservatism may lead the administration of justice. If the mischief had gone no further, common law pleading would not have been suddenly overthrown, as it was overthrown in America, because of a popular demand for a free administration of substantial justice. But, as I have said,[1] there were other causes at work, causes which grew out of this same inveterate incongruity between our procedure and our substantive rights; and these causes were so deep-seated in the common law system that an attempt to eradicate them threatened the life of the whole system. To them we shall now give some attention.

Leading special causes of the overthrow of common law pleading.

Sec. 42. The chief among the special causes just referred to may be grouped under the following heads:

(1) The separation, in procedure, of equitable from legal relief.

(2) The many distinct and arbitrary forms of action at law.

(3) The artificial restrictions of the common law as to the joinder of different causes and as to the joinder of parties in one action.

(4) The subtle, complex, and artificial verbiage, or the vague generality of common law pleadings.

[1] Ante, §17.

(1) *The separation, in procedure, of equitable from legal relief.*

Sec. 43. There is a natural distinction in substantive law between the rights which are known as "equitable" and those which go under the name of "legal". B's right to compel C to pay him a certain sum of money due and unpaid has very different characteristics, in the nature of things, from B's right to require C to refrain from doing an act which if done will work B an injury. So, in the rights which arise out of contract there are natural distinctions between those which may be redressed through pecuniary damages alone, and those which permit of redress through specific performance.

Distinctions of this kind, although properly belonging to substantive law, must, of course, come within the view of remedial justice. It does not follow, however, that the law of procedure should raise an impassable barrier between them. Indeed, it would seem that they could hardly fail of adequate recognition in a case if the pleading made a clear and true statement of the material facts of the controversy. Such a statement should of itself reveal these distinctions in the theory of the law to the trained mind of a judge, and the final form of relief could vary accordingly. But this was quite beyond the philosophy of our ancient law.

Abuse of the distinction between law and equity by our older procedure.

Sec. 44. The peculiar development of English jurisprudence was such that natural distinctions in the theory of substantive law became of vital importance in the application of adjective law. The procedure to enforce legal rights was separated and kept apart from the procedure to enforce equitable rights. He who sought relief of an "equitable" nature was required to apply to a different court from that to which he must resort if his proper relief was of a "legal" nature; and the two jurisdictions which thus arose followed widely different rules of procedure.

Theoretically, the line of division between legal and equitable relief was clearly defined; but in practice there was often a difficult question which of the two jurisdictions should grant relief on the facts of the case. To enter the wrong tribunal was fatal to the whole proceeding. A court of equity could not entertain the suit if the plaintiff had an adequate remedy at law; a court of law knew no "equity". Equitable pleas, it was said, carried no sound to the ears of a law judge.

The origin and nature of so wide a difference in procedure required, logically, the existence of two distinct tribunals. But, while some of the American Colonies and States, following the example of England, did in fact vest the powers of equity in courts which were entirely distinct from the courts of law, the tendency in America was to delegate both the equitable and the legal jurisdiction to the same judges. Nevertheless, no attempt was made to fuse the two systems of remedial justice into one. The same judge would sit at one time as a court of law, at another as a court of equity; but, as a court of law he could not enforce an equitable right, however closely connected with the case before him; as a court of equity he could not enforce a right for which his court of law afforded an adequate remedy. In either case, and at the end, perhaps, of protracted and expensive litigation, the unfortunate seeker for justice was thrown out of court because he had mistaken his form of remedy. He might try again, but only in a new proceeding, in a distinct court, and under a very different form of procedure, although on the same material facts, and often before the same judge. In some cases neither law nor equity would attempt to give full relief, and the aid of both jurisdictions was invoked, through distinct proceedings, to settle one controversy.

Moreover, and because of the limitations imposed by the law of procedure, justice was sometimes one thing in a court of law, another thing in a court of equity. A man might be sure of succeeding, might actually have succeeded, at law and yet be forbidden by equity, under pain of imprisonment, to go on with his action or to reap the fruits of it. There were cases in which it was possible to behold the same judge giving solemn judgment as a court of law, and then, as a court of equity, in a separate suit between the same parties and on the same subject matter, solemnly enjoining the enforcement of his correct legal judgment. We had a court of law, it was said, and a court of equity, but no court of justice.

(2) *The many distinct and arbitrary forms of action at law.*

Sec. 45. Even when it was clear that a plaintiff's relief should come from law, and not from equity, he still ran the risk of delay and defeat in selecting his action. For, while courts of equity had but one form of suit, the forms of action at law were many and arbitrary, and dominated the substantive rights of the parties. A plaintiff was required to show and follow a technical formula, recognized as suited to his case; otherwise he had no standing in the court.

These formulae were not merely convenient or approved modes of stating a plaintiff's case; nor were they the result of a logical or a merely convenient classification applied to existing material. They were organically separate actions —distinct, historical entities. They had arisen here and there out of the urgency of the time. They had lived each its own life, and each bore the marks of its peculiar development. Their specific differences were not those of scientific arrangement, but those which had been imposed by time and circumstance. And so it came about that actions which sought substantially the same end might differ essentially in procedure. For instance, the action of mort d'ancestor and the action of cosinage, or *de consanguineo*,[1] were very near akin in their purposes. If B claimed seizin of his uncle, the former action would lie; if B claimed seizin of his first cousin, the other action was to be used. But the procedure of the two was very different. The explanation appears to be that the one belonged to the latter half of the twelfth, the other to the middle of the thirteenth century.

In many instances the reason for a distinction was quite lost in the mists of antiquity. And generally each action was distinguished from every other by points of difference which, whether they could be explained or not, were minute and technical; yet were they none the less vital. There were, it is true, some states of fact in which the plaintiff could select from two or three actions and recover in either; but here again peculiar technical advantages or disadvantages commonly attached to whatever action was selected. In many cases there was only one action in which the plaintiff could succeed—one right action with several other actions which were very similar to it in appearance, but fatal if tried.

Fatal consequence of a mistake in the selection.

Sec. 46. If a wrong action was adopted, the error was fatal to the whole proceeding, however clearly the facts of the controversy might have been brought before the proper court. The plaintiff may have served his adversary in due time, and may have given as full information as to the material facts of the case as could be given in any other

[1] Cf. 3 Bl. Com. 186.

action; he may have proceeded openly and fairly in all matters; there may have been no question as to the substantial justice of his claim; but all this would not avail if his action was not technically the proper one. He must pay the costs and go out of court. If he chose he could begin again, but under like conditions. At his peril he must select the appropriate formula. It was not enough that he stood within the temple of justice, he must have entered through a particular door. Or, to change the figure, chancery, the so-called *officina justitiae*, was like an armory. To it every man who would contend with another in the courts comes to choose his weapon. The choice is large. All the weapons of juridical warfare are here. But every weapon has its proper use, and can be put to no other. Moreover, only one weapon can be chosen at a time;[1] and once chosen it can not be exchanged for a different weapon in the progress of the combat. If the fight is to go on, it must be with such a weapon as was first chosen, and according to its special rules. A sword being selected, the rules of sword-play must be strictly followed. A crossbow may not be used as a mace.[2] The issue of the combat must not be determined by mere brute force—not even by the brute force of indisputable facts arrayed before the court. It is a contest of skill; success depends upon observing the formal rules of the combat.[3]

[1] Cf. Bracton's explanation of why a defendant had only a single plea in bar—otherwise it would be "like a man's defending himself with several cudgels, which ought not so to be." Brac. De Leg. f. 400 b.

[2] Cf. 2 Pollock & Maitland, Hist. Eng. Law, 559.

[3] Perhaps it is the wandering spirit of this archaic principle which has inspired some of our code decisions upon the necessity of keeping to the "theory of the action."

The difficulty in making a selection.

Sec. 47. To choose between the different actions was hardly less difficult than important. The number of those in common use was considerable, and they were characterized by nice and artificial distinctions, which often baffled the skilled attorney as well as his bewildered suitor. On scarcely any other subject in the law was there so much curious and technical learning.

The full number of common law writs and actions is not clearly known. As late as 1831 a commission in England reported that "there is at present no authentic enumeration of actions in the law of England, but the register contains a variety of writs, and is said to comprise most of those for which authority is to be found". Including some which had become part of our legal system by virtue of early statutory enactment, the register fell little if any short of sixty different actions. If variations rather than essential differences are made a test, the number might be run into the hundreds. Many of these, however, became obsolete at an early day; many never came into extensive use. There appear, however, to have been in common use thirty or forty actions which were largely different.[1] And the names of twenty or more are still like the names of childhood in the memory of living practitioners.

The common forms of action.

Sec. 48. It may be of service at this juncture to call some of these venerable shapes back into the light for a moment, as showing more clearly the nature of the change which has been wrought by the single civil action of code pleading.

A variety to "real actions" lay to recover land. If a plaintiff sought to regain possession of a freehold, he could

[1] Cf. 2 Pollock & Maitland, Hist. Eng. Law, 563 et seq.

choose, according to the circumstances of his case, between the *writ of entry*, the *writ of assize*, the *writ of forcible entry*, the *writ of unlawful entry*, or the *writ of unlawful detainer*—all "possessory" actions, as they were called. If he had lost not only the possession, but the right of possession to his freehold, and had merely a right of property, the plaintiff could resort to one or the other of four "droitural" actions, the *writ of quod ei deforceat*, the *writ of right of dower*, the *writ of formedon*, and the *writ of right*. To recover not only the land, but damages for its unlawful detention, resort was had to a "mixed action," as *ejeetment*, the *writ of waste*, the *writ of dower unde nihil habet*.

Possession of a specific chattel was recovered through certain "personal actions" ex delicto—*replevin* when the chattel had been unlawfully taken, *detinue* when the chattel, having been lawfully taken, was unlawfully withheld. *Trover and conversion*, another "personal" action of this class, lay to recover the money value of a chattel unlawfully withheld. Other torts gave rise to still other personal actions ex delicto, notably to *trespass vi et armis*, or *trespass*, as it was commonly called, which lay to recover for injuries caused directly by force and violence; and *trespass on the case*, or, shortly, *case*, which lay when the injury was not the immediate result of force.

A breach of contract was redressed through various "personal" actions ex contractu, as *debt*, ro recover a specific sum of money due by contract express or implied, *covenant*, to recover damages for a breach of contract under seal, *assumpsit*, to recover damages for a breach of contract not under seal, and *accompt*, to settle mutual accounts when there was a privity between the parties, and to recover the amount due.

A typical pitfall.

Sec. 49. Until but the other day, the current volumes of decisions were full of cases showing the pitfalls which awaited the practitioner among these forms of action. It is beyond the province of this work to examine them, but the technical nature of their distinctions and the practical danger which they involved may be illustrated from a little reminiscence by Mr. David Dudley Field, of the period which immediately preceded the enactment of the New York Code of 1848. "I came near losing a case," said he, "on a policy of insurance by declaring in *assumpsit.* When the policy was produced at the trial, the defendant's counsel insisted that it *had a seal.* If so the action should have been covenant. There was, indeed, a mark on the paper as if it had been stamped with a seal or something like it, but the impression was faint, and the judge, *looking at it without his glasses*, said he could see no seal, and denied the motion for a nonsuit."[1]

(3) *The artificial restrictions of the common law as to the joinder of causes and the joinder of parties.*

Sec. 50. Naturally connected with this hard and fast formulary system of actions was another cause of embarrassment in common law pleading—its artificial restrictions as to joining in one proceeding such different causes of action as might be subsisting at the time between the plaintiff and the defendant, and also as to joining in one suit all the different parties who might be necessary to a complete determination of the controversy before the court. Many things in our older procedure will be the clearer if we remember that the common law, in its earlier stages, was intolerant of judicial discretion, and that this intolerance acquired a definite and permanent shape in the fossilized

[1] 25 Am. Law Rev. 518 (1891).

formalism which dominated our courts of law for more than five centuries of their later history. Its tendency in all questions of joinder was to break up a composite cause of action into different proceedings according to real or fancied distinctions of logic. It mattered little or nothing that the whole controversy could, in fact, be considered by a trial court in one proceeding, or that all the parties were before the court and desirous of settling their dispute in one action, or that time and money would be saved both the parties and the public by permitting a joinder. The different aspects of the controversy were carefully and logically distinguished by the common law. In theory they were distinct things, and the procedure was resolutely differentiated upon this same theory. Questions of convenience, even questions of substantial justice, were not permitted to interfere with the process.

Joinder of causes.

Sec. 51. As to the joinder of different causes in one proceeding, the general principle, as laid down in later times, was that all causes of action between the plaintiff and the defendant might be and should be joined, provided *they were of the same nature, and the same judgment could be given in each.* The rule is sometimes cited in the older books as an instance of the liberality of common law procedure; and, indeed, it is liberal in its terms. But applying it we must not forget the fossilized artificiality of the common law's classification of actions. Whether two causes of action between the same parties were of the same nature depended at common law on very nice distinctions; and its rule as to joinder, although rational enough in its appearance, resulted in many irrational and inconvenient restrictions.

The joinder of equitable with legal causes was, of course, not to be thought of. But the rule went much further than this, much further even than prohibiting the joinder of legal causes of action in tort with legal causes of action in contract. For, among causes of action at law, it forbade the joinder even of some which were wholly ex contractu and the joinder of some which were wholly ex delicto. An example or two may be of service. P claims damages from D because of his alleged breach of a contract under seal and also because of his alleged breach of another contract not under seal; P desires to join his claims in one suit and there make an end of the matter; D has no material objection to offer; the convenience of both parties, of the courts, and of the public will be subserved by a joinder. Nevertheless such a joinder was not permissible at common law. The two claims must be fought out separately; such was the rule of the game. For the action on the one cause was *covenant* and on the other cause, *assumpsit;* and these two actions were different in their nature. Likewies *debt* and *account* could not be joined, although both were actions ex contractu. Nor, among actions ex delicto, could *trespass* be joined with *case;* "for they were actions of distinct natures, and the judgments were different, that in tresspass being in strictness "*quod capiatur*," and that in case being "*quod sit in misericordia.*"

It is significant of the artificial nature of these distinctions that the common law itself departed from them in one instance, and this without apparent reason; *debt* might be joined with *detinue*, although the former was an action ex contractu and the latter an action ex delicto.[1]

[1] The reason suggested is that both actions supposed a detention, the one of money, the other of some collateral chattel: 1 Chit. Pl. 229; 4 Minor's Insts. 367; and the reason was worthy of the distinction.

Joinder of parties.

(a) Suing in conjunction at law.

Sec. 52. A like narrow and technical range of application characterized the common law rules as to the joinder of parties. That one who had an equitable interest in the subject matter of a controversy might join in the action of one who had merely a legal interest in the same subject matter, and thus dispose of the whole question in one proceeding, lay, of course, far beyond the scope of common law procedure; but in the joinder of parties, as in the joinder of causes of action, the common law carried its inflexible differentiation very far among actions of a purely legal nature. It could not give effect to the threefold principle which slowly made its way into courts of equity, (1) that all who have an interest in the subject of the action and in obtaining the relief demanded may properly be joined as plaintiffs; (2) that all who have or claim an interest in the controversy adverse to the plaintiff, or who are necessary parties to a complete determination or settlement of the question, may be joined as defendants; and (3) that if the consent of one who should join as a plaintiff can not be obtained, he may be joined as a defendant. Such a doctrine is now accepted as of course; in England at least, code pleading has gone beyond it. But the courts of law regarded all such questions from a different point of view. Applying a punctilious logic to the definitions of legal rights, and treating these rights as entireties, they relentlessly carried merely logical distinctions into the practical question of who might join in asserting or opposing a legal right. In some cases it was required that all should join even when such joinder was impracticable. In other cases the courts of law forbade a joinder which, while seemingly illogical, would yet have served the real interest of all.

Joinder of plaintiffs.

Sec. 53. If the right was one which the common law defined as *joint*, those who were jointly interested in its enforcement must unite as plaintiffs. There was no way by which a party to such a right could enforce it, either in its entirety or to the extent of his own interest, without the formal cooperation of all who were joined with him in interest. The right must be asserted by all, otherwise it ceased to be joint. It was not enough that all the parties were before the court—that some consented to assert it while the others were brought in among the defendants.

This joint interest had another feature which illustrates very well the doctrine in hand. If one of two or more joint obligees, covenantees, partners, or others having a joint legal interest in a contract, died, the executor or administrator of the deceased could not join the surviving obligee. The whole right of action remained in the survivor or survivors. Nor could the executor or administrator sue alone, even when the deceased alone was entitled to the whole beneficial interest in the contract. To obtain his share the representative must go into equity with a distinct suit against the surviving obligee.[1] And the principle, it will be observed, did not apply merely to such joint interests as are found in a partnership or a trusteeship, where the legal interest is joint in fact and the survivorship is real. It was the general rule.

If, on the other hand, the legal right was such as the law defined as *several*, those who had each a several interest could not join in one suit, however willing they might all be to act together; nor could any of them join. Each must sue alone, otherwise the right was not truly several. The right and interest of each obligee being regarded by the common law as a unit, no two obligees should nullify

[1] 1 Chit. Pl. 11.

this logical character of their respective claims by making them the subject of a single action. Accordingly, when A, B, and C were appointed assignees under a commission of bankruptcy, and A and B each paid half of the solicitor's bill, it was decided that A and B could not maintain a *joint* action against C for his proportion of the money so paid out, but each must bring a separate action against him; and having sued C jointly, A and B were non-suited.[1]

If, however, the right was *joint or several*, the parties jointly or severally interested might all unite in bringing one action or might all sue severally. But they must do the one thing or the other. It was not permissible that some join and others sue separately. The very definition of the right forbade.

Joinder of defendants.

Sec. 54. Essentially the same doctrine governed the joinder of defendants in actions ex contractu. When the promise was joint, all the promisors who were alive, whether principals or sureties, must be sued jointly; when the promise was several, each must be sued separately, even if all the suits were brought at the same time and in the same court; if the promise was joint and several, the action must be against all jointly, or against each separately, but not against *some* of the promisors, or of their survivors, jointly. As in the case of joint right, so in the case of the joint obligation ex contractu—the death o. one of those who were jointly bound left the whole obligation intact as against the survivors. The representative of the deceased could not be made a defendant in an action at law on the promise.

[1] Brand v. Boulcott, 3 B. & P. 235 (1802); Graham v. Robertson, 2 D. & E. 282 (1788). 1 Chit. Pl. 9.

In this connection it is worth noticing that the inflexibility of the common law procedure did not cease with the selection of the parties; in all actions of contract it was inexorably required that the plaintiff should prove his contract against *all* whom he made defendants; he must recover against all or none.

(*b*) *Suing in the alternative, whether at law or in equity.*

Sec. 55. These technical restraints upon the freedom of procedure did not prevail in courts of equity; but there was one respect in which equity also refused to follow the argument of convenience, and fell behind the statutory reforms which our own day has witnessed, at least, in the latest reforms of code pleading.[1] Neither law nor equity would permit two plaintiffs to sue *in the alternative*—to come into court and say, in effect: "One or the other of us is entitled to maintain this action against the defendant; if one is not, then the other is". But the older procedures rigorously enforced the principle that if there were more than one plaintiff, the right of action must be alleged to be in them in conjunction. It often happened, however, in cases in which no question could arise concerning the defendant's liability to one or the other of two persons, in one and the same state of facts, that there was a grave doubt which of the two should bring the action. For example, a sale is made by an agent. It is certain that the defendant is liable on the contract, but to whom? If he is not liable to the agent, he is to the principal; but he is not liable to both. By whom, then, must the action be brought, by the agent or by the principal?

Sec. 56. There are various contingencies in which the

[1] Cf. the provision under the English Judicature Acts (Order XVI, rule 1): "All persons may be joined as plaintiffs in whom the right to any relief claimed is alleged to exist, whether jointly, severally, or *in the alternative.*"

answer to such a question may be involved in doubt. And the same thing is true of several other important and common relations of fact. Thus a doubt frequently arises whether the bailor or the bailee of particular chattels is entitled to sue for an injury to them, whether the consignor or the consignee of goods delivered to a carrier should bring the action concerning them, whether the heir or the devisee should sue with reference to the land. But, in all such cases, the older procedure would not permit the two parties interested in asserting the claim to appear as plaintiffs in the same action and, setting out the facts, claim relief alternatively, that is, pray that, if one is held not entitled to recover, the judgment shall be given for the other. The only thing to be done was for the one or the other to risk an action alone. He was liable, of course, to meet the defense that the action should have been brought by the other, and, if this defense succeeded, the action failed, and nothing remained but for the other to bring a new action. But here, again, the defense might be that the plaintiff in this second action was not entitled to sue—that the action should have been brought by him who had already sued as plaintiff in the first action. "And this result could very well be brought about, that for one matter you might have two actions and a different result in each on the same point." [1]

(4) *The verbiage or the vagueness of common law pleading.*

Sec. 57. Another complaint against common law pleading was that the modes of statement which prevailed in it, even when no question arose as to the form of action, tended to conceal the real facts of the case. It was often difficult and sometimes impossible to discover from a com-

[1] Cunningham & Mattinson, Precdts. 3.

mon law declaration what case *in fact* the other side was required to meet. The defendant, the court, the jury might all be at fault. For, instead of a plain and concise statement of the material facts of the plaintiff's claim there was, in some instances, a complex, abstruse, and technical verbiage, which concealed these facts in overflowing measures of chaff; in other instances there was a vague generality of abstract statement which disclosed nothing. Who, it was asked, in the first half of the nineteenth century, would read a common law declaration to a court or a jury with any expectation of acquainting them with the real facts of the plaintiff's controversy? The same thing held true of other pleadings of fact. If not merely abstract, they were commonly involved "in all that perplexity could suggest or prolixity supply". Not only did common law pleading fail of its chief end, that of "rendering the fact plain and intelligible and bringing the matter to judgment with convenient certainty,"[1] but, through this verbiage or this vagueness, it commonly brought about just the opposite result. It became a positive embarrassment to the administration of justice.

Sec. 58. These faults, however, are hardly to be regarded as innate in common law pleading. In large part they were a parasitical growth which, springing up under the influence of a passing fashion in discourse, fastened itself upon common law pleadings, and flourished there when it had withered elsewhere. They were far from being characteristic of our earlier formal pleading, as we find it six centuries ago. And so it came about that, in later times, the *theory* of the common law left little to be desired in this respect, although its *practice* afforded such rare instances of a plain and concise statement of the substantive facts of a case.[2]

[1] So laid down by Sir Matthew Hale, Hale Hist. Com. Law. 212.

[2] Infra, §63.

The short, nervous, and perspicuous statements of the earlier common law.

Sec. 59. The earlier formal pleadings were, it is true, very technical. They bristled with words of art, with sacerdotal terms vital to the case. Their scope was restricted by the limitations of the writ system. But within such bounds, their mode of statement was simple and direct. Lord Coke looked back to the reigns of Edward the Second, Edward the First, and upward, as to a time when "the pleadings were plain and sensible, but nothing curious, evermore having chief respect to matter and not to forms of words".[1] The same fact was pointed out more than once by Sir Matthew Hale. In the time of the first Edward, says he, pleadings were "short indeed, but excellently good and perspicuous—very short, but very clear; neither loose or uncertain, nor perplexing the matter either with impropriety, obscurity, or multiplicity of words".[2]

Sec. 60. There was a special reason for this. Through the reigns of the first and the second Edward, and possibly as late as the middle of the fourteenth century,[3] pleading was still viva voce. The litigants stood opposite each other at the bar of the court, and the plaintiff stated his case by his own mouth or that of his pleader. Apparently everything advanced in this oral altercation was treated as a matter in fieri. It might be amended, upon discussion and consideration at the bar, or wholly abandoned and other matter resorted to until the pleader felt himself upon safe ground.[4] When settled, however, the plaintiff's statement

[1] Coke, Littleton, 304*a*. "But even in those days, the forms of the register of original writs were punctually observed, and matters in law excellently debated and resolved." Ib.

[2] Hale's Hist. Com. Law, 190, 195, 211.

[3] Stephen suggests a date "about the middle of the reign of Edward III." (1326–1377). Stephen, Pl. (Tyler's ed.), 59.

[4] For an illustration, see 3 Reeves' Hist. Eng. Law, 61 et seq.

of his case—his *narratio*, as it was called in Latin, his *conte*, in French, his *tale*, in the English of that day—was often noted down upon the roll of the court in a clear and direct statement of fact, "short indeed, but excellently good".[1]

Such was the original of a common law declaration. And, when this viva voce pleading at the bar of the court was supplanted by written pleadings, the latter naturally followed for a time the short and pithy forms of statement which characterized the only existing precedents — the records, in the plea rolls, of a suitor's final statement of his case in the oral altercation at the bar.

Illustrations from the plea rolls.

Sec. 61. The simplicity and directness with which these plea rolls often set out the concrete nature of a case, as distinguished from its abstract nature, or merely legal aspect, is well worth noticing. It indicates very clearly that the verbose, artificial, and complex modes of statement which afterwards impeded common law pleading, which, under the influence of the common law, still clog the pleading in more than one code state, were due to causes operating from without, rather than to anything peculiar to our legal nomenclature.

They indicate still another thing, that a plain and concise statement of the material facts of a case was possible and usual even in the midst of the intense formalism of our early procedure; a priori, should such pleadings be possible and desirable in our own day, which has dispensed with formalism. It is a curious fact that, within certain limits, these ancient precedents of pleading are often near

[1] In some instances the Plea Rolls make no further record of the nature of a plaintiff's claim than the name of his writ—as, "One Adam brought the Novel Disseism against his elder Brother," or "One Adam brought the Mordancester against B."

akin, in their simplicity and directness of statement, to what code pleading is expected to be. Their modern tone in this respect may be illustrated by a few close translations from the Plea Rolls. The three following, taken at random, date from about the year 1292:

"One Alice brought a writ of debt against B., for that she gave him twenty pounds worth of chattels by reason that he was to marry her; and he did not marry her."

"A man and his wife Isabelle brought a writ of Waste against B. and Joan his wife, and said that whereas they held certain tenements as the dower of the said Joan, and whereof the reversion belonged to Isabelle, they had wasted there oaks and pear trees and apple trees, each of the value of, etc., to their damage, etc."

"The Abbat of Reading and his men brought the attachment against the bailiffs of Hereford, and said that, whereas King Richard, ancestor of our Lord the King who now is, did by his charter grant to the Abbat of Reading and his men that they should be quit throughout all England of all manner of tolls and payments and from all liability to repairs, there came the aforesaid bailiffs, and by grievous distress extorted from the Abbat and from his men toll and pavage and murage; whereupon, the Abbat Robert, predecessor of this same Abbat, brought the prohibition of our Lord the King to the aforesaid bailiffs, directing them not to distrein for toll, etc.; but not for that did they cease, but after the prohibition they went on as before, in opposition to the commands of our Lord the King, and to the despite of our Lord the King £20, and to the damage of the Abbat and his men £10."

More ancient than the foregoing, but no less modern in its directness of statement, is this case of boycotting in the year 1200: "Matilda, who was the wife of Roger le Passur, complains that John de Mewic had deforced her of her land in Fransham which she recovered against him by judgment of the court, so that no one dare till that land because of him, nor can she deal with it in any way because of him."

Theory and practice of the later pleading.

Sec. 62. Similar instances of a clear and definite statement of the material nature of a plaintiff's case can be found here and there in the reports through all the later history of English procedure. And, through all this period, the common law theory with respect to the nature of the statements in pleading left little to be desired. In point of theory the chief end of common law pleading in this respect was clear enough, and most excellent. It was, indeed, all that the codes themselves seek to obtain. Then and now, according to the mere doctrine of the law, the material nature of a claim should be so stated that, in the first place, the other party may know what ultimate facts he is called upon to meet and thus may be enabled either to deny them as facts or, admitting them to be true, to deny his legal liability under them, and, in the second place, that the court may be able both to discern the facts on which, if admitted to be true or established by evidence, it must declare the law, and to keep the trial and the judgment within the limits of certain material facts affirmed on the one side and denied on the other. Sir Matthew Hale, as we have seen, had carefully pointed out that "the use, nature, and design of pleading is only to render the fact plain and intelligible, and to bring the matter to judgment with a convenient certainty";[1] nor could a law reformer have asked for anything better. In 1779 also, Buller, J., declared no less happily that "it is one of the first principles of pleading that you have only occasion to state facts, which must be done for the purpose of informing the court, whose duty it is to declare the law arising upon those facts, and to apprise the opposite party of what is meant to be proved, in order to give him an opportunity to answer or

[1] Hale's Hist. Com. Law, 212.

traverse it".[1] Here, again, the reformers of the common law could hardly take exception. And so it was laid down by Bacon[2] that "the declaration is an explanation of the plaintiff's writ, in which he expresses at large his complaint, setting forth the nature and quality of his case more fully than in the writ; and, as it is the foundation of his suit, the law requires that it contain certainty and truth, that the defendant may be able to make a proper answer thereto, and the court be enabled to give a right judgment thereon".

Practice in derogation of theory.

Sec. 63. But, while the theory of the common law in these matters was so excellent, it was largely nullified in fact. For, as it happened, the formative period of our written pleadings fell in an age which was given over to pedantic subtleties. The philosophy of the times was a war of words. Naturally enough, the courts of that day, when construing a pleading, applied exceedingly narrow and strict rules of verbal criticism, requiring that the proof correspond to the allegations in the most exact and literal sense. From this arose a host of complex forms of statement, wearisome repetitions of the same state of facts in varying phraseology, and a mixed multitude of other redundancies and verbal niceties. Nor did these narrow artificialities pass away with the fashion of those times. The fear of a variance was ever before the mind of the pleader. A wasteful learning of words and phrases, approved in precedents, continued to burden the administration of justice long after other sciences had resorted to more simple and direct methods.

Involved in all that perplexity could suggest or prolixity

[1] King v. Lyme Regis., 1 Doug. 159 (1779).
[2] Abridg. Pleas and Pleading, B.

supply, these "special pleadings," as they were called, frequently became masses of verbiage in which the grain of fact was concealed even from the eyes of trained and learned judges. And this held true not only of the practice in England and the older states of the Union, but in its western states as well, where the woodchopper's axe still echoed around the courthouse. "There are no judges, no matter how learned," declares a formal report of able lawyers to the legislature of Ohio, in 1853, "to whom a statement of facts according to the rules of special pleading will not oftentimes be obscure and difficult to understand;" and the fault thus complained of was no new growth in Ohio, but its inheritance from the common law.

Sec. 64. In strong contrast with special pleading was the practice of pleading generally, by means of "common counts" and "general issues". This, it will be observed, was the opposite of special pleading, and the work of courts and legislatures in their efforts to get away from it. A more complete departure from the true principles of pleading could hardly be devised. It averred the pleader's conception of his abstract legal right in the matter, but disclosed to the court, to the jury, and to the parties, almost nothing of the material nature of the controversy. While special pleading, with its verbiage, subtlety, and abstruseness, often concealed the facts of a case under a multitude of special and technical allegations and repetitions, general pleading often carried brevity so far that it failed to state the facts at all. Yet it became the more popular mode of pleading, so inconvenient was the other.[1] And to remove

[1] The New York Commissioners who framed the Code of 1848 reported that out of eighty-nine cases taken at rendom from the records of New York courts eighteen had the common counts alone and forty-two others the same counts with a copy of a note or bill of exchange annexed. Report, 1848, p. 141.

It is to be noticed also that there were various statutes, previous to the enactment of the reformed pleading, which were intended to prevent the objection that general pleading disclosed nothing material, or to ascertain the real matter in dispute, the courts had resort to a patchwork expedient. The plaintiff was required to furnish a bill of particulars of his claim, the defendant was required to give notice under the general issue of the defense which he intended to make.

the mischief of special pleading; but the tendency was rather towards general pleadiug than towards a plain and concise statement of the material facts. The convenience of general pleading has always appealed to the favorable notice of practitioners. It gained steadily on special pleading; nor perhaps is there matter for surprise that something very near akin to these common counts and general issues has forced its way into the practice of code pleading.

CHAPTER III.

PRELIMINARY MOVEMENT IN ENGLAND AND AMERICA FOR A STATUTORY REFORM OF THE PLEADING.

1. EARLY EFFORTS.
   1. STATUTE OF WESTMINSTER II., C. 24.
   2. CROMWELL'S ATTEMPT AT LAW REFORM.
   3. SUBSEQUENT EFFORTS, PRIOR TO THE AMERICAN REVOLUTION.
2. THE NEW MOVEMENT IN ENGLAND.
   1. ITS RISE—JEREMY BENTHAM.
      1. THE BEGINNING OF THE MOVEMENT.
      2. BENTHAM'S LATER INFLUENCE.
   2. ITS FIRST FRUITS.
      1. PARLIAMENTARY COMMISSIONS.
      2. A SPIRIT OF CRITICISM.
      3. RULES OF HILARY TERM.
3. THE PRELIMINARY MOVEMENT IN THE UNITED STATES.
   1. ITS GENERAL CHARACTER.
   2. ITS PREMATURE EXPRESSION IN THE LIVINGSTON CODES.
   3. THE RISE OF THE NEW YORK CODE.
      1. THE BILLS OF 1842.
      2. THE CONSTITUTIONAL CHANGES OF 1846.
      3. ITS RELATION TO A CODIFICATION OF THE WHOLE LAW.
      4. THE COMMISSION ON PRACTICE AND PLEADINGS.
      5. NATURE OF THE TASK.
      6. DRAFTING THE CODE OF 1848.

Early efforts—Statute of Westminster II.

Sec. 65. These and other faults and defects in our older procedure often resulted in a practical denial of justice. It was no new problem which the American codes of civil procedure and the English judicature acts attempted to solve—the harmonizing of adjective and substantive law. Parliament had essayed it on a liberal scale as early as the year 1285, when one of the famous enactments of Westminster the Second provided for the framing of new writs whenever no existing writ was found in a case which fell under a recognized right and required a remedy like one already existing, "lest it happen that the court of our Lord the King be long deficient in doing justice to the suitors".[1] And but for the illiberality of the following century, this statute might have been the magna charta of a new pleading which, spontaneously developing with the development of substantive rights, would have been adequate to the needs of modern civilization. The archaic spirit, however, which ever sacrifices substance to form, was too strong in the fourteenth century for a development of this sort.

Cromwell's attempt at law reform.

Sec. 66. In the middle of the seventeenth century, with the unsettling of ancient institutions in the days of the Commonwealth, a door seemed to be opened for radical reforms in the law. Oliver Cromwell was earnest for it. Parliament was active toward the same end. A commission was appointed "to take into consideration what inconveniences there are in the law, and how the mischiefs that grow from the delays, the changeableness, and the irregularities in law proceedings may be prevented, and the speediest way to reform the same". Many reformatory acts were drafted. A general code of laws was compiled. The movement even went so far as to threaten the separate existence of chancery. For the Little Parliament, finding in the administration of the law "grievances greater than could be borne, finding, for one thing, twenty-three thousand

[1] 13 Edw. I., c. 24, (1285).

causes, from five and thirty years' continuance, lying undetermined in chancery, was of the opinion that some court ought to be contrived which would actually determine these and like causes; and that, on the whole, chancery would be better for the abolition''. A vote to this effect passed in 1653. But, in this as in most other respects,[1] the promise or threat of the time exceeded its performance, and largely because of opposition by the lawyers.[2] ''These sons of Zeruiah,'' said Cromwell, ''are yet too strong for us; and we can not mention the reformation of the law but they presently cry out we design to destroy propriety.''

Subsequent efforts prior to the American Revolution.

Sec. 67. Nevertheless, among the lawyers both before and after this time, there were some who pointed out the urgent need for a change. A very little this side of Oliver Cromwell's day, about a century before the American Revolution, Sir Matthew Hale recalled the thought of the profession to the true aim of pleading. ''Its nature and design,'' said he, ''was only to render the fact plain and intelligible, and to bring the matter to judgment with a convenient certainty.'' The learned judge was very clear

[1] One innovation which was effected was the change from Latin to English as the language of judicial records. It is significant that even this was premature. After the restoration the courts went back to Latin, and so continued until 1730. Cf. Stats. 4 Geo. II., c. 26; 3 Bl. Com. 322. Cf. White's Outlines, p. 102.

[2] "It was mainly by this attack on the lawyers, and attempt to abolish chancery, that the Little Parliament perished. Tithes helped, no doubt; and the clamors of a safely settled ministry, presbyterian-royalist, many of them. But the lawyers exclaimed: 'Chancery? Law of the Bible? Do you mean to bring the Mosaic Dispensation, then; and deprive men of their properties? Deprive men of their properties; and us of our learned wigs, and lucrative long-windedness,—with your search for "single justice" and "God's law," instead of learned-sergeant's law?' There was immense carousing in the Temple when this parliament ended; as great tremors had been in like quarters while it continued." —Carlyle's Oliver Cromwell, Nov. 1653.

in his conviction that pleading had long since "begun to degenerate from its true use and end, and to become a piece of nicety and curiosity"; and he added with some irony that the improvement which his own day had effected in the matter was only too much witnessed by "the length of the pleadings, the many unnecessary repetitions, and the many miscarriages of causes upon small and trivial niceties in pleading".[1]

Nor did legislation in England or America omit all efforts to relieve the suitors. But there was little substantial progress. As formerly, so now, the task of change, when approached at all, was approached with trembling hands. In the four hundred years which preceded the American Revolution, in the seventy years which followed it, the reformatory statutes were comparatively few in number and all were timid in spirit. So timid and imperfect were they that the root of the evil remained untouched. The real causes of a mischief which was felt by all lay embedded in the foundation of a great and venerable system. They were not easily reached; their removal was not to be dreamed of. Meanwhile, our substantive rights steadily grew in number and complexity, and the art of pleading tended more and more to impede the practical administration of justice. "What would Sir Matthew Hale have said had he lived in these times of nicety and curiosity?" queried a learned English lawyer in 1820—"times in which pleading seems to be involved in all that perplexity can suggest or prolixity supply."[2] And what was true in England was true also in most of the American states, for the English precedents, brought to this country at the time of their most "sterile exuberance," had been copied by our practitioners with painstaking care. On both sides of the Atlantic delays and ex-

[1] Hale, Hist. Com. Law, 212.

[2] Hale, Hist. Com. Law, 212, Runnington's note.

penses continued to wear out the patience of litigants and to confiscate their property. A steadily increasing number of suitors, driven to and fro from law to equity and from equity to law, entangled in a labyrinth of actions, or lost in a wilderness of words, suffered what they felt and knew to be a practical and substantial injustice. The demand for relief became more and more urgent, and slowly took form and movement.

The new movement in England.
Its rise—Jeremy Bentham.

Sec. 68. This growing demand was not a formless clamor of ignorance. Here and there among the lawyers were critical minds who saw the need for a change; and the cause of reform found a champion—as able, bold, and tireless as any reform could wish—in Jeremy Bentham.

His entrance into the history of English and American law is one of its dramatic incidents. He had been a pupil of Blackstone. In the year 1769, when Bentham was but twenty-one, the first complete edition of Blackstone's Commentaries was published. High as Blackstone still stands in the esteem of lawyers on both sides of the Atlantic, the excellence of his book as a popular exposition of law is probably underrated among us. It is not only the typical achievment of the eighteenth century, in the history of our law,[1] but it was the first book in which the general system of English law had been set forth in an attractive form, even with consummate literary skill. For the first time in our history the study of legal rules was not repellant. And the work had a further claim upon contemporary popularity. Our ancient legal doctrines, thus placed as in the gladsome light of jurisprudence, were also treated by Blackstone with the reverent spirit in which the rank

[1] Cf. remarks of Pollock, in 3 Law Quar. Rev. 344 (1887).

and file of the profession then delighted to consider them, as worthy of their highest veneration. For Blackstone was an excellent representative of the legal mind of his day — that conservative mental attitude which regards whatever is established law as an immutable principle of justice; and he had expressed this spirit of the times more clearly, more elegantly, than it had ever been expressed before.

Sec. 69. But hardly had Blackstone's able and splendid laudation of the common law been heard than his pupil, Bentham, sounded a rude blast of opposition. It was the beginning of a long-continued assault upon entrenched abuses in the administration of justice. It was the first note of a contest whose end is not yet, but which has already accomplished the greatest revolution known in our law within the last six centuries.

The year for the beginning of this revolution, if a precise date can be given to so gradual a movement, may be said to have been 1776. It was the year of Bentham's first book, his "Fragment on Government," which, in general, was a criticism of Blackstone's Commentaries at large and in particular was an attack upon his "Introduction".[1] Bentham himself has described his pamphlet—it

[1] How clearly this little book struck the keynote of Bentham's opposition to Blackstone, appears in the preface to the first edition. "If," says Bentham, "it be of importance and of use to us to know the principles of the element we breathe, surely it is of not much less importance, nor of much less use, to comprehend these principles, and endeavor at the improvement of our *laws*, by which alone we breathe it in security. If to this endeavor we should fancy any author, especially any author of great name, to *be*, and as far as could in such case be expected, to *avow himself*, a determined and persevering enemy, what should we say of him? We should say that the interests of reformation, and through them the welfare of mankind were inseparably connected with the downfall of his works: of a great part, at least, of the esteem and influence which these works might, under whatever title, have acquired. Such an enemy it has been my misfortune (and not mine only) to see, or fancy at least, I saw, in the anthor of the celebrated

was hardly more than that—as "the very first publication by which men at large were invited to break loose from the trammels of authority and ancestor-worship on the field of law". But Bentham's effective work came later. It continued for half a century, steadily growing in intensity, and ceased only when death stayed his hand in 1832.[1]

Bentham's later influence.

Sec. 70. For many years Bentham's was the only voice raised against "ancestor-worship on the field of law". His bold and vigorous attacks, however, set men to thinking. Slowly thoughtful lawyers gathered about him. His influence was felt on both sides of the Atlantic.[2] His cherished plans, often radical to the extreme, were indeed never to be realized in full, at least within his century. Many of them were impracticable even according to present standards; nor have Anglo-Saxon peoples been able to cut loose from their historical development. But Bentham's criticisms and those of his followers gave point and force to demands for relief which were founded on something more than theory—on a long-felt, substantial failure of justice. In some measure, also, the suggestions of Bentham's analytical school supplied lines of action for reformers who urged less radical changes. "I do not know a single law reform effected since Bentham's day," said

Commentaries on the Laws of England: an author whose works have had, beyond comparison, a more extensive circulation, have obtained a greater share of esteem, of applause, and consequently of influence (and that by a title on many grounds so indisputable) than any other writer who on that subject has ever yet appeared. It is on this account that I conceived, some time since, the design of pointing out some of what appeared to me the capital blemishes of that work, particularly this grand and fundamental one, the *antipathy to reformation.*"

[1] It is a curious coincidence that the year of Bentham's death is the year of the flood tide of the movement towards common law reform in England.

[2] See the note in Dillon's Laws and Jurisprudence, 337.

Sir Henry Maine in 1874, "which can not be traced to his influence."[1] By slow degrees the movement grew until, about the year 1825, it assumed more than respectable proportions in both England and America.

Its first fruits.
(a) Parliamentary commissions.

Sec. 71. Excepting the sporadic case of the Livingston codes in Louisiana,[2] the first tangible results of this movement appeared in England. Beginning in 1828—four years after the appearance of Stephen on Pleading—parliament appointed a series of commissions to inquire into the law of procedure, and other subjects, and report such changes as should be enacted. Very radical suggestions were considered by these commissions, but their recommendations to parliament, especially as to matters of pleading, were at first extremely conservative. It was still a prevailing doctrine that the existing rules of common law pleading were founded "in strong sense and in the soundest and closest logic, and so appear when well understood and explained". The venerable system, it was said, could be adapted to the demands of modern times without impairing its integrity. Any attempt to erect a new system would cause greater mischief than the retention of the old.

Sec. 72. This halting conservatism in the earlier stages of the movement is well shown in a report made in 1831 by the commissioners on common law practice and procedure. "An opinion," say these commissioners in their third report, "is entertained by some persons that all distinc-

[1] Maine, Early Hist. Institutions, 397. "If the analytical jurists [Bentham and his school] failed to see a great deal which can only be explained by the help of history, they saw a great deal which, even in our day, is imperfectly seen by those who, so to speak, let themselves drift with history." Ib.

[2] Infra, §76.

tion as to Form of Action should be abolished and that the plaintiff should be allowed to state the circumstances of his claim, or complaint, in ordinary language, free from all restraint of technical method; and there are others who, without rejecting forms of action altogether, think that those which are now established should be resolved into more convenient and simpler divisions. We can not, however, persuade ourselves that, with respect to the forms now in common use, any considerable change would be expedient, with the exception only of the new shape which in our second report we have proposed to give to the action of ejectment. It is not that we are insensible to certain imperfections and inconveniences incident to these forms, for we feel that their classification is arbitrary and otherwise defective. But in this, as in so many other cases, we are presented with a choice of difficulties. To those who have observed the inconveniences which in other systems of judicature are found to flow from the want of fixed forms of action, it will scarcely be doubtful that they are an invention of real merit and importance. They tend most materially to secure that certainty in the right of action itself, which is one of the chief objects of jurisprudence; they form a valuable check to vagueness and prolixity of statement; and in this and other respects they are essential to the convenient application of the rules of pleading."

Whether the other great evil, the separate administration of law and equity, should be abolished was hardly deemed a practical question at this time. It was apparently the general impression that the distinct systems for the administration of legal and equitable rights were founded in the nature of eternal entities. Nor was the question of their fusion brought to an issue in England until about thirty years later.

(*b*) *A spirit of criticism.*

Sec. 73. Apart from actual legislation, these commissions and the movement of which they were a part had this result, at least: they shook the self-satisfied conservatism of the English bench and bar. A spirit of criticism was abroad in the land. Many became questioners of things established, even in the province of the law. So marked, indeed, was this new spirit among English lawyers that it presently attracted attention on the other side of the Atlantic, and roused a similar spirit there. "The zeal and activity with which the reform in the law has been conducted in England within the last few years," said an American law writer in 1832,[1] "present a strong contrast to the indifference with which the subject had for a long time previously been regarded in that country by the great body, both of the profession and the public. Till recently the lawyers, with very few exceptions, appeared to feel themselves bound, on all occasions, to stand forward in defence of the system under which they had been brought up. But now they are among the most busy in examining the law, pointing out its defects, and suggesting remedies."

(*c*) *Rules of Hilary Term.*

Sec. 74. The time, however, was not yet ripe for a radical reform. The official recommendations made by the parliamentary commissions referred to above fell far short of the suggestions considered by them; and the legislation which followed was no less conservative. It found its chief expression in the Rules of Court of Hilary term—the "New Rules" of 1834.[2] But these hardly touched the

[1] 7 Am. Jurist, 80.

[2] They were framed by the judges in pursuance of the statute of 3 & 4 Wm. IV., *c.* 24—an elaborate act which is as remarkable for its latitude in some questions as for its restrictions in others.

weightier matters of reform. Fear of plunging into a chaos brought the movement to a pause at the very threshold of its work. The "new rules" were a compromise—a lame and unhappy compromise, as it turned out—between the conservatism of six centuries and the demand of modern criticism, of modern convenience; and they had a marked professional leaning towards the past rather than the future. Their chief aim was to remedy what were essentially but incidental defects and faults in the existing systems, the vagueness of general pleading, the prolixity of special pleading, the necessity of certain formal allegations. However well intended and highly praised, the "new rules" amounted to little more than "an attempt to stave off an immediate pressing difficulty by a patchwork scheme of modification and suspension". And, like most such attempts, they not only fell behind the real needs of the day, but tended to retard the progress of reform. Through them the real reform of common law procedure in England was put off for twenty years.

The preliminary movement in the United States.

Sec. 75. Meanwhile, a similar movement had begun in America and, after some delay, was making startling progress here. Once fairly under way, the reform movement in several of the United States went at a leap beyond the boldest designs then entertained in England. The most radical schemes of reform were hastily vested with the authority of law. And it is to be remembered that the enactment of what was then appropriately enough called the "American system" preceded and, in a large measure, inspired the sweeping changes which characterize the English legislation of 1873.

Its premature expression in the Livingston codes.

Sec. 76. But just here it is worth while to go back a little in the history of American law and notice the curious episode of the Livingston codes. Speaking generally, the movement towards a statutory reform of common law procedure assumed a definite and aggressive shape in the United States at a somewhat later day than in England; but the new critical spirit whose earlier effects in England have been noticed had one tangible result of moment on this side of the Atlantic at a very much earlier day than these parliamentary commissions. It occurred in Louisiana under conditions which were quite out of the ordinary. Shortly after the acquisition of that territory by the United States, the question arose whether the provisions of the federal constitution as to the right of trial by jury and procedure according to the common law did not at one stroke impose upon Louisiana the whole system of English legal practice, unknown and repugnant although it was there. In 1804 a test case was made up. After earnest discussion the court held that, although the constitution of the United States required trial by jury, and made obligatory the observance of common law rules in appellate proceedings in federal courts, yet the people of Louisiana were free, in much the greater part of their legal procedure, to follow a different system. The way was thus opened for a liberal and rational treatment of the whole subject of judicial procedure. It was such an opportunity as Bentham dreamed of—such a result as, in 1804, was to be found nowhere else in the United States or in England. And, as it happened, a man worthy of the occasion was at hand. Edward Livingston had removed from New York to Louisiana shortly before the case just referred to came up for trial. He appeared for those who opposed the adoption of the common law procedure; and, following up his success in the courts, he recommended to the legislature a simplification of the existing system, which was a medley of civil and Spanish law. His suggestion meeting with approval, Livingston promptly drafted what was in effect a new code of procedure. It was adopted by the Louisiana legislature in 1805.[1] Nor did the impulse cease with this. Fifteen years later the legislature provided for the appointment "of a person learned in the law" who should prepare and present a code of criminal law, "designating all criminal offenses punishable by law, defining the same in clear and explicit terms, designating the punishment to be inflicted on each, laying down the rules of evidence on trials, directing the whole mode of procedure, and pointing out the duties of the judicial and executive officers in the performance of their functions under it".[2]

Sec. 77. A little later this very comprehensive task was entrusted by the legislature to the hands of Mr. Livingston. With characteristic thoroughness he prepared complete codes of crimes and punishments, procedure, and evidence, and explained the nature of each with an elaborate introduction. His plan had been reported in advance to the Louisiana legislature; he had been earnestly requested to complete it, and he did complete it. But the codes when completed were not enacted in Louisiana. Their influence, however, both at home and abroad, was hardly the less for that. They were received with the

[1] Act of April 10, 1805. In many respects this code anticipated the codes of half a century later. "Under it, all suits were commenced by petition, addressed to the court and filed with the clerk, stating the names and residence of the parties, the cause of action, with places and dates, without prolixity, scandal, or impertinence, and concluding with a prayer for relief. The defendant was brought into court by citation, issued by the clerk, and served by the sheriff. On proof of service, and of failure to answer, judgment was entered in favor of the plaintiff. The defendant appearing and answering, either party could demand a jury." Hunt, Life of Livingston, 117.

[2] Act of February 10, 1821.

highest praise in America and in Europe, and that by recognized leaders in the law. They have since proved "an unfailing fountain of reforms" on both sides of the Atlantic. Their influence was especially noteworthy in this respect: they went far towards demonstrating the advantages of codification "in giving precision, specification, accuracy, and moderation" to a system of law.[1] They appeared, indeed, before the times were ripe for such a reform, but in no small measure they prepared the minds of men for the great changes which came a quarter of a century later. It is worth noting also, as indicating the intimate, mutual bearings of the reform movements in England and America, that Livingston looked to Bentham as his teacher in all these things.[2]

Rise of the New York code.

Sec. 78. Important and interesting as they were, the Livingston codes can hardly, however, be regarded as directly influencing the rise of code pleading in this country. The agitation which was immediately connected with that event began a little after the year 1826. It was most conspicuous in the State of New York, where the legal procedure had been modeled very closely after the English system, and where the relations with the mother country had continued to be both constant and intimate.[3] By 1842 the movement had made such progress that a bill was introduced into the New York legislature "for the more simple and speedy administration of justice in civil cases in the courts of common law"; and, since law and equity were

[1] "You have done more in giving precision, specification, accuracy, and moderation to the system of crimes and punishments than any other legislator of the age, and your name will go down to posterity with distinguished honors." Chancellor Kent to Livingston, in February, 1826. Hunt, Life of Livingston, 281.

[2] See 11 Bentham Works (Bowring ed.) 23, 51; Hunt, Life of Livingston, 96*n*.

[3] Cf. remarks of David Dudley Field, 25 Am. Law. Rev. 515, 519, (1891.)

then separated by the New York constitution, another bill was introduced to bring about a like result in the courts of equity. These measures failed of their intended effect at the time, but, four years later, when the New York constitution was revised, the demand for a radical reform found more emphatic expression, and a remedy was attempted. The new constitution, adopted in November, 1846, abolished the court of chancery, created a court "having general jurisdiction in law and equity,"[1] and required that the next legislature should provide for the appointment of three commissioners, whose duty it should be "to revise, reform, simplify, and abridge the rules and practice, pleadings, forms, and proceedings of the courts of record of this state, and to report thereon to the legislature".[2]

Sec. 79. This contemplated reform, even at its outset, was part of a larger plan, that of codifying the whole law, both substantive and adjective. For the New York constitution of 1846 provided also that the legislature, at its first session after the adoption of the constitution, should appoint three commissioners "to reduce into a written and systematic code the whole body of the law of this state, or so much and such parts thereof as to the said commissioners shall seem practicable and expedient".[3] The commission thus appointed was distinct from the one referred to above and differently constituted.[4] Its members were designated in the New York statutes as "Commissioners of the Code," while the members of the other bore the statutory name of "Commissioners on Practice and Pleadings". The two commissions so divided the entire work between them that one took the codification of the law of procedure, and the other, the "Commissioners of the Code," took the

[1] Art. XIV., § 5, Art. VI, § 3, N. Y. Const. of 1846.

[2] N. Y. Const. of 1846, Art. VI, § 27.

[3] N. Y. Const. 1846, Art. 1, § 17.

[4] Act of April 8, 1847, N. Y. Laws, ch. 59, § 8.

codification of the rest of the law. The work of this commission will be noticed hereafter; it is with the commission on practice and pleadings that we have now to do.

Sec. 80. When it came to the appointment of the latter commissioners, the legislature prescribed their duty somewhat more explicitly, instructing them, in accordance with a memorial from fifty lawyers of New York, "to provide for the abolition of the present forms of action and pleadings in cases at common law; for a uniform course of proceedings in all cases whether of legal or equitable cognizance, and for the abandonment of all Latin and other foreign tongues, so far as the same shall by them be deemed practicable, and of any form and proceeding not necessary to ascertain or preserve the rights of the parties".[1]

Nature of the undertaking.

Sec. 81. Most of the lawyers and many of the general public were hostile to so radical a change.[2] The task imposed was, indeed, unparalleled in the history of English or American jurisprudence. A great and venerable system, deep-rooted in the past of a conservative profession and

[1] Act of April 8, 1847, N. Y. Laws, ch. 59, § 8.

[2] Whenever any considerable amelioration has been obtained, either in the form or in the substance of the law, in procedure or in doctrine, it has come from a minority of lawyers supported by the voices of laymen. I do not complain of this. It is the nature of the profession. The lawyer becomes wedded to old things by the course of his daily avocations. He reposes upon the past. He is concerned with what is, not with what should be. The rights he defends are old rights, grounded, it may be, in the ages that have gone before him. Nor is this conservative tendency altogether to be regretted. Rooted in the past, and covered with the branches of many generations, the legal profession may be said to stand like the oak as a barrier and shelter in many an angry storm, though it may at the same time dwarf the growth beneath. With its innumerable traditions and its sentiments of honor, it is one of the strong counteracting forces of civilization, and we should hold fast to it, with all its good and in spite of its evil, though we may have occasion to combat and overcome its resistance to reforms as often as new wants and altered circumstances make them necessary." David Dudley Field, 1 Jurid. Rev. 18, 20 (1889).

overshadowing the land, was to be supplanted in a day. The prejudices of thousands of practitioners must be disregarded and the habits of their daily lives reversed; the active opposition of many able men recognized as profoundly learned in the law must be overborne; a community accustomed, especially in such matters, to be led by their lawyers must be assured of safety in turning aside to follow a few reformers. In the face of such obstacles the three commissioners were asked to design and construct a new system which they could recommend as capable of doing all the work of the old, and doing it better.

Drafting the code of 1848.

Sec. 82. One member of the commission resigned rather than comply with the command of the statute. The other two, Mr. Arphaxed Loomis and Mr. David Graham, had publicly expressed themselves against changes so sweeping as those contemplated; but, disregarding opinions no longer held, they now accepted the appointment in the spirit in which it was made. Most opportunely, also, Mr. David Dudley Field, who at first had been thought too radical in his plans of reform to hold a place on the commission, was chosen to fill the vacancy, and the three united in the promptest execution of the work.

Some portions of the proposed code were already formulated in the two bills which had been submitted to the legislature in 1842, "for the more simple and speedy administration of justice in civil cases". But, with all allowances, it is seldom that so great a work is accomplished in so short a time. The commission was first appointed by the legislature in April, 1847, and reorganized, as indicated above, in the following September; five months later it reported the draft of an act, in fifteen chapters, and nearly four hundred annotated sections, "to simplify and abridge the practice, pleadings, and proceedings of the court of this state".

PART II.

ENACTMENT OF THE DIFFERENT CODES, AND THEIR RELATIONS INTER SE.

CHAPTER IV.

General Aspects of the Change.

1. Its rapid movement.
    1. Its impetuous haste in New York.
    2. Its course in other states and countries.
        1. The real significance of the New York enactment.
        2. The result in five years.
        3. The result in twenty-five years.
2. Distinctions in its order of treatment.
    1. The distinction between codes of the United States and codes of the British Empire.
    2. The three aspects of the change within the United States.
        1. "Code" states.
        2. "Quasi-code" states.
        3. Partial conformity in federal courts.

Impetuous haste in New York.

Sec. 83. So far we have dealt with code pleading in its formative state; we now come to its realizations. The official draft of the New York code, framed and filled in, as we have seen, with astonishing rapidity, was passed into an operating law no less quickly. The commissioners' bill, "to simplify and abridge the practice, pleadings, and proceedings" of the New York courts, having been reported to the legislature about the beginning of March, 1848, was considered, amended in some eighty of its three hundred and ninety-one sections, and passed before the middle of the following month.[1] And the new law, revolutionary as it was in theory and in its practical effects, went into operation on the first day of the following July.

Less expedition might have imperiled the whole enterprise. Opposition to the measure was bitter and intense, among both lawyers and laymen. Given time for organization, the "sons of Zeruiah," it was feared, might again, as in Cromwell's day,[2] have been too strong for the spirit of law reform. But, being once clothed with the authority of actual, operating law, the new movement was better able to make head against that "antipathy to reformation" which lawyers feel, and, perhaps, are bound to feel.

The course in other states and countries.

Sec. 84. If the legislation thus begun had gone no further, the result would still have been among the great events in the history of modern law. But the really significant thing here is that the enactment of this New York code opened, as it were, the floodgates of reformatory legislation, and determined the course of its progress. Within five years after 1848, the older systems of pleading at law and in equity had been dispossessed of their inheritance by similar codes in Missouri, California, Iowa, Kentucky, Minnesota, Indiana, and Ohio; the civil procedure of Mississippi, Massachusetts, and Alabama had been largely reformed upon somewhat similar lines; the procedure of the English courts of law and of equity had been simplified by the acts of 1852. Within twenty-five years, that is, by the end of 1873, the New York code of 1848 had been enacted in substance, and often in its very letter, by sixteen other American commonwealths — Oregon, Washington, Nebraska, Wisconsin, Kansas, Nevada, Dakota, Arizona, Montana, Idaho, North Carolina, Wyoming, Arkansas,

[1] New York Laws, 1848, ch. 371, Act of April 12.

[2] Ante, §66.

South Carolina, Florida,[1] and Utah; the procedure on the law side of the federal courts had been brought into conformity with these same principles, wherever they prevailed in the state courts; and in England the great Judicature Act of 1873 had prescribed for our most ancient courts of law and of equity a more radical change of this same general nature than any which had preceded it in America—a greater change withal than any other in English law for six centuries.

Distinction in the order of treatment.

Sec. 85. In the pages which follow I shall attempt to trace, as briefly as may be, the progress of this legislation from state to state, from commonwealth to commonwealth, among the English-speaking peoples of the new world and the old. I shall endeavor also to point out, in passing, such of the characteristic features of the different codes which make up the general system of code pleading as relate to this historical development. But, in considering it, two or three distinctions are to be kept in mind—primarily, the distinction between the codes of the United States and the codes of the British Empire. They belong, indeed, to one movement, but the latter are a more recent development of code pleading. Their influence, however, is apparent in one or two of our later codes, that of Connecticut, for instance. The British codes, moreover, are the result of a gradual movement, whereas with us code pleading came *per saltum*. But the beginnings of the movement in both cases are not far apart. The year 1848 may be fixed as the date in America; the year 1852, as the date in England.

Sec. 86. Within the United States also a distinction is to be kept in mind. Here the reform has three aspects.

[1] Which state, however, presently receded from this advanced position.

A majority of all the states have followed the lead of New York with more than common unanimity. For convenience we may call them the "code states," which in fact is their more common designation in our legal nomenclature. Some states, however, while reforming their procedure upon similar lines, have not ventured quite so radical a change. These can not be called common law states—their departure from the older procedure is too radical for that. They are more nearly code states, but it is confusing to refer to them as such. Perhaps the most convenient way will be to group them under a distinct head, as "quasi-code states". The progress of the change has affected also the procedure of the federal courts, but in a different and altogether unique way—their procedure at law being made to conform to that of the state in which the court is sitting, while their procedure in equity remains independent. The enactment of the reformed procedure in the United States has, therefore, these three heads, (1) Its progress in the "*code states*"—the procession, as it were, of the codes, their uniformity, and their stability; (2) Its progress in the *quasi-code states*; (3) Its progress in the *federal courts*.

Sec. 87. In the British Empire the reform movement has been kept more closely within one path. The mother country leads the way; the colonial legislatures follow in her footsteps. The model here is found in the Judicature Acts and Rules of 1873 and 1875.

CHAPTER V.

THE CODES OF THE UNITED STATES.

Procession of the codes.

(1) *The New York code*, 1848.

Sec. 88. The enactment of the New York code referred to above, the first of all our operating codes of civil procedure, dates, as I have said, from April 12, 1848. Its statutory name, given by a supplementary act of that date, was wider than its terms, the "Code of Procedure".[1] To distinguish it from the amendments and revisions which presently followed in New York with quick succession, it is commonly referred to as the "code of 1848".

Its characteristic features were those which now serve to distinguish "code pleading" in general, namely, the demolition of the forms of action and suits, with the abolition, in that respect, of the distinction between proceedings for legal and proceedings for equitable relief, and the substitution of a single form of action for the enforcement or protection of private rights; the substitution of concise and plain statements of the substantive facts of a case for the technical and verbose pleadings of the older systems; the granting of authority to the court to bring in all persons who are necessary for a complete determination of the controversy, and to frame its judgment, in this single action, according to the rights, whether legal or equitable, of all the parties, and of each of them.

[1] N. Y. Laws, 1848, chap. 380, 1. The name given was significant of the purpose of the commissioners—"to make full provision for every proceeding in the judicial tribunals from the beginning to the end of every controversy"—rather than of the scope of the act itself, which related only to the proceedings and pleadings in civil actions in courts of record, and to corresponding changes in the jurisdiction and functions of the civil courts. A code of criminal procedure was submitted in 1850, but was not adopted in New York until 1881. The code of civil procedure retained its very comprehensive name on the statute book of New York until 1877.

(2) *The code of Missouri*, 1849.

Sec. 89. The example thus set by New York was followed first of all by Missouri. Early in 1849 the legislature of that state, declared it expedient that the present forms of actions and pleadings in cases at common law should be abolished, that the distinction between legal and equitable remedies should no longer exist, and that a uniform course of proceeding in all cases should be established; and thereupon an elaborate act was passed to reform the pleadings and practice in courts of justice in Missouri.[1] It corresponded closely to the New York statute of the previous year. It was approved on February 24, 1849, and patriotically went into effect on the succeeding fourth of July.

In 1855, the provisions of this code, with amendments here and there, were carried into and distributed among the one hundred and seventy-one chapters of a "Revised Statutes of Missouri". Under the alphabetical arrangement of this work, the newly codified law of pleading lost something of its individuality in Missouri; but most of its essential principles were grouped in one chapter, designated in 1855 as the chapter on "Practice in Civil Cases,"[2] and now officially styled the "Code of Civil Procedure".[3]

(3) *The code of California*, 1850.

Sec. 90. A little over a year after the enactment of the Missouri code of 1849, the California legislature, in its first session, passed a similar act "to regulate proceedings in civil cases in the district court, the superior court of the

[1] Missouri Laws, 1849, p. 78.

[2] Rev. Stats. Missouri, 1855, chap. 128.

[3] Rev. Stats. Missouri, 1889, chap. 162. This chapter is coordinate with one hundred and seventy-four other chapters, on topics great and small, and arranged alphabetically.

City of San Francisco, and the supreme court".[1] This statute was repealed in 1851, when its place was taken by a more elaborate act of wider scope but of the same general tenor and effect.[2]

It is commonly referred to as the "Practice Act," by which name it is distinguished from the California "Code of Civil Procedure."

Its extensive revision.

Sec. 91. The latter is the outcome of a very elaborate revision entrusted to two commissions, one appointed in 1868,[3] the other to complete the task, in 1870.[4] A draft code framed by this second commission was enacted, under the formal designation of the "Code of Civil Procedure," on March 11, 1872, a year which saw the adoption by California of three other elaborate codes, a "Penal Code," a "Political Code," and a "Civil Code".[5] The Code of Civil Procedure ran to more than two thousand sections.

Scarcely had it been established when it was itself subjected to a searching revision. Apparently the motto of the legislature was, Enact first, amend afterwards. Eleven days after its adoption the revised code was put into the hands of a "Revision Commission,"[6] charged, among other

[1] Cal. Laws, 1849–1850, chap. 142, p. 428, Act of April 22, 1850. The relation between New York and California in these matters was closer than appears on the surface. From 1841 to 1848, which was within the period of Mr. David Dudley Field's greatest activity in the cause of law reform, he had as law partner his brother, Mr. Stephen J. Field, now of the Supreme Bench. In 1848 the latter removed to California, and became a member of the judiciary committee of the first California legislature. As such, he was very influential in shaping the progress of California legislation. Nor did this influence cease with this. Other commonwealths in the west looked to California for guidance.

[2] Cal. Laws, 1851, ch. 5, pp. 51–153. Act of April 29.

[3] Cal. Stats., 1867–68, ch. 365, Act of March 28, 1868.

[4] Cal. Stats., 1869–70, ch. 516, Act of April 4, 1870.

[5] Adopted respectively on February 14, March 12, and March 21. The four codes are four statutes, each a distinct act.

[6] Cal. Stats., 1871–2, ch. 350, sec. 13.

things, with the duty of drawing up for the next legislature a bill which would "obviate any conflicts or incongruities" appearing in the code just adopted, and supply whatever was needed to give it completeness. The result, as respects the code of civil procedure, was a hundred pages of proposed amendments, which were adopted in 1874. As thus amended, the California code has preserved its integrity, and has greatly influenced the elaboration of other codes. In essentials, however, it is in line with the codes of the states which came before it.

(4) *The code of Kentucky*, 1851.

Sec. 92. In 1851, also, the new system was established in Kentucky, Iowa, and Minnesota, and its speedy enactment in Indiana and Ohio was provided for by constitutional amendments.

The Kentucky code, drafted by a commission appointed in February, 1850,[1] was enacted on March 22 of the following year, under the statutory name of the "Code of Practice in Civil Cases". It was an act of seventeen titles and seven hundred and forty-five sections. The new law went into effect on August 1, 1851.[2]

Its distinction between law and equity.

Sec. 93. In the main it conformed closely to the New York statute. But there was one important, although not vital, departure. The Kentucky enactment retained a distinction in procedure between the administration of law and the administration of equity—a distinction which was adopted, wholly or partly, in several other codes, and still prevails in Kentucky, Oregon, Iowa, and Arkansas. The code expressly declared that "the forms of all actions and suits heretofore existing are abolished," and that there

[1] Ky. Laws, 1850, p. 28.
[2] Ky. Laws, 1851, pp. 106–212.

should be thenceforth in Kentucky "but one form of action for the enforcement or protection of private rights and the redress or prevention of private wrongs, which shall be called a civil action";[1] but the proceedings in this civil action were to be formally distinguished according as they sought legal or equitable relief.[2] Under the terms of the statute, a plaintiff might prosecute his action by equitable proceedings in all cases where courts of chancery, before the adoption of the code, had jurisdiction, and he must so proceed in all cases where such jurisdiction was exclusive. In all other cases, the action was required to be by "ordinary" proceedings.

This distinction, however, was hardly an essential departure from the spirit of the new procedure. It amounts to little more than a rule of practice, that equity cases shall be tried on separate dockets from cases at law. The general provisions of the code applied to both classes of proceedings; the pleadings in both were framed alike, except that the title of the petition in an equitable proceeding bore a distinctive name; a mistake in going into equity was readily corrected.

In the main, the Kentucky code has continued unaltered in substance and in form despite some revision. It has kept its name, "Civil Code of Practice," and preserved its identity as a distinct body of law. Unlike a number of the codes, it has not grown greatly in bulk.[3]

[1] Ky. Laws, 1851, p. 107; cf. Ky. Civil Code of Practice, 1895, §§ 4, 5.

[2] The earliest provisions of the Kentucky code made a somewhat nicer distinction on this point than do the present terms. The latter declare that "there shall be but one form of action"; and that "*actions* are ordinary or equitable," which might seem to involve a difference of form. The earlier provision was that "the *proceedings* in a civil action may be of two kinds: 1, ordinary; 2, equitable."

[3] In 1851 this Kentucky code comprised seven hundred and forty-one sections; in 1895 it comprised eight hundred and thirty-nine sections. However, one title of the original act, that on "the time of commencing civil actions," has been transferred to the General Statutes.

(5) *The code of Iowa*, 1851.

Sec. 94. The inception of the Iowa code antedated the code of Kentucky. As early as 1848 the first general assembly of Iowa appointed a commission of three to prepare "a complete and perfect code of laws, as nearly as may be, of a general nature only".[1] The labors of this commission resulted in the Iowa "Code" of 1851, of which Part Third,[2] relating to "courts and the procedure therein," was in effect a code of procedure, derived from the New York act, and agreeing with it in substance. But the terms of the parent act were so far departed from that it was often difficult to apply the decisions of other code states to the illumination of the Iowa law. In 1860 a new statute, formally designated as a "Code of Civil Practice," was substituted for the earlier act, and forms the basis of the existing procedure in Iowa.[3]

This code of civil practice, like the Kentucky code, from which it was largely derived, made a formal distinction in procedure between a demand for legal and a demand for equitable relief. The departure was founded upon a supposed requirement of the Iowa constitution, "not conceded by the code commissioners, but deferred to because so fixed in the legal mind of Iowa". It was followed in a number of territorial codes. The distinction has vanished from most of these, or their successors, but it is still retained in the Iowa statutes.

Individuality of the Iowa code.

Sec. 95. Besides the somewhat uncommon feature mentioned above, the Iowa code is readily distinguished in another respect. It has more of an individuality than is

[1] Iowa Laws, 1848, p. 42.

[2] Iowa, Code of 1851, §§ 1543–2564.

[3] Iowa Laws, Rev. of 1860, Part Third, §§ 2605–4187; Code of 1873, Part Third, §§ 2504–3844; McClain's Annotated Code (1888), §§ 3709–5124.

found elsewhere among the codes of civil procedure, excepting only the recent practice act of Connecticut. While the essential principles of the reform were carefully observed, and many sections of the existing codes were copied, with literal exactness, into the Iowa statute of 1860, no one of these codes was adopted, either wholly or for the most part. The act of 1860 was rather a revision and adaptation, not only of all the other codes then in force in the Union, but of the reformatory legislation in Maryland and Massachusetts, and of the English common law procedure acts of 1852 and 1854. "To New York, and England, and Kentucky," say the commissioners of 1860, "we are most largely indebted for our act; but every state which has adopted the new system has contributed something." The act, however, contained considerable new matter, the result of decisions in other code states on questions of civil procedure.

(6) *The code of Minnesota*, 1851.

Sec. 96. In Minnesota, a code of procedure for actions at law was enacted in 1851, as chapters in "the Revised Statutes of the Territory of Minnesota," which were passed by the legislature in its second session.[1] So far as it went, this act followed substantially the provisions of the New York code. But a distinct jurisdiction "in all matters of chancery" was retained for a time; and the term "civil actions," it was expressly declared, was not intended to include suits in chancery.[2] This incongruity was of short duration. In 1853, the court of chancery was abolished, and the suits and proceedings in equity were brought within the provisions of the code, as "civil actions".[3] The Minnesota code was revised in 1866.[4] Altered in a number

[1] Minn. Stats., 1851, ch. 70, et seq.

[2] Ib. ch. 94, §§ 1, 2.

[3] Minn. Stats., 1853, ch. 1, Collated Stats., ch. 9, p. 19.

[4] Gen. Stats., Minn., 1866, ch. 66.

of instances and considerably expanded, it was still not changed in essentials. It retained, and still retains, its form as merely coordinate with a multitude of other chapters in the general body of statute law. As revised in 1866, it has continued to be the foundation of the Minnesota procedure in civil causes.[1]

(7) *The code of Indiana*, 1852.

Sec. 97. In the year 1851, again, the State of Indiana adopted a constitution which required that the next general assembly should appoint a commission "to revise, simplify, and abridge the rules, practice, pleadings, and forms of the courts of justice," and, in particular, made it the duty of this commission to provide for the abolition of the distinct forms of actions at law then in use, and for the administration of justice in a uniform mode of procedure, "without distinction between law and equity".[2] For the discharge of these duties three commissioners were selected by the legislature under a special act, approved on January 5, 1852. It was made an urgent matter that they "report to the present general assembly the result of their labors at the earliest practicable period".[3] And the commission responded so readily that a code of forty-eight articles and eight hundred and three sections, framed on the lines of the New York act, was reported, considered, and passed within six months after the appointment of the commission.[4]

The code thus enacted was embodied in the "Revised Statutes" of 1852, as the first chapter of their second part. It has passed through one revision by the legislature, that

[1] Cf. Compilations of 1878, ch. 66, and 1894, ch. 66.

[2] Ind. Const., 1851, Art. VII, Sec. 20.

[3] Indiana Laws, Special Acts, 1852, pp. 99, 100.

[4] The code was approved June 18, 1852.

of 1881,[1] when, as in later years, it sustained a number of changes; but it has not been materially altered.

(8) *The code of Ohio*, 1853.

Sec. 98. The state of Ohio, likewise, adopted in 1851 a new constitution which required the speedy appointment of a commission to "revise, reform, simplify, and abridge the practice, pleadings, forms, and proceedings of the courts of record," and, "*as far as practicable and expedient*, to provide for the abolition of the distinct forms of action at law now in use, and for the administration of justice by a uniform mode of proceeding, without reference to any distinction between law and equity".[2]

This commission was appointed in March of 1852, and made their first report to the legislature in January of 1853. It was a carefully drawn bill of six hundred and six annotated sections, "to establish a code of civil procedure for courts of record". While the terms of their appointment gave the commissioners some latitude as to abolishing the forms of distinct actions at law, their recommendations to the legislature went to the full extent of the new movement. In its preparation, the bill was affected more or less by the recent enactments on pleading and practice in Kentucky, Missouri, Indiana, and Massachusetts; but it followed in most instances the report of the New York commissioners. It passed the Ohio legislature on March 11, 1853, and went into effect on the first day of the following July.[3]

Sec. 99. With the rest of the Ohio statutes this code was revised in 1879. It underwent a considerable number of minor changes in language and arrangement. It was,

[1] See Laws of 1881, p. 240, Act of April 7; Rev. Stats., 1881, §§ 249, et seq.

[2] Ohio Const., 1851, Art. XIV.

[3] Ohio Laws, 1853, pp. 57-166.

moreover, incorporated into the general body of Ohio statute law; it ceased to be formally designated as a "code of civil procedure, and became Title I of Part III of the "Revised Statutes of Ohio," a work which, its framers declared, might be known, "with equal propriety, as the Ohio Code". But in essentials the code of civil procedure remained as it had been. It has so continued in later years, although the changes have been somewhat frequent. Its distinctive name also survives in popular usage, but the custom is rather to shorten it into the inaccurate designation "Civil Code".[1]

(9) *The code of Oregon*, 1854.

Sec. 100. In 1854 the New York code, in so far as it related to actions at law, was adopted, word for word, by the fifth legislative assembly of the territory of Oregon.[2] A separate act was passed to regulate proceedings in equity.[3]

In 1862 the Oregon state legislature in its second session substituted a more extensive act, of eleven hundred and sixty-seven sections, and officially designated as a "Code of Civil Procedure". It related both to legal and equitable remedies, but the distinction between actions at law and suits in equity was retained in a measure. The pleading in the two jurisdictions was, however, brought under substantially the same principles.[4] The new code was approved on October 11, 1862, and went into effect on June 1, 1863.

[1] That a "code of civil procedure" is not a "civil code," see latter title in index.

[2] Act to regulate proceedings in Actions at Law in the Supreme and District Courts, Ore. Stats., 1854, p. 64.

[3] Ore. Stats., 1854, p. 173.

[4] Ore. Code of Civ. Pro., ch. I, ch. V, et passim.

(10) *The code of Washington*, 1854.

Sec. 101. In 1854, also, a civil practice act, containing the essential provisions of the New York code, was adopted by the territorial legislature of Washington at its first session.[1] Like other codes, it has been considerably amended and supplemented, but not essentially changed. As revised in the "code of 1881," it forms the basis of the present procedure in the State of Washington.[2]

(11) *The code of Nebraska*, 1855.

Sec. 102. The more important provisions of the reformed procedure, selected from the Iowa "Code" of 1851, were formally adopted in 1855 by the first territorial legislature of Nebraska.[3] These enactments were somewhat fragmentary. In 1857 they were recast and supplemented in an act known as the "Code of Nebraska,"[4] the details of which also failed to give satisfaction. In the latter part of 1858 almost all its provisions were repealed, and the Ohio code of civil procedure was adopted in their stead.[5] Most of the terms and divisions of the Ohio statute were followed with literal exactness; but there was one noteworthy departure. As in some other territorial codes, a formal distinction between law and equity was retained in matters of procedure; and a title on chancery practice was subsequently incorporated into the code.[6] But the distinction vanished in 1867, being then expressly abolished by the first legislature under the state constitution.[7]

1 Wash. Laws, 1854-56, pp. 129-221.

2 Wash. Code of 1881, Civil Proced., pp. 35-156; 2 Hill's Ann. Stats. and Codes of Wash., Code of Proced.

3 Neb. Laws, 1855, pp. 55, 56, et seq.

4 Neb. Laws, Act of Feb. 13, 1857, pp. 41-127.

5 Neb. Laws, 1858, pp. 110-214, Act to establish a code of civil procedure, Nov. 1, 1858.

6 Neb. Rev. Stats. of Territory, 1866, p. 520, Title XXIV.

7 Neb. Laws, 1867, p. 71, cf. p. 32.

(12) *The code of Wisconsin*, 1856.

Sec. 103. Two months before the enactment of the New York code of 1848, provision was made by the first state constitution of Wisconsin for the immediate appointment of a commission "to enquire into, revise, and simplify the rules of practice, pleadings, forms, and proceedings, and arrange a system adapted to the courts of record of this state".[1] This task was assigned to three commissioners who had been charged by the same legislature with the duty of revising all the general laws of Wisconsin.[2] The work was hastily begun and hurriedly executed within a year. The result was the "Revised Statutes" of Wisconsin, adopted in 1849. A considerable number of important modifications of the existing rules of pleading appear in this compilation, but it shows no such radical changes as those which characterize the New York code of 1848.[3] Seven years later, however, these enactments were repealed for the most part, and the New York code was adopted by Wisconsin, in substance and often in the letter, by an act approved on October 9, 1856.[4]

This code was revised in 1858, and then once more became part of the Revised Statutes of Wisconsin.[5] It went through another revision in 1878, but without essential change.[6]

[1] Wis. Const., Feb. 1, 1848, Art. VII, § 22.

[2] Wis. Laws, 1848, first session, p. 181, Act of Aug. 19; cf. p. 24, Act of July 13.

[3] Wis. "Rev. Stats.," 1849, Part III.

[4] Wis. Laws, 1856, ch. 120; cf. § 364.

[5] Cf. Rev. Stats. Wis., 1858, Title XXIII.

[6] Cf. Rev. Stats. Wis., 1878, Title XXV; cf. the same title in the admirable compilation of 1889, known as the "Annotated Statutes of Wisconsin."

Other codes in the virgin West, and their general features.

Sec. 104. In the six years from 1859 to 1864, inclusive, the new procedure was established in six recently organized territories, Kansas, Nevada, Dakota, Arizona, Montana, and Idaho. No material innovation was attempted, nor any important changes of form. Each of the new acts was, in the main, a close copy of some code already established, the code of Ohio or New York, but chiefly the code of California. And this, it should be said, holds true generally of the later codes in the West.

(13) *The code of Kansas*, 1859.

Sec. 105. In Kansas the Ohio code was adopted by the fifth territorial legislature, through the act of February 11, 1859, "to establish a code of civil procedure".[1]

Eight years thereafter a commission was appointed, pursuant to an act approved February 18, 1867, "to revise and codify the civil and criminal codes of procedure, and all laws of a general nature of this state". The result was "The General Statutes of Kansas," arranged alphabetically and published October 31, 1868. The code of civil procedure suffered no essential change in the process, and, in spite of the alphabetical arrangement of the work, has preserved its identity, even to its formal designation in the statute book as a code of civil procedure".[2]

(14) *The code of Nevada*, 1861.

Sec. 106. The first act of the first territorial legislature of Nevada adopted "the common law of England, so far as it is not repugnant to or inconsistent with the constitution or laws of the United States, or the laws of the terri-

[1] Kans. Gen. Laws, 1859, ch. 25.

[2] Kans. Gen. Stats., 1880, ch. 80, "Procedure;" Gen. Stats., 1889, ib.

tory of Nevada"; the same legislature adopted also the California practice act of 1851.[1] This code passed through a revision in 1869, and now appears as a chapter of almost nine hundred sections in the General Statutes of the state.[2]

(15) *The code of the Dakotas*, 1862.

Sec. 107. The Ohio code of civil procedure was substantially adopted by the first territorial legislature of Dakota, through an act approved in May, 1862.[3] This act, however, was repealed in 1868, and the New York code of civil procedure was adopted in its place, by a statute which took effect on June 1 of that year.[4] The new code had been adopted with only such revision and adaptation as could be given in the hurried work of legislative committees. There were obvious defects. In 1875 the legislature directed the appointment of a commission to revise all the statute law of the territory. In the progress of this undertaking, which continued for rather more than a year, the code of civil procedure was "completely revised, amended, enlarged, and reenacted," as a distinct code in the "Revised Codes of Dakota". The changes, however, did not affect the essence of the new pleading. After the creation of the States of North Dakota and South Dakota, there was a further revision of this code by the legislature of the former state, but with few material alterations.

(16) *The code of Idaho*, 1864.

Sec. 108. The civil practice act of Idaho dates from February 1, 1864.[5] It was revised in 1875, but suffered few material changes.[6] Twelve years later there was an-

[1] Nevada Laws, Nov. 29, 1861, p. 314.

[2] Nev. Gen. Stats., 1885, ch. XX.

[3] Dakota Laws, 1862, ch. 8.

[4] Dakota Laws, 1867–68, pp. 1–119.

[5] Laws of Idaho, Title I, pp. 77–233.

[6] Rev. Laws of Idaho, 1875, pp. 80–236.

other revision, when this practice act became Part III of the "Revised Statutes of Idaho". It retained, however, a more distinctive name in the statute book, being formally designated also as the "Code of Civil Procedure". In arrangement and classification it has kept close to the California code of civil procedure. One departure, however, is worth noting as being of a very general aspect. To the provision of the California code that there shall be but one form of civil action, the Idaho code adds the express declaration that "in all matters not regulated by this code, in which there is any conflict or variance between the rules of equity jurisprudence and the rules of the common law, with reference to the same matter, the rules of equity shall prevail".[1]

(17) *The code of Montana*, 1865.

Sec. 109. Montana also has received its legislation very largely from California. Early in 1865 the provisions of the California practice act were substantially adopted by the first legislature of Montana in an act to regulate proceedings in civil cases.[2] There was a revision in 1879, when a code of civil procedure framed on the lines of the California statute was adopted, as part of a general body of laws.[3] In 1895 the fourth regular session of the state legislature revised and reenacted this code, along with the other codes of Montana, but in all this the lines of the California codes were carefully observed.

[1] Rev. Stats. Idaho, § 4020; Cal. Code of Civ. Proc., § 307. Cf. Code of Connecticut, and English Judicature Acts and Rules.

[2] Laws of Montana Territory, 1866, Title I.

[3] Revised Statutes, Montana, 1879, Division I.

(18) *The code of Arizona*, 1864.

Sec. 110. The Arizona code of civil procedure sprang into being in 1864 as part of a larger "code". The first act of the first territorial legislature of Arizona authorized the governor "to appoint a commissioner to prepare and report a code of laws for the use and consideration of the legislature of said territory".[1] A code was speedily forthcoming. The wants of the territory had been anticipated in an elaborate bill which the legislature speedily enacted, with a formal vote of thanks, as a single statute. As a further mark of approbation, both houses resolved that the new code should bear the name of its author,[2] and be officially designated as "the Howell Code". One chapter of this general code dealt with the subject of "Proceedings in Civil Cases," and repeated the California practice act. These provisions reappear in the compiled laws of 1877 with apparently few amendments. In 1887 a commission was appointed to revise the laws of the territory, and in particular to eliminate "all crude, useless, imperfect, and contradictory matter, and insert such new provisions as they might deem necessary and proper". The outcome was "The Revised Statutes of Arizona," of 1887, a work of alphabetical arrangement and containing as one of its titles a "Code of Civil Procedure". This has recast the provisions of the older act, and departed somewhat from the now familiar classification and phraseology of the codes. But there appear to be no violent changes. In some instances, indeed, the Arizona code gives a clearer and more concise statement of a principle common to all the codes than is to be found in most of them.

[1] Arizona Laws, 1864, p. 1, Act of Oct. 1, 1864.

[2] William T. Howell, an associate justice of the Supreme Court of the Territory, and formerly a resident of Michigan.

Code pleading in the South, and the peculiar circumstances of its enactment.

Sec. 111. In the three years which followed 1867 the new system spread into the South, as well as further into the West, being adopted by North Carolina, South Carolina, Florida, Arkansas, Wyoming, and Utah. Here also there was no attempt to recast the principles of the reform, or to adapt it to the special needs, if any, of the state; but the code of some other state was adopted bodily, except for a few omissions, additions, or alterations of a minor character.

The three southern states mentioned above adopted the New York code. Its appearance here, closely connected with the "reconstruction" which followed the civil war, was not under favorable auspices. So adverse, indeed, were the conditions that the Florida code suffered a repeal after a three years' trial, and the former system was reestablished with, however, a number of changes.[1]

(19) *The code of North Carolina*, 1868.

Sec. 112. The inception of the North Carolina code of civil procedure dates from March 16, 1868, when a constitutional convention adopted, as part of a new constitution, the familiar provision that "the distinction between actions at law and suits in equity, and the forms of all such actions and suits shall be abolished, and there shall be in this state but one form of action, for the enforcement or protection of private rights or the redress of private wrongs, which shall be denominated a civil action".[2] This constitution required also the appointment of commissioners to report to the general assembly "rules of practice and procedure"

[1] Fla. Laws, 1873, pp. 15-18; cf. ch. 162, p. 807; cf. McClellan's Digest (1881). See infra, Stability of the Codes.

[2] N. C. Const., 1868, Art. IV, § 1.

in accordance with these provisions. The result was a "code of civil procedure," framed after the model of the New York code, and enacted within the year. It has become part of a more general "code," whose topics have an alphabetical arrangement, but it keeps its original name, and appears to have suffered few substantial changes.[1]

(20) *The code of South Carolina*, 1868–1870.

Sec. 113. The South Carolina code also found its first expression in a constitutional provision. "That justice may be administered in a uniform mode of pleading without distinction between law and equity," ran the constitution of 1868,[2] "the General Assembly, at its first session after the adoption of this constitution, shall provide for abolishing the distinct forms of action, and for that purpose shall appoint some suitable person or persons whose duty it shall be to revise, simplify, and abridge the rules, practice, pleadings, and forms of the courts now in use in this state." A commission thus appointed reported a code of procedure in 1869. It was enacted in 1870, embodied in the "Revised Statutes of South Carolina" in 1873,[3] and made part of another revision in 1893; but it has sustained no essential change. In the process, indeed, it has acquired a somewhat more exact name, being now formally designated as a "Code of Civil Procedure".[4]

(21) *The code of Arkansas*, 1868.

Sec. 114. In the year in which North Carolina adopted the New York code of procedure, 1868, Arkansas adopted the Kentucky "code of practice in civil cases," as amend-

[1] N. C. Code, Vol. I, ch. 10, "Code of Civil Procedure."
[2] S. C. Const., 1868, Art. V, § 3.
[3] Ch. 122.
[4] S. C. Revised Stats., 1893, Part IV, "Code of Civil Procedure."

ed and supplemented in 1854.[1] The new statute followed the provisions of the Kentucky act not only in substance, but very often in the letter. Among other things the formal distinction of the Kentucky code between legal and equitable proceedings was retained.

Appearing in 1869 under the erroneous designation of the "Civil Code," the act has since been carried into an alphabetical digest of all the statute law of Arkansas. But it has been kept intact for the most part as a chapter on "Pleading and Practice".[2]

(22) *The code of Wyoming*, 1869.

Sec. 115. In 1869 the first legislative assembly of Wyoming Territory adopted in substance the Ohio code of civil procedure.[3] There was, however, one notable departure. The Wyoming act did not abolish the distinction between actions at law and suits in equity; and a chapter on "Chancery" was put into the code.[4] Although more formal than real, this distinction held a place in the law of Wyoming for a considerable time. It disappears in the revision of 1886, when the Ohio code of civil procedure was followed with even more literal exactness than before.[5]

(23) *The code of Florida*, 1870.

Sec. 116. In 1870 the State of Florida, it will be remembered, followed the example of North Carolina and South Carolina and adopted the New York code, apparently under the stress of reconstruction. But in this—the one

[1] Ark. Laws, 1868, Act of July 22; cf. provision in Arkansas Const., 1868, Art. 15, sec. 11.

[2] Ark. Dig. Stats., 1894, ch. 122.

[3] Wyo. Laws, 1869, ch. 75.

[4] Wyoming Laws of 1869, Code of Civil Procedure, Title 31; Laws of 1873, p. 146, et seq.

[5] Wyoming Laws, 1886, ch. 60; Rev. Stats., Wyoming, 1887, §§ 2337 et seq.

instance out of many—the new pleading proved so unpopular that it was presently overthrown, and the older pleading ostensibly reestablished. Still there were some statutory changes in this reestablished procedure, which tend to place Florida with the code states, as will appear a little further on.[1]

(24) *The code of Utah*, 1870.

Sec. 117 In Utah, code pleading had an early beginning. The first legislature of the territory passed a brief act at the end of 1852, "regulating the mode of procedure in civil cases".[2] This statute, of less than four pages in length, established in Utah a number of the principles which characterize the reform procedure; but the act was essentially primitive and very incomplete. In 1870 it was supplanted by an elaborate law framed upon the lines of the California practice act of 1852.[3] It has since been brought into closer accord with the California code of civil procedure.[4]

Influence of the English reforms of 1875.

Sec. 118. In the twenty-two years which elapsed between 1848 and 1870, the enactment of new codes in the United States had been with an impetuous vigor. The average was at least one new code each year. But, with the code of Utah in 1870, the movement came to a pause. Seven years elapse before the next code, that of Colorado, appears; it is followed by the Connecticut practice act in 1879, and by the code of Oklahoma in 1890.

Meanwhile, word had gone forth in England for an even more radical departure from common law pleading, and

[1] Infra, Stability of the Codes.

[2] Utah Laws, p. 132, as printed in 1855, Act of Dec. 30, 1852.

[3] Utah Laws of 1870, p. 17.

[4] Utah, Compiled Laws, Part 10, "Code of Civil Procedure."

the Judicature Acts of 1873 and 1875 with their Rules of Court had come into operation.[1] It was natural that this new system of pleading, comparatively simple and flexible as it evidently was, and the slow work of cautious hands, should attract the favorable attention of legislators in English commonwealths who sought to simplify the older procedure. Its influence is very marked in the Connecticut act. But the other two codes keep well within the now beaten path of American codification.

(25) *The Colorada code*, 1877.

Sec. 119. Most of the territories, as has been seen, adopted the new system very speedily and almost at the outset of their career; but Colorado, although organized as a territory as late as 1861, held to the common law and equity pleadings for sixteen years, until the inauguration of the state government. The older practice was, however, modified by statutes in many particulars.[2] In 1877 the first general assembly of the state passed an act of four hundred and forty-seven sections, providing a system of procedure in civil actions in the courts of justice. The customary forms of code legislation were carefully observed, and, in its scope and phraseology, the act suggests the earlier rather than the later statutes.[3] Unlike the codes of many states, the Colorado code has not yet been incorporated as part of the general laws or of the general statutes of the state, and still appears as a distinct volume.

(26) *The code of Connecticut*, 1879.

Sec. 120. The code which was next enacted, the practice act of Connecticut, made a wide and notable departure from the traditions of code legislation. Nevertheless, the

[1] In November, 1875, see infra.

[2] Col. Laws, 1861, pp. 172, 181; Rev. Stats., 1868, pp. 91, 498.

[3] Colo. Laws, 1877, Code of Civil Procedure.

principles of the reform were carefully observed and clearly expressed. This statute, which was passed in March of 1879, under the title of "an act to simplify procedure in civil causes and to unite legal and equitable remedies in the same action," [1] ran to but thirty-four short sections. It was devoted chiefly to the fundamental principles of the new system. Many of the details of procedure being found sufficiently provided for in general statutes already enacted were adopted for use under the new act.

While very comprehensive, the terms of this Connecticut code are admirably plain and concise. Nor do they depart essentially from the principles of the reform. They reflect the cardinal provisions of both the American codes and the English judicature acts, but are rarely a literal copy from either. Some of them, as the provision "that wherever there is any variance between the rules of equity and the rules of common law, in reference to the same matter, the rules of equity shall prevail," prevent the occurrence in Connecticut of questions which have caused grave difficulties in the practice under more elaborate codes.

(27) *The code of Oklahoma*, 1890.

Sec. 121. The next code of procedure was that of Oklahoma, hurriedly enacted by the first legislative assembly of the territory in 1890,[2] and hurriedly revised by the second legislature in 1893.[3] In its revised form the act is a very close copy of the Kansas code, with its amendments as late as those of 1889.[4]

[1] Conn. Public Acts, 1879, ch. 83.

[2] Okl. Stats., 1890, ch. 70, et seq.

[3] Okl. Stats., 1893, ch. 66, §§ 1–759.

[4] Cf. Kan. Gen. Stats., ch. 80, §§ 4078–4846. The Kansas Code is of special value in the new territory, being fully annotated, while the Oklahoma Code has no annotations.

The uniformity of the codes—(1) *Their accord in general.*

Sec. 122. These seven and twenty codes were enacted under different titles, more or less appropriate. "Codes of procedure," "codes of civil procedure," "codes of practice," "practice acts," "civil practice acts," such are the more common forms. In a few instances the misleading name of "civil code" has been given somewhat formally; and the term is frequent in the parlance of the courts.[1] A few codes have no distinctive name in the statute book, and save for a numerical designation are now well nigh merged in the general mass of statute law.

But, whatever their title, and even when they bear no title as a whole and their provisions are scattered in disjointed chapters through an alphabetical digest of statutes, these codes are evidently framed after one design. They do not merely seek substantially the same ends in substantially the same way; they have a similarity of detail, a uniformity in phraseology, and in classification and arrangement. They repeat, with occasional exceptions, the spirit and the letter of one code—that of New York in its earlier form. They are framed out of the same materials. They are designed for the same purpose, that of filling the place occupied for so many centuries by our two great systems of procedure, pleading at law and pleading in equity. Distinct although the codes are, and independent each of the other, they stand together as one system—and that the most wide-spread system of pleading known in English and American jurisprudence.

Their agreement in respect to substance and in respect

[1] This loose and improper application of "civil code" is approved by popular usage in some states, as Ohio, even by statute in some, as New York. (See New York Laws, 1892, p. 1491.) Strictly the term is applied only to a code of substantive law. The California "Civil Code" and the "California Code of Civil Procedure" are very different things. And so in a few other states.

to word and form has already been noted; but it will be worth while to advert with a little more particularity to some of the weightier matters in which these distinct codes are at one.

(2) *Cardinal points of agreement among the codes.* *The single civil action.*

Sec. 123. With two exceptions[1] all concur in the express declaration that there shall be but one form of civil action; and the exceptions here are more seeming than real.[2] In substantial effect every code provides for a single civil action. Moreover, while less than half now abolish in express terms the old distinction between actions at law and suits in equity, such an abolition is a plain and necessary inference from the terms which are expressed in all the codes.

Proper party plaintiff.

Sec. 124. All agree also in their provisions as to the party by whom an action shall be brought. It must be in the name of the real party in interest, excepting certain well-defined cases, when convenience dictates a relaxation of the rule. These modifications are almost as uniform among the different codes as is the rule itself. They agree in permitting an executor, an administrator, a trustee of an express trust, and a person expressly authorized by statute, to sue without bringing in the beneficiary as a party.

Joinder of parties.

Sec. 125. The codes are at one again in their rules as to the joinder of parties. Parties are declared to be either plaintiffs or defendants. All who have an interest in the

[1] Arizona and Oregon.

[2] It will be remembered that a few other codes distinguish the *proceedings* in the single civil action according as they are at law or in equity.

subject of the action and in obtaining the relief demanded should be plaintiffs. All who have an adverse interest to the plaintiff are to be made defendants; and with them may be joined any who should join with the plaintiff but will not. If the complete determination of the controversy in hand requires still other parties, the court may order them to be brought in.

Joinder of causes of action.

Sec. 126. Much the larger number of the codes concur in the substance and wording of their rules concerning the joinder of causes of action. In brief, all causes of action, whether they are such as were formerly denoted legal or equitable or both, may now be joined, provided they affect all the parties, do not require different places of trial, and are all comprised within some one of the following classes:

1. Causes of action which arise out of the same transaction, or transactions connected with the same subject of action.[1]

[1] Fifteen codes concur. The exceptions are Arizona, Arkansas, California, Colorado, Indiana, Iowa, Kentucky, Montana, Nevada, Oregon, Utah, Washington. But these exceptions are often due to minor differences in classification. The elaborate classification in the California Act has been followed in several of the codes referred to above. The provision in Iowa is very general, namely: "Causes of action of whatever kind, where each may be prosecuted by the same kind of proceedings, provided that they be by the same party, and against the same party in the same rights, and if suit on all may be brought and tried in that county, may be joined in the same petition; but, the court, to prevent confusion therein, may direct all, or any portion of the issues joined therein, to be tried separately, and may determine the order thereof." Iowa Rev. Stats. (McClain's ed.), § 3836. So the Arizona code provides very generally that "the complaint may contain several different causes of action, and the answer may contain several different defenses." (Rev. Stats. § 659). On the suggestive principle of the English judicature acts see references in the index.

2. Causes of action arising out of contract, express or implied.[1]

3. Injuries, with or without force, to person and property or either.[2]

4. Injuries to character.[3]

5. Claims to recover real property, with or without damages for the withholding thereof, and the rents and profits of the same.[4]

6. Claims to recover personal property, with or without damages for the withholding thereof.[5]

7. Claims against a trustee by virtue of a contract or by operation of law.[6]

New names for pleadings.

Sec. 127. All the codes agree in abrogating most of the older names for the different pleadings. In nineteen codes the first pleading on the part of the plaintiff is a "complaint"; in eight it is a "petition".[7] The codes which permit a second distinct pleading of fact on the part of the plaintiff agree in designating it as a "reply". The defendant's first pleading of fact is an "answer" in all the codes. And all concur again in the name "demurrer" for a pleading intended to raise an issue of law.

[1] Twenty-four codes concur. The exceptions are, Arizona, Colorado, and Indiana. Here again the disagreement is often very slight. Thus, the Indiana Code refers to causes of action arising out of "money demands on contract," which has been held to mean any action arising out of contract that seeks the recovery of money. Roberts v. Nodwift, 8 Ind. 339, 341 (1856).

[2] Twenty codes concur. The exceptions are Arizona, California, Idaho, Indiana, Montana, Oregon, Utah.

[3] Twenty-four codes concur. The exceptions are Arizona, Iowa, Nevada.

[4] Twenty-five codes concur. The exceptions are Arizona and Iowa.

[5] Twenty-five codes concur. The exceptions are Arizona and Iowa.

[6] Twenty-two codes concur. The exceptions are Arizona, Colorado, Indiana, Iowa, and Kentucky.

[7] Iowa, Kansas, Kentucky, Missouri, Nebraska, Ohio, Oklahoma, Wyoming.

Limited series of pleadings.

Sec. 128. The code of Kentucky, like the later English code, permits "such additional pleadings by way of rejoinder and rebutter as may be necessary to form a material issue of fact";[1] the code of Connecticut provides that "further pleadings subsequent in their nature may be had if necessary by leave of court";[2] but, with these exceptions, our codes concur in limiting the pleading to two or three steps. In most codes the "petition," or "complaint," and the "reply" are the only pleadings of fact upon the part of the plaintiff.[3] A few codes do not provide for a reply.[4] In all codes the "answer," running on occasion, in some states, into a "cross complaint," or "cross petition," is the defendant's one pleading of fact. And in almost all each pleading of fact may be met by a "demurrer". But, at the utmost, the common theory of code pleading calls for a speedy conclusion of the judicial altercation.

Production of an issue.

Sec. 129. The codes agree also in a partial retention of the common law *issue*; but the differences between the old and the new pleading here are many and important. Their more important aspects will be noticed further on in connection with the later development of code pleading in

[1] Ky. Civ. Co. Prac., § 89.

[2] Conn. Gen. Stats., § 875.

[3] Twenty-three codes concur.

[4] California, Nevada, Idaho, and Utah. A "replication" was permitted under the California Code by Act of April 28, 1860, but was soon abandoned. In 1872 the commissioners remark: "We have been urged to restore the 'reply,' and the arguments in favor of its restoration are convincing. Were we making the law, instead of drafting a bill to be passed upon by the law-making power, we would feel no hesitation whatever as to our course. The 'reply' once formed a part of our system of pleading, and after a short time it was abandoned. Were we to restore it we would be met with this fact as an objection. After careful consideration we have determined not to move in the premises."

England. As between themselves, however, the codes are in no less accord here than elsewhere. They have followed one model. They all set out to require that the questions to be decided shall be defined not by the court from the parties' statements at large, but by the parties themselves through their mutual altercation in the pleading. But our codes, unlike the common law, do not keep to this principle strictly. As the limited series of pleadings indicates, the altercation is cut short at a certain stage—the answer in some codes, the reply in some; and if a natural issue has not been already evolved, a constructive issue is compelled. The material new matter alleged in this last permitted pleading is *deemed* to be denied. On the other hand, the codes, like the common law, treat the natural distinction between an issue in law and an issue in fact as a hard and fast matter of procedure. The two issues can be raised only in separate and distinct pleadings, the *demurrer* being retained for the issue in law, the *answer* and the *reply* being provided for the issue in fact. And, as at common law, we can not demur *and* answer, or demur *and* reply, to the same matter at the same time.

Sec. 130. Most of the codes follow substantially and very often literally the terms of the New York code of 1849;[1] but here and there a variation is to be found.

It is a very frequent declaration that issues arise upon the pleadings when a fact or a conclusion in law is maintained by the one party and controverted by the other; and that issues are of two kinds, "of law," and "of fact". It is also frequently declared that an "issue of law arises upon a demurrer to a complaint, answer, or reply, or to some part thereof".[2] Most of the codes agree further in declar-

[1] See its sections 248 et seq. These sections contain several amendments to the code of 1848 on this point; cf. its sections 203 et seq.

[2] This description has been omitted from some codes, but is evidently to be inferred. We are sometimes told that the common phraseology

ing that an issue of fact arises (1) upon a material allegation in the petition or complaint controverted by the answer; or (2) upon new matter in the answer controverted by the reply; or (3) upon new matter in the reply, except an issue of law be joined thereon. But in some codes, as we have seen, there is no "reply," so that their definition of the issue stops one stage short of the foregoing, and the issue of fact arises upon uncontroverted new matter in the *answer* unless it is demurred to. Other codes require a reply not to all new matter in the answer, but only in response to a setoff, or counterclaim. In such instances the issue is declared to arise upon the setoff, or counterclaim denied by the reply, and, without express denial, upon all other new matter in the *answer*, and upon all new matter in the reply.

Frame and contents of petition or complaint.

Sec. 131. Excepting the codes of Arizona and Connecticut, which differ slightly in their phraseology from the other codes on this point, all agree as to the frame and contents of the petition, or complaint. It shall contain (1) the title of the case; (2) a plain and concise statement of the facts which constitute each cause of action; (3) a demand for the relief sought. And here it will be observed that, while six codes[1] still provide in express terms for the abolition of "all fictions in pleading," this express abolition is unnecessary. It follows as an unquestionable inference in all the codes, from their express requirements as to the facts which should be stated in a petition, or complaint.

of the codes here is faulty, that a demurrer does not raise an issue "*of* law," but an issue "*in* law"; as to which see Phillips, Code Pl., § 35.

[1]Iowa, Kansas, Ohio, Oklahoma, Oregon, Wyoming.

Grounds of demurrer by defendant.

Sec. 132. There is a very general agreement as to the grounds on which a defendant may demur. It must appear on the face of the petition, or complaint, either (1) that the court has no jurisdiction of the person of the defendant or of the subject of the action; or (2) that the plaintiff has not legal capacity to sue; or (3) that another action is pending between the same parties for the same cause; or (4) that there is a defect of parties, plaintiff or defendant;[1] or (5) that several causes of action have been improperly united;[2] or (6) that the complaint, or petition, does not state facts sufficient to constitute a cause of action.[3]

Sec. 133. Some further grounds of demurrer are specified in a few codes—as, that the action was not begun within the time limited by law;[4] that there is a misjoinder of parties *plaintiff*;[5] that there is a misjoinder of parties plaintiff or defendant;[6] that the complaint is ambiguous, unintelligible, or uncertain.[7] But these are minor grounds, and do not change the general character of the demurrer in the states referred to.

Contents of the answer.

Sec. 134. The codes agree also that the answer must contain: (1) a general or specific denial of every material allegation in the petition, or complaint, which is contro-

1 Twenty-five codes concur in these four grounds of demurrer. The exceptions are Arizona, which does not recognize the demurrer in its series of pleadings, and Connecticut.

2 Twenty-three codes concur. The exceptions are Arizona, Arkansas, Connecticut, Iowa.

3 All concur except Arizona.

4 So Iowa, Oregon, Washington, Wisconsin.

5 A later provision in New York and Ohio, and found also in Wyoming.

6 So California, Colorado, Idaho, Missouri, Montana, Nevada, Utah.

7 So California, Colorado, Idaho, Montana, Nevada, Utah.

verted by the defendant, or of any knowledge or information thereof sufficient to form a belief; (2) a plain and concise statement of any new matter constituting a defense, or counterclaim, or setoff. And the codes are at one in abrogating the common law rule that a defendant could allege but one defense, however numerous his grounds of defense might be. For, excepting three states,[1] all the codes provide expressly, and with slight variations in phraseology, that the answer may set forth as many defenses and counterclaims, or setoffs, as the defendant may have, "whether they be such as have been heretofore denominated legal or equitable, or both".

With two or three exceptions the codes concur also in the provision that a plaintiff may demur to the answer or to any defense or counterclaim in it, when it appears on the face thereof that it does not state facts sufficient to constitute a defense or a counterclaim, or setoff.

No less common is the provision that every material allegation of a complaint, or petition which is not controverted by an answer, or of a counterclaim which is not controverted by a reply, shall be taken to be true.[2]

Principle of interpleader.

Sec. 135. Almost all the codes agree in adopting the equitable principle of interpleader, and in certain cases make it a much simpler process than the old bill of interpleader. Twenty-four codes permit the defendant to interplead a stranger in actions to recover specific personal property;[3] twenty-three permit it in actions upon contracts.[4]

[1] Arizona, Connecticut, Iowa.

[2] Four states, it will be remembered, do not embrace the reply in the series of pleadings, California, Nevada, Idaho, Utah.

[3] The exceptions are Arizona, Connecticut, and Missouri.

[4] The exceptions are Arizona, Connecticut, Missouri, Oregon.

Scope of the motion.

Sec. 136. Some twenty of the codes provide that when the allegations of a pleading are indefinite, ambiguous, vague, or uncertain a "motion" to make definite and certain should be resorted to; and commonly a motion, not a demurrer, is provided for a fault or defect of form.[1]

Principle of construction.

Sec. 137. The rule of the common law that a pleading is to be construed most strongly against the pleader is abrogated very positively in almost all the codes through a provision that, in the construction of a pleading for the purpose of determining its effect, the allegations shall be liberally construed with a view to substantial justice between the parties.

Rule of amendment.

Sec. 138. One and the same rule as to the amendment of pleadings is found in nearly every code. Any pleading may be once amended by the party as of course, without costs and without prejudice to prior proceedings, at any time before the period for the adverse party's response has expired, or within certain days after the service of the answer or demurrer to such pleading. Upon the trial or at any other stage of the action, before or after judgment, the court may, in furtherance of justice and upon such terms as may be just, amend any process, pleading, or proceeding, by adding or striking out the name of a party or by correcting a mistake in the name of a party, or a mistake in any other respect, or by inserting other allegations material to the case, or, when the amendment does not change substantially the claim or defense, by conform-

[1] Exceptions are found among the lesser grounds for demurrer, noted above.

ing the pleading to the facts proved. No less common is the provision that errors which do not mislead or affect the substantial rights of the party are to be disregarded.

Rules of convenience.

Sec. 139. The codes commonly agree also in their leading devices of convenience, as in the rule that when the real name of a party is unknown he may be sued by a fictitious name, and the true name inserted thereafter by amendment. So they concur in the provision that the performance of a condition precedent may be alleged generally, and the details proven if denied.

(3) *Relation of the codes to the New York code.*

Sec. 140. Such are some of the points of substantial agreement between the codes. It would be easy to add to the list. And it will be remembered that this similarity is heightened by a more formal similarity in arrangement and phraseology. But while the procession of the codes has thus followed carefully in the footsteps of the earlier New York enactments, it is not to be understood that the New York code was everywhere repeated in the very shape in which it was enacted in 1848. This code was itself presently amended by the New York legislature in 1849,[1] in 1851,[2] and in 1852;[3] and these amendments were considered in the drafting of later codes. There were also substantial additions to the provisions of the New York act, made by the legislatures of other code states, and some departures from it in matters of detail. Many of these departures, however, came from New York—from its proposed "code of civil procedure" of 1850.

[1] N. Y. Laws, 1849, ch. 438.
[2] N. Y. Laws, 1851, ch. 479.
[3] N. Y. Laws, 1852, ch. 392.

The proposed New York "code of civil procedure" of 1850.

Sec. 141. The code of 1848, it will be remembered, was confessedly incomplete. It went no further than the proceedings and pleadings in the ordinary remedies in courts of record. The immense mass of special proceedings, prerogative and remedial writs, arbitrations, processes against absent and insolvent debtors, probate proceedings, civil proceedings before justices of the peace, and other matters were left untouched for the time being. In 1850 the three commissioners who had drawn up the code of procedure of 1848 reported to the New York legislature the draft of a proposed act for a complete "Code of Civil Procedure," eo nomine.[1] This act was never adopted by the New York legislature—rather it was rejected in 1876 for the "Code of Remedial Justice"; but being published and widely circulated the provisions and the name of this code of civil procedure were adopted by other states whose legislatures sought to enact codes which would make full provision for every proceeding in the judicial tribunals, from the beginning to the end of every controversy.[2]

[1] A code of criminal procedure was reported at the same time, thus completing the commissioners' design "to prepare a code of procedure which shall comprehend the whole law of the state"—a complete code of adjective law.

[2] This point and some other matters will be the clearer from comparing the main divisions of the New York Act of 1848 with those of one or two other leading codes, for example, with the Ohio Code of 1853, and the California Code as amended in 1874.

New York Code, 1848: PART I—Of the courts of justice and their jurisdiction. PART II—Of civil actions. TITLE I—Form of civil actions. II—Time of commencing them. III—Parties. IV—Place of trial. V—Manner of commencing them. VI—The pleadings. VII—Provisional remedies. VIII—Trial and judgment. IX—Execution of the judgment. X—Costs. XI—Appeals. XII—Miscellaneous proceedings and general provisions.

Ohio Code of Civil Procedure, 1853; TITLE I—Form of civil actions. II—Time of commencing them. III—Parties to civil actions. IV—County in which to be brought. V—Commencement of. VI—Joinder

(4) *The hesitation of some codes over the "fusion" of law and equity.*

Sec. 142. There is one point, however, at which a number of the codes seemed to diverge widely from the general scheme of the New York act. In several instances they retained a formal distinction between actions at law and suits in equity. A chapter on chancery practice was now and then incorporated into the new act, to the derogation, in appearance at least, of the cardinal principle that there should be but one form of civil action. The distinction was most frequent in the territorial codes where it was due to excessive prudence in construing the federal statute under which several territories were organized. This law required that the principal courts of the territories should

of. VII—Pleadings in. VIII—Provisional remedies. IX—Trial. X—Evidence. XI—Judgment. XII—Survival and abatement. XIII—Revivor. XIV—Executions. XV—Miscellaneous provisions. XVI—Error in civil cases. XVII—Costs. XVIII—Actions and proceedings in particular cases. XIX—General provisions applicable to the whole code.

California Code of Civil Procedure, 1872: PART I—Of courts of justice and their jurisdiction. PART II—Of civil actions. TITLE I—Form of civil actions. II—Time of commencing them. III—Parties. IV—Place of trial. V—Manner of commencing them. VI—Pleadings. VII—Provisional remedies. VIII—Trial and judgment. IX—Execution. X—Actions in particular cases. XI—Proceedings in justices' courts. XII—Civil actions in police courts. XIII—Appeals. XIV—Miscellaneous provisions. PART III—Special proceedings of a civil nature. TITLE I—Certiorari, mandamus, and prohibition. II—Contesting elections. III—Summary proceedings. IV—Enforcement of liens. V—Contempts. VI—Voluntary dissolution of corporations. VII—Eminent domain. VIII—Escheated estates. IX—Change of names. X—Arbitrations. XI—Proceedings in probate courts. XII—Proceedings by married women to become sole traders. XIII—Proceedings in insolvency. PART IV—Evidence. TITLE I—General principles. II—Kinds and degrees. III—Production of evidence. IV—Effect of evidence. V—Rights and duties of witnesses. VI—Evidence in particular cases and miscellaneous provisions.

The procedure in probate courts and in courts of justice of the peace is regulated in Ohio by separate acts, passed, however, in the same year as the code of civil procedure. (See Ohio Laws, 1853, p. 167; Ib. p. 179.)

have both a common law and a chancery jurisdiction;[1] and doubts were entertained whether these jurisdictions must be exercised separately, or could be exercised together in the same proceeding. Some contended that a statute authorizing a uniform course of proceeding in all cases, legal and equitable, would be repugnant to the fundamental law of the territory, and so far void. It was held, indeed, in a few cases that chancery jurisdiction being thus granted to the territorial courts a territorial legislature could not abolish the distinction between actions at law and suits in equity.[2]

The doubt removed through an act of congress.

Sec. 143. The doubt continued until 1874; and the date is significant, being a year after the first judicature act had prescribed "fusion" of law and equity in England.[3] An act of congress then provided in express terms that it should not be necessary for the territorial courts to exercise their common law and chancery jurisdictions separately; "that the several codes and rules of practice adopted in said territories respectively, in so far as they authorize a mingling of said jurisdictions or a uniform course of proceedings in all cases whether legal or equitable, be confirmed"; and that "all proceedings heretofore had or taken in said courts in conformity with said respective codes and rules of practice, so far as relates to the form and mode of proceeding, be, and the same are hereby, validated and confirmed".[4]

[1] Cf. U. S. Rev. Stats., § 1868; "The Supreme Court and the District Courts, respectively, of every Territory shall possess chancery as well as common law jurisdiction."

[2] Stevens v. Baker, 1 Wash. Ter., 315, 318 (1871).

[3] See infra; but it is before this act had come into effect.

[4] Act of April 7, 1874; 18 Stats., L. 27, 1 Sup. Rev. Stats., ch. 80. The act has some provisions which, however, do not affect materially the nature of the reform so established in the territories.

Nature of the distinction when made.

Sec. 144. In the meantime, several territorial legislatures, out of abundant caution, had incorporated into their codes a formal distinction between proceedings for legal and proceedings for equitable relief. A like distinction was made by state legislatures in the codes of Kentucky, Iowa, and Arkansas, where it is still retained; but it has been abolished elsewhere, Oregon excepted.

The nature of the distinction has already been noticed.[1] It does not restore the old wall of separation between legal and equitable procedure. It amounts, indeed, to little more than a classification of actions according as they are to be tried by a jury or the court, a classification which is recognized, of course, in all code states, but is commonly regulated by rules of practice rather than of pleading.

Stability of the codes—In general.

Sec. 145. Drafted in haste and hurriedly enacted, as most of the codes were, they have naturally enough suffered frequent alteration at the hands of the legislatures. Change begot change in some codes with startling rapidity. But, in view of the character of the original legislation—its novelty, its wide scope, its varied application, the changes have been less radical and scarcely more frequent than might fairly have been expected. It held true of the codes as of legislation in general that a system complete and perfect in all its parts can not be struck out at a heat by the most able law-giver that ever lived. "No code," says Austin, "can be perfect."[2] Almost all the codes,

[1] Ante, § 93.

[2] Note his suggestion, that every code should contain a "perpetual provision for its amendment." Juris. 697. Cf. Gibson, J., in Pennock v. Hart, 8 S. & R. (Penn.), 368, 378 (1822). Cf. Provision under English Code for alteration without resort to the legislature.

however, passed through the experimental stages and became established systems without material departure from the form in which they were first enacted. But there are two notable exceptions in New York and Florida.

The two exceptions—(1) *The experiment in New York.*

Sec. 146. After twenty-five years of amendatory legislation[1] and judicial construction, the New York code had reached, as its friends hoped, a definite and secure position. It had, indeed, sustained five hundred and fifty-one changes; the aggregate of its amendments had exceeded the total number of its sections. But many of these amendments were formal, and many were repeated attempts to frame the same section in a satisfactory form. Of the four hundred and seventy-three sections in the revised code of 1849, nearly one-half had never been amended in 1876. And among them were found the more important and substantial features of the original act. Moreover, the code as a whole had received extended judicial discussion; the practice provided by it had become fairly well understood. All reasonable criticism, it was believed, had been answered or was in process of being answered, without another revolutionary change.[2]

[1] The original code, that of 1848, remained in force until May 1, 1849, when it was reenacted with a host of amendments and supplements (N. Y. Laws, 1849, ch. 438, Act of April 11), the new act running to four hundred and seventy-three sections. In a little over two years this amended code was greatly changed by the amendatory act of July 10, 1851 (N. Y. Laws, 1851, ch. 479). Presently the latter act was itself amended in a large number of its sections (N. Y. Laws, 1852, ch. 392, Act of April 16). Other amendments followed, but in less volume, until the "revision" referred to in the text.

[2] Up to this point the history of the New York code is significant as being that of many codes, and not of the New York code alone; but from this on the story is rather a prophecy of what may happen in other codes if the noble art of statutory revision goes mad.

The New York revision in 1876.

Sec. 147. But at this point the spirit of innovation attacked the code, with serious results. In 1870 the New York legislature appointed a commission of three to revise and simplify all the general statutes of the state.[1] Six years later this commission reported a bill for a new code of procedure, covering the ground of the existing code; and the bill was presently passed in an act of thirteen chapters and fourteen hundred and ninety-six sections, relating to the jurisdiction of the courts and the ordinary proceedings in courts of record. To this new code the statute gave a new name, the "Code of Remedial Justice," for which, however, the popular phrase, the "Code of Civil Procedure," was soon substituted by another enactment.[2]

Its characteristics.

Sec. 148. While retaining the fundamental requirements of its predecessor, the new code differed from it widely in phraseology and in the nature of its provisions. It was reactionary in spirit. It showed a vast increase in bulk—a figure of Falstaffian proportions among the other codes. It was "built up under a microscope". Its requirements ran into the most minute and trivial details of practice.[3] So smothered in details were its principles that New York practitioners have since been working under a civil procedure which scarcely any approve, and which is

[1] N. Y. Laws, 1870, ch. 33, p. 100.

[2] N. Y. Laws, 1876, chs. 448, 449; N. Y. Laws, 1877, ch. 416, § 1. The term "Civil Code" may also be used; cf. Laws of 1892, p. 1491, Statutory Construction Law.

[3] "When we get into court on a motion to vacate an attachment, or an order of arrest, or an order for an examination before trial, five out of six of the orders we obtain are set aside because they do not state something that the code says they should state—for instance, we have failed to put in the address of the attorneys. All this is procedure run mad." Wm. B. Hornblower, 53 Alb. Law Journ., 152 (1896).

far enough from the ideal of those who framed the original code, and from what they succeeded in constructing. However defective and faulty the code of 1848 may have been, the faults of this code of 1876 are greater still. Such degree of clearness as the old code possessed is obscured; its conciseness is rendered diffuse; its simplicity is made intricate; its authority, settled by thirty years of judicial construction, was destroyed, and the task of reconstruction again became necessary.[1]

Sec. 149. Like the "Code of Procedure" in 1848, the "Code of Remedial Justice" in 1876 was but part of a proposed code of civil procedure. The remainder of the commissioners' draft was reported in 1877 in the form of a bill containing nine chapters to be added to the thirteen chapters of the new code. This bill, however, met with such persistent opposition that it did not become a law until 1880.[2] In the meantime the first thirteen chapters had been repeatedly amended. And from 1880 down "The Completed Code of Civil Procedure," now numbering twenty-two chapters and almost four thousand sections, has been amended or supplemented at every session of the legislature no less copiously than before. With its annotations, the revised code makes "three gigantic volumes which appall the legal mind, and fill the lay mind with awe and dismay".[3]

The proposed New York revision of 1896.

Sec. 150. Hasty, unsystematic, and piecemeal, these multitudinous changes only confirmed the character of this New York code of civil procedure as a "Brobdignagian conglomeration of heterogeneous rules of law and practice". The evil grew to such proportions that in June,

[1] See remarks of Irving Browne, 3 Green Bag, 51 (1891).

[2] N. Y. Laws, 1880, ch. 178. Another chapter was added in 1890.

[3] Cf. 53 Alb. Law Journ., 151 (1896).

1895, the legislature passed an act requiring the governor of New York to appoint a commission to "examine the code of procedure of this state and the codes of procedure and practice acts in force in other states and countries, and the rules of court adopted in connection therewith, and report thereon to the next legislature in what respects the civil procedure of this state can be revised, condensed, and simplified".[1] This commission was appointed at once. It speedily ascertained that the "very decided preponderance of opinion" among New York lawyers was in favor of a general revision of their code. The commissioners themselves were clear in the conviction that the civil procedure of New York could "doubtless be revised, condensed, and simplified, and the administration of justice thereby greatly improved.

The commissioners' recommendations, and the attitude of the bar.

Sec. 151. In December, 1895, they made a preliminary and suggestive report, looking to a thorough revision upon an historical basis. "The civil procedure in the courts of this state," say they, "is the product of many years of slow and halting growth, and a revision, such as might be justified by the terms of this law, should be the result of close study of principles and methods, and much deliberation. A commission should study not only the whole subject of procedure, historically and scientifically, but the comparative merits of different systems which are, or have been, in force in different states and countries. We are unwilling to submit a revision which does not embody substantially the result of such care and study, and hence, at this time, we deem it proper to suggest only general recommendations, with an outline of the changes proposed, together

[1] N. Y. Laws, 1895, ch. 1036, Act of June 15.

with a brief statement showing the development of civil procedure and the systems of practice in use in other states and countries."[1]

Sec. 152. In August, 1895, the commission sent to the judges and to nearly ten thousand other lawyers of New York a circular defining the possible scope of the proposed revision, and asking for the bar's opinion upon the subject. The suggestions thus evoked have been many and varied. That the New York code of 1876 stands in need of revision appears to be taken for granted. "It is universally and properly condemned as the product of unskilled workmen, ill equipped for the task."[2] But some members of the New York bar, constrained by that "antipathy to reformation" which shows itself so quickly when a change in the law is proposed, urge that the code be let alone. Their argument is the argument of inconvenience. They would "avoid the uncertainty in practice which may be created by a new code," and are far from claiming that the existing code is as systematic and convenient as it should be. Others suggest that the code of 1848 be restored as it stood in 1876, before the adoption of the "code of civil procedure". Others point to the English reforms of 1873 and 1875—the judicature acts and rules[3]—as in the true line of progress. Others are still more radical, and recommend an assimilation to the German or French practice. But the prevailing tone, at large as in the commission, appears to be in favor of a conservative reform upon an historical and comparative basis, with a view to embodying the best which the experience of other states and countries has to offer on the subject of a codified civil procedure.

[1] For the report in detail see 52 Albany Law Journal, 390, 408 (1895); 53 Ib. 6 (1896).

[2] Cf. Article in 54 Alb. Law Journ., 202 (1896).

[3] As to which see infra.

The conservatism of the new movement.

Sec. 153. This aspect of the present reform movement in New York—its conservatism, but with reference to the results attained not in New York alone, but in all other commonwealths which have tried the experiment of codification—is very significant, so marked is it among some who recognize most clearly the faults of the present system of code pleading. "While our code needs revision," says the Albany Law Journal in September, 1896,[1] "our bar and the public demand a careful, searching, painstaking examination as to its defects and methods by which they can be remedied, and deprecates anything like undue haste or work prepared by others than those specially fitted for the task, and who will give the necessary time and attention demanded by its importance. The sentiment of the bar as voiced by the state association requires that suitable provision shall be made for a thorough examination and analysis of the methods of procedure adopted in this country and abroad, and a selection of what is best and omission of what is most objectionable in our present code. We should either have the best work of the most thoroughly trained minds, which shall embody the best results of all human experience on the question, or we should let code revision remain a thing of the future, when such a result may be accomplished."

Sec. 154. "My first notion of the best method of revising this Brobdignagian conglomeration of heterogeneous rules of law and practice," says Mr. Wm. B. Hornblower, of the New York City bar, referring to the code of 1876,[2] "was to abolish it out of hand; substitute in its place a few general provisions as to pleading and procedure; authorize the courts to regulate by rules all other matters of prac-

[1] 54 Alb. L. J., 193.
[2] In 53 Alb. Law Journ., 151 (1896).

tice, and relegate to other portions of the statutes the provisions of substantive law. Reflection, however, has satisfied me that this radical course would be unwise and inexpedient. This body of statutory rules, built up with so much care, although not with the most skillful workmanship, ought not to be ruthlessly destroyed. It has become the chart of our professional navigation in practice; many of its provisions have been judicially construed by the courts, and I am constrained to the conclusion that to abolish it out of hand would be a great mistake.

"The work of revision should be placed in the hands of men who can give, and who shall be required to give, their entire time to this business. It can not be done in fragmentary intervals of an active professional practice. Men who are to do the work should have salaries equal to those of the justices of the supreme court in the state at large, and they should be prohibited from practicing law during their term of office as commissioners. . . . The co-operation of the various bar associates throughout the state should be actively and earnestly sought by the commissioners, and their proposed revision should be submitted to these bodies in such shape and at such times as will enable them to carefully consider and criticise before the work of the commissioners is submitted to the legislature. There is always great danger in any work of this kind that we may take a step backward instead of forward. On general principles it is best 'to let well enough alone,' unless we are very sure that we are substituting for the 'well enough' a distinctly better thing. We can afford to wait and bear the ills we know rather than plunge ahead into ills that we know not of."

The possible effect of the new movement.

Sec. 155. It is a strange sight to see these conservative forces of the bar, so long and so bitterly opposed to the New York code, thus arrayed in its support. But if this conservatism does not result in stagnation, if it merely keeps the movement to the lines of cautious progress, the outcome may be of far-reaching benefit, although it fall short of "embodying the best results of all human experience on the question".

The effect on other states is, of course, very problematical. General legislation by New York seldom fails to influence legislation far and wide in the Union. But the "code of civil procedure" which New York enacted in 1876 is without a following in the states which so readily adopted the New York "code of procedure" of 1848. Moreover, "the completed code of civil procedure" which became a law in New York in 1880 has been far less productive of similar legislation by other states than the proposed code of civil procedure which was submitted, *eo nomine*, to the New York legislature in 1850 and ultimately was rejected by that state. Apparently the impulsive movement of the early fifties has largely spent its force. The states which eagerly accepted the earlier results of codification in New York show no great readiness to adopt its later results.

The general tendency towards a uniform system of procedure in all the states.

Sec. 156. On the other hand there appears to be a leaning in all the states towards a uniform system of procedure. The remarkable degree of uniformity now to be found in the twenty-seven code states is a striking illustration—all the more striking if we consider how far legislatures separated by continental distances might have diverged when once they cut loose from the common law. And this tendency has recently found further and very significant expression. In 1895 the American Bar Association appointed a committee of five "to inquire into and collate the facts relative to the movement now in progress to further a uniform system of legal procedure, and the study of comparative legislation on that subject throughout the English-speaking world".[1] In August, 1896, the committee made a suggestive report, dealing with the procedure in the different state and federal courts, and "the workings of the supreme court of judicature act of 1873 in the mother country".[2] The committee favor a continued and systematic effort towards the end of a uniform procedure. They make a strong plea for cooperation and communication. "Enactments," say they, quoting from a circular issued by the Society of Comparative Legislation,[3] "may be proposed and adopted by one English-speaking community in ignorance of the fact that similar measures have, after trial, been abandoned or modified in another. Much it is conceived might be learned with advantage both as to the substance and the form of legislation, and many mistakes might be avoided if precedents derived from the experience of other countries were collected and studied."

[1] Reports Am. Bar Ass'n, 1895, p. 33. The wide scope of the movement will be clearer from the remarks of Mr. J. Newton Fiero, offering the resolution for the committee's appointment. "During the past few months," said he, "a very active movement has been on foot in England with a view to bringing about what is termed a Uniformity in Methods of Procedure in English-speaking countries, and I have been communicated with by persons interested in that movement abroad, with a view to learning whether it would not be well, by way of correspondence, to take up the matter and ascertain what could be done. I am further led to this view by the suggestions which were made in the admirable address of the President, with reference to the present state of procedure, and, I need not say, by my own experience with regard to the matter." Ib. p. 32–33.

[2] Report of Committee on Uniform System of Legal Procedure, Am. Bar Ass'n, August 21, 1896: 54 Alb. Law Journ., 198.

[3] Organized in England in December, 1894.

Sec. 157. It appears, indeed, from the committee's investigations that we have given "little or no study to the system adopted in England under the Act of 1873 and its amendments"; that "no systematic study of the question has been made in any of the states, either those adhering to common law methods, or those which have adopted the reformed procedure"; and that not much if any "attention has been given in any state to the workings of the system or systems adopted by the others". But the committee finds also that responses from forty-three states are almost unanimous in expressing a decided opinion in favor of assimilating the practice of the state courts and the federal courts by rules regulating procedure. And, with a view to effective action, the committee recommends "the passage by congress of an act authorizing judges of the higher federal courts to select from the bar of the country a limited number of lawyers, familiar with the procedure in this and other countries, for the purpose of drafting and presenting to congress and to the federal courts such statutes and rules as shall tend to simplify the procedure in the courts of the United States and render it uniform, and eventually tend toward assimilating the practice in the superior courts of the states to a common standard". Such a course, it is suggested, "will give an opportunity for a close, careful, and painstaking investigation into the methods of procedure which are or have been in use throughout the English-speaking world, and avoid the trial of experimental methods already found insufficient, and secure the adoption of such as are the results of the best thought and widest experience of all courts administering the common law".

In view of these surroundings, it would seem to be not quite unreasonable to hope that this new reform movement has not sprung up from stony places where it has not much earth and must wither in the first heat of the day, but that it will take root in good ground and bring forth fruit a hundredfold. It may be that these efforts in 1896 are the beginnings of a greater system of code pleading, more simple and more elastic than the present; possibly the lawyer of 1946 may look back to them as we look to the efforts of 1846.

(2) *The reaction in Florida.*

Sec. 158. The code of Florida was the victim of a speedy and positive reaction. Adopted in 1870, it was repealed in 1873, and the former system was reestablished by a statute "to repeal an act to simplify and abridge the practice, pleadings, and proceedings of the courts of this state, approved February 19, 1870, and to revive the practice, pleadings, and proceedings existing at the date of the passage of said act, and to provide additional rules of practice and pleading".[1] But this revival of the older pleading was accompanied with many and important statutory modifications. They established in effect several of the fundamental principles of the new system.[2] They tend to bring Florida within that class of states, presently to be noticed, in which some of the leading principles of the new pleading, but not all, have been substantially adopted—the class of quasi-code states.

Historical relation of code pleading to codification in general.

Sec. 159. The inception of the New York code of procedure of 1848, as has already been indicated, was part of a much more ambitious design—that of codifying the substantive law as well as the law of procedure. Both purposes found expression in the New York constitution of

[1] Fla. Laws, 1873, p. 15.

[2] Cf. Fla. Rev. Stats. 1892, Div. II, §§ 967–1791; and in particular §§ 981–1076.

1846; and the outcome was that the codification of the substantive law was entrusted to three "commissioners of the code," while the codification of the procedure was assigned to three "commissioners on practice and pleadings".

The former commission accomplished very little; but the movement which resulted in its appointment had far-reaching effects further on. In 1857 a new commission was appointed, with Mr. David Dudley Field, then for some years prominent in the commission on practice and pleadings, at its head.[1] Its instructions were to reduce the substantive law of the state to a systematic code consisting of three parts, a "political," a "civil," and a "penal code". The political code was completed in 1860; the other two were reported to the legislature in 1865. Only one of these codes has as yet become a law in New York—the penal code, and this after sixteen years of waiting.[2] The civil code, however, has on two occasions been almost in touch of its goal, having twice passed both branches of the New York legislature and failed of ultimate adoption only for want of the governor's approval.

Complete and partial codification.

Sec. 160. But, while failing of effect at home, this code of substantive law and the others have had great influence abroad. Their career has been something like that of the New York "code of civil procedure," which was proposed at the beginning of the fifties. In the far West especially the results have been noteworthy.

Thus the civil code and the penal code drafted by the New York commissioners were adopted as early as 1865 by

[1] N. Y. Laws, 1857, ch. 266, Act of April 6.

[2] N. Y. Laws, 1881, ch. 676, Act of July 26. Cf. ch. 680. The same session of the legislature established, after a delay of thirty-one years, the New York Code of Criminal Procedure, reported by the first Commission on Practice and Pleadings; see N. Y. Act of June 14, 1881, ch. 504.

the territory of Dakota, the first English commonwealth to venture upon a codification of its substantive law.[1] The state of California has had a full suit of codes since 1872—a political code, a civil code, a code of civil procedure, and a penal code, which includes a code of criminal procedure as its second part. Each of the four was a separate act and is commonly published as a distinct volume.[2] A similar series of codes has been completed in the Dakotas, whose activity in codifying has been quite remarkable,[3] and in Montana.[4]

Sec. 161. Besides these instances of all-round codification, the half century since 1848 has seen many instances of partial codification, in addition to the codes of civil procedure. The latter, indeed, make not quite half the total list of codes now extant in the United States. Notably and naturally there has been great activity in codifying the

[1] This first operating civil code in America would make an octavo volume of some three hundred and eighty pages, including its short schedule of forms for deeds to land, bills of lading, etc. It numbers two thousand and thirty-four sections. It went into effect from the date of its approval, January 12, 1866. The Penal Code, an act of seven hundred and eighty-eight sections, went into effect a year earlier.

[2] The official designations of these codes and the order of their enactment are as follows: "The Penal Code of California," Feb. 14, 1872, numbering with the amendments of the next year 1,614 sections; "The Code of Civil Procedure of California," March 11, 1872, numbering 2,104 sections; "The Political Code of the State of California," March 12, 1872, numbering 4,460 sections; "The Civil Code of the State of California," March 21, 1872, numbering 3,543 sections.

[3] During the first ten years of Dakota's existence as a Territory scarcely a session of its legislative assembly was passed, and the sessions were annual, without one or more codes being introduced and adopted out of hand. "These codes were taken either from those prepared by the New York Commissioners, or from other states in which codes based on the work of the New York Commissioners had been adopted." (Cf. Preface of "Revised Codes of North Dakota, 1895.") To make room for these activities it was found necessary now and then to *repeal* a code in short order.

[4] "Codes and Statutes of Montana in force July 1, 1895." The work is complete in four volumes, even to a translation of Magna Charta.

law of criminal procedure. It began in 1850, with the enactment of a penal code in California;[1] and nineteen other codes of criminal procedure have followed.[2] By the same showing the codes of *substantive* law are still few in number. But it is to be remembered that piecemeal changes of the common law here have been very numerous. The result lacks the system of a code; but the repeated incursions of legislatures into the domain of the substantive common law have very greatly diminished its extent. Many of its doctrines have been overthrown, many have been brought within the statute book.

Section II. Quasi-code states—Their aspects in general.

Sec. 162. The causes which brought on the codes of civil procedure were not peculiar to any one state. They operated more or less strongly through all the Union, with the exception of Louisiana. The result is that the older systems of pleading have been greatly modified by statute even in that minority of our commonwealths which have not adopted the new pleading. In no state of the Union has common law pleading preserved its integrity. But in some states the modified system is more nearly that of the common law than the code system. These states, for convenience of reference, we may call "common law" states. There are other non-code states, however, in which the statutory changes have gone very far in the direction of "code pleading," as that term is commonly understood. And these states, for the sake of a better term, we may call "quasi-code states". They comprise Mississippi, Massachusetts, Alabama, Maryland,

[1] Cal. Laws, 1849-50, ch. 119, Act of April 20, 1850. The statute runs to 746 sections.

[2] Cf. 25 Am. Law Rev., 515, 526 (1891); 1 Jurid. Rev., 18, 22 (1889); 35 Am. Law Rev. and Reg. (N. S.), 548, 549 (1896); Anderson's Dict., "Codifier."

Tennessee, Georgia, and Texas. Historically considered, the changes in their procedure rank with those in the earlier code states. And they show in a partial yet very suggestive way the impetus and general character of the reform movement in the early fifties. Its causes and effects appear in nearly every state in the Union, and on both sides of the Atlantic. The surprising thing is that, with so brave a start, the movement has gone no further than it has, either in these "quasi-code" states, or in the larger field of the "code" states.

Individual aspects of the quasi-codes.
(1) *In Mississippi*, 1850.

Sec. 163. The influence of the reform movement brought tangible results in Mississippi within two years after the enactment of the first New York code. In March of 1850 an act was passed to remodel the pleading, but not the rest of the procedure, in the circuit courts of Mississippi upon the lines of the new system.[1] The statute was a close copy of that portion of the New York code of 1848, as amended in 1849, which related to "pleadings in civil actions,"[2] and went far towards making Mississippi a code state. All existing forms of pleading were expressly abolished so far as inconsistent with the provisions of the act. A plaintiff's first pleading was required to be a complaint, which "shall contain a statement of the facts constituting the cause of action, in ordinary and concise language, without repetition, and in such a manner as to enable a person of common understanding to know what was intended". The only pleading by the defendant was to be "either a demurrer or an answer". The court was required "in every stage of the action to disregard any error or

[1] Laws of Miss., 1850, ch. 4, p. 57; Act to change the forms of pleading in the Circuit Courts of this state.

[2] Being Title VI, comprising six chapters and thirty-seven sections.

defect in the pleadings or proceedings which shall not affect the substantial rights of the adverse party''.

The reaction of 1857.

Sec. 164. This act was soon modified, the state returning, in the revised code of 1857, more nearly to the form of common law pleading. But several characteristic principles of the codes were retained in a slightly altered form, and, with other principles from the same source, have long been established in Mississippi by legislative enactment.[1] Thus it is now required that "the declaration shall contain a statement of the facts constituting the cause of action, in ordinary and concise language, without repetition; and, if it contain sufficient matter of substance for the court to proceed upon the merits of the case, it shall be sufficient; and it shall not be an objection to maintaining any action, that the form thereof should have been different''.[2] Likewise a bill in equity "must contain a statement of the facts on which the complainant seeks relief, in ordinary and concise language, without repetition or needless prolixity, and conclude with a prayer for relief, without a charge of combination or confederacy by the defendants, or the insufficiency of the remedy at law, or other merely formal matter or similar useless averment''.[3]

[1] Cf. the elaborate acts "to establish Circuit Courts, to define their jurisdiction, and to regulate the practice therein," and "in relation to Chancery Courts," chs. 61, 62, of the Revised Code of 1857, pp. 471–568.

[2] Miss. Code, 1892, 671; cf. Miss. Code, 1857, art. 78, p. 491. Under the Revised Code litigants are not held to the strict technical rules of pleading. All that is required is to state, in ordinary and concise language, the facts constituting a substantial ground of action or defense. Lamkin v. Nye, 43 Miss. 241, 249 (1870).

[3] Miss. Code, 1892, § 527. "A bill in chancery should set out in plain, positive, and perspicuous language the nature of the complainant's case." Perkins v. Sanders, 56 Miss., 733, 737 (1879). The statute further declares that "it shall not be a ground of objection to a bill that it contains all the parts of a bill according to the former practice in chancery pleadings." Miss. Code, 1892, § 527.

(2) *In Massachusetts*, 1851.

Sec. 165. In 1851 several of the guiding principles of code pleading were substantially adopted in Massachusetts by a sweeping, yet conservative statute, which is commonly known as the Practice Act.[1] Under its provisions the personal actions were reduced to one or the other of three general forms, an action of contract, an action of tort, or an action of replevin.[2] This partial abolition of the forms of action went further than appears at first sight. For while, as a rule, actions of contract and actions of tort can not be joined, yet the statute provided also that, "when it is deemed doubtful to which of these classes a particular cause of action belongs, a count in contract may be joined with a count in tort, averring that both are for one and the same cause of action".[3] Nor does it appear to be material in such a cause, at least as a question of pleading, whether the action is entitled as of contract or of tort.[4]

Sec. 166. The title of "declaration" is retained for the plaintiff's first pleading at law, but the character of its statements is regulated by an enactment which is in close accord with the codes. Their leading principle, indeed, as to stating a cause of action is embodied in the Massachusetts act, and admirably expressed by it. "No averment need be made which the law does not require to be proved. The *substantive* facts *necessary* to constitute the cause of action may be stated with substantial certainty, and without unnecessary verbiage."[5]

[1] Act to amend some of the Proceedings, Practice, and Rules of Evidence of the Courts of this Commonwealth. Mass. Acts and Resolves, 1851, ch. 233, May 22.

[2] Mass. Acts, 1851, ch. 233, § 1. Publ. Stats., 1882, ch. 167, § 1.

[3] Mass. Pub. Stats., 1882, ch. 167, § 2 (5).

[4] Hulett v. Pixley, 97 Mass., 29, 30 (1867).

[5] Mass. Pub. Stats., 1882, ch. 167, § 2.

Distinction between law and equity.

Sec. 167. A distinction between law and equity was also retained, but no longer as a vital matter in procedure. Rather it is the shadow cast by the natural difference between legal and equitable rights under the substantive law. Excepting the allegations which confer jurisdiction in equity, the plaintiff's first pleading is substantially the same as at law. "The material facts and circumstances relied on by the plaintiff shall be stated with brevity, omitting immaterial and irrelevant matters."[1] A mistake in selecting the tribunal will not defeat the proceeding. When it becomes necessary to enable a plaintiff "to sustain the action or suit for the cause for which it was intended to be brought," amendments may be allowed changing the action at law into a suit in equity, or the suit in equity into an action at law."[2]

(3) *In Alabama*, 1852.

Sec. 168. In 1852 a statutory procedure was enacted as part of the "Code of Alabama".[3] The portion which related to proceedings in civil cases, an elaborate act of eight hundred and thirty-nine sections, wrought many important changes in the older practice; and some of its provisions were in notable accord with the very spirit of the

[1] Mass. Pub. Stats., 1882, ch. 151, § 7. Of the chancery rules of the Supreme Court, rule VII provides that "all prolixity and repetition in the pleadings shall be avoided." A general form for a bill in equity under the Massachusetts practice may be found in Crocker's Notes to Public Stats., of Mass., 2d ed. (1891), p. 434.

[2] Mass. Publ. Stats., 1882, ch. 167, § 43. For an example see Loring v. Salisbury Mills, 125 Mass., 138, 142 (1878).

[3] By acts of the Alabama Legislature of 1850 three commissioners were appointed to draft a complete code of law, and in that connection, "to prepare a code, simplifying and regulating the practice in the several courts of this state." Acts of 1849–50, Feb. 5, 1850, Feb. 9, 1850, pp. 43, 47. The code so prepared was adopted in February of 1852.

reform movement in the northern states. A "complaint" was substituted for the common law declaration.[1] A civil action was, as a rule, to be commenced by the service of a summons accompanied by the complaint, setting forth the cause of action.[2] It was further provided that "all pleadings must be as brief as is consistent with perspicuity and the presentation of the facts, or matter to be put in issue, in an intelligible form," and that "no objection can be allowed for defect of form if facts are so presented that a material issue in law or fact can be taken by the adverse party thereon".[3]

(4) *In Maryland*, 1856.

Sec. 169. A like reform in procedure was authorized by the Maryland legislature in 1856, through an act "to simplify the rules and forms of pleading and practice in the courts of law".[4] This statute, which ran to one hundred and thirty-eight sections, made very extensive changes in the older system of pleading. It was in the nature of a "code," by which term, indeed, it is commonly referred to in its own provisions.[5]

Many sections of this Maryland statute are evidently taken at first hand from the English common law procedure act of 1852—a more elaborate and extensive statute on the whole than that of Maryland.

It greatly simplified the classification of actions at common law and went far towards abolishing their distinctive forms. Just how far the reform was intended to go in this

[1] Ala. Code, 1852, § 2234; Ib., 1886, § 2671.

[2] Ala. Code, 1852, § 2160; Ib., 1886, § 2651.

[3] Ala. Code, 1852, § 2227; Code, 1886, § 2664.

[4] Md. Laws, 1856, ch. 112.

[5] As such it is to be distinguished from the compilation of the general statutes of Maryland, now often cited as the "Code." Sometimes the "Act of 1856" and the "Code" are given in contrast; cf. Canton Ass'n v. Weber, 34 Md., 669, 670 (1871).

direction is not clear from the act itself. Its requirements lacked the positive force of the New York act, and in effect left the question to the construction of the courts, which, having a choice between the new and the old, preferred the old.[1]

In matters of pleading, however, the act of 1856 and its amendments established in Maryland one of the fundamental principles of the codes, that a pleading must be a plain and concise statement of the facts which constitute the cause of action. "Whatever facts," declared the original statute, "are necessary to constitute the ground of action, defense or reply, as the case may be, shall be stated in the pleading, and nothing more; and facts only shall be stated, and not arguments, or inferences, or matter of law, or of evidence, or of which the court takes notice ex officio."[2] By amendments it was further provided that it should be unnecessary to state any formal commencement or conclusion to any declaration or other plea, and that "any declaration which contains a plain statement of the facts necessary to constitute a ground of action shall be sufficient, and any plea necessary to form a legal defense shall be sufficient, without reference to mere form".[3]

(5) *In Tennessee*, 1858.

Sec. 170. In 1858 the state of Tennessee enacted an elaborate "code" in four parts, relating respectively to "Public Rights," "Private Rights," "The Redress of

[1] See Farmers' Bank v. Allen, 18 Md., 468, 474 (1862); Canton Ass'n v. Weber, 34 Md., 669, 670 (1871).

[2] Act of 1856, ch. 112, § 52; Maryland Code, 1888, Art. 75, § 2.

[3] Md. Laws, Acts of 1870, ch. 421; Acts of 1872, ch. 346; Code, 1888, Art. 75, §§ 3, 4. "Substance is to be considered the purpose of the pleading—whilst the forms prescribed by the Code, or any other of like character, to suit the facts of the case, may be used; the courts must have regard to the substance of the pleading—facts only are to be stated." Per Stewart, J., in Gott v. State, 44 Md., 319, 336 (1875). Cf. Consolidated Coal Co. v. Shannon, 34 Md., 144, 158 (1870).

Civil Injuries," and "Crimes". The third part formed a compact system of pleading, based upon the common law, but with many of the essential requirements of the codes of civil procedure.

Under it all contracts "may be sued upon in the same form of action," and torts "may be redressed in an action on the facts of the case".[1] All pleadings, as a rule, must state only material facts, without arguments or inference, as briefly as is consistent with presenting the matter in issue in an intelligible form. And a pleading is sufficient when it conveys a reasonable certainty of meaning and when, by a fair and natural construction, it shows a substantial cause of action or defense.[2]

Distinction between law and equity

Sec. 171. A formal distinction is retained between the administration of law and the administration of equity, but the pleadings are closely assimilated. In all actions at law, the declaration must state the cause of action "clearly, explicitly, and as briefly as possible";[3] while the bill in equity "should contain a clear and orderly statement of the facts on which the suit is founded, without prolixity or repetition". It is expressly provided also that there need be no averment of any combination or confederacy by the defendants or others, of the insufficiency of the remedy at law, or of other mere formal matter.[4] Nor is any action allowed to fail because of a defect in form. In short, while derived from the common law, this code, in effect, abolished forms of action so far as to obliterate the technical

[1] Tenn. Code, 1858, §§ 2746, 2747; Ib., 1884, §§ 3440, 3441.

[2] Tenn. Code, 1858, §§ 2881, 2884; Ib., 1884, §§ 3593, 3596. If defective in the first of the above particulars the court, on motion, shall direct a more specific statement; if in the latter, it is ground for demurrer. Code, 1858, § 2885; Ib., 1884, § 3597.

[3] Tenn. Code, 1858, § 2751; Ib., 1884, § 3445.

[4] Tenn. Code, 1858, § 4314; Ib., 1884, § 5057.

distinctions between them, and saves the action when the material facts are stated, in whatever form, subject, however, to some power in the court to require amendment when the terms of the code are not substantially complied with.[1]

(6) *In Georgia*, 1860.

Sec. 172. In 1860 the state of Georgia enacted a "Code of Practice," whose provisions also were often in substantial accord with the leading doctrines of code pleading. This "code" formed the Third Part of the more general Code of Georgia, which was drawn up in pursuance of an act of the general assembly in 1858, providing for a commission of three "to prepare for the people of Georgia a code, which should, as near as practicable, embrace in a condensed form the laws of Georgia, whether derived from the common law, the constitution of the state, the statutes of the state, the decisions of the supreme court, or the statutes of England of force in this state".[2]

Partial accord with code pleading.

Sec. 173. In particular, the Georgia code of practice abolished "all distinctions of actions into real, personal, and mixed";[3] declares in express terms that "for every right there shall be a remedy, and every court having

[1] Cf. Remarks of Hammond, J., in Whittenton Mfg. Co. v. Memphis Packet Co., 19 Fed. Rep., 273, 281 (1883).

[2] Georgia Laws, 1858, Act of Dec. 9, p. 95, 202. The other main divisions of the Code of Georgia—"Part First, the Political and Public Organization of the State;" "Part Second, the Civil Code," and "Part Fourth, Penal Laws"—suggest the "Political," the "Civil," and the "Penal" Codes of the New York codifiers of 1850 and later years. "But the preparation of the Georgia Code," says Mr. Field, "was not known to the New York commissioners while they were engaged in their labors, owing, it is supposed, to the breaking out of the civil war." The resemblances between the recommendations of the two commissions were in substance and not in form.

[3] Code of Ga., 1860, § 3176; Code, 1882, § 3252.

jurisdiction of the one, may, if necessary, frame the other'';[1] and, while maintaining a distinction between law and equity, provided that ''no suitor is compelled to appear on the equity side of the court, but he may institute his proceeding for an equitable cause of action upon the common law side of the court at his option, and the court may allow the jury to find a verdict, and a judgment be rendered thereon, so molded and framed to give equitable relief in the case, as verdicts and decrees are rendered and framed in equity proceedings''.[2]

The pleading was further regulated by the provision that ''ordinary suits in the superior and inferior courts shall be by petition to the court, signed by the plaintiff or his counsel, plainly, fully, and distinctly setting forth his charge or demand, and no want of form shall be cause of delay if this article is substantially complied with''.[3]

(7) *In Texas*, 1840.

Sec. 174. The system of pleading which prevails in Texas, although distinct from that of the codes, is in remarkably close accord with it. Civil pleading in Texas has never been encumbered with the technical distinctions and obsolete forms of a scholastic age. The common law of England was, indeed, adopted generally by the Republic in 1840, but the common law system of pleading was expressly excluded form the scope of the statute; and it was then enacted that the proceedings ''shall, as heretofore, be conducted by petition and answer''.[4]

[1] Code of Ga., 1861, § 3174; Code of 1882, § 3250.

[2] Code of Ga., 1861, § 3015; Ib., 1882, § 3082. Cf. Cox v. Cox, 48 Ga., 619, 621 (1873).

[3] Code of Ga., 1861, § 3245; cf. § 4087 as to equity proceedings. Ib., 1882, § 3332. The rule of conciseness which is lacking here was presently supplied by the Supreme Court. Martin v. Barton Iron Works, 35 Ga., 320, 322 (1867).

[4] Act of March 16, 1840; cf. Laws of Tex., 1850, p. 121. A code of civil procedure was reported to the legislature of Texas in 1856, but it was never adopted. On the advanced position early taken by Texas in its system of pleading see 30 Am. Law Rev. 813 (Nov.-Dec., 1896).

Under this system, as molded by various statutes and the unwritten practice of the state, there is no distinction in Texas between legal and equitable procedure,[1] nor any distinctive forms of civil action. Ordinary proceedings in private causes are by a "civil suit," which must be commenced by filing a petition. "The pleadings," it is further provided, "shall consist of a statement, in logical and legal form, of the facts constituting the plaintiff's cause of action or the defendant's ground of defense."[2] As construed by the courts, this statement of facts should be full, clear, and concise.[3] "Our petition," said the supreme court in an early decision, "was designed to be a plain, straightforward statement of the cause of action, without repetition or circumlocution."

Section III.—Code pleading in the federal courts—Twenty-five years of discord.

Sec. 175. Since 1872 the leading principles and rules of code pleading have had an important though limited authority in the federal courts. For twenty-five years after the inauguration of the new procedure, common law pleading was adhered to by the circuit and district courts of the United States, even in districts where state courts followed the simpler forms of the code. It was, indeed, within the power of a federal court to adapt its procedure at law to that of the state in which it sat;[5] but the federal judges, preferring the familiar paths of the common law,

[1] Cf. Johnson v. Davis, 7 Tex., 173-175 (1851).

[2] Tex. Civ. Stats., § 1187. "Pleadings, with the exception of those presenting issues of law, must be a statement of facts, in contradistinction to a statement of evidence, of legal conclusions, and of arguments." Rule 2, 47 Tex., 615.

[3] Cf. Morrison v. Ins. Co., 69 Tex., 353, 359 (1887); Miles v. Mays, 4 App. C. C., 110.

[4] McClelland v. Smith, 3 Tex., 215 (1848).

[5] Amy v. Watertown, 130 U. S., 301, 303 (1888).

seldom ventured upon the new highway of the codes. As the new procedure spread through the Union many of the profession, in a steadily increasing number of states, found it necessary to become familiar with systems of remedial law which were not only distinct but widely different, and to meet in practice the very dissimilar requirements of both. The inconvenience was great and wide-spread, amounting, in the view of the Supreme Court, to a serious evil.[1]

The practice conformity act.

Sec. 176. With a view to remedying this state of things, congress in 1872 enacted that "the practice, pleadings, and forms, and modes of proceeding in civil causes, other than equity and admiralty causes, in the circuit and district courts, *shall* conform, as near as may be, to the practice, pleadings, and forms, and proceedings existing at the time in like causes in the courts of record of the state within which such circuit or district courts are held, any rule of court to the contrary notwithstanding".[2] The purpose of this statute, as declared by the supreme court, was to bring about a convenient uniformity in the law of procedure in federal and state courts of the same locality by "assimilating the pleadings and the procedure in common law cases in the federal courts to the pleadings and procedure used in such cases in the courts of record of the state within which the federal courts are held".[3]

Its peremptory character when applicable.

Sec. 177. Within its limitations, presently to be noticed, the act is peremptory. It requires in general terms what formerly was merely permitted. When the statute applies,

[1] Nudd v. Burrows, 91 U. S., 426, 441 (1875).

[2] Act of June 1, 1892, 17 Stats., 196, ch. 255, § 5; U. S. Rev. Stats., § 914.

[3] Lamaster v. Keeler, 123 U. S., 376, 387 (1887); Nudd v. Burrows, 91 U. S., 426, 441 (1875).

whatever belongs to the three categories of practice, pleading, and forms and modes of proceeding in common law actions must conform to the state law and the practice of the state courts.[1]

It is not merely unnecessary to follow the common law pleading in an action at law brought in the federal courts of a code state, but such pleading is inadmissible there, except as it may be deemed to be substantially in compliance with the code of that state. If it appears that there is no such substantial compliance, the pleading will be set aside.[2]

The codes as part of the federal system.

Sec. 178. Whether a pleading is sufficient under a code depends upon the construction by the federal courts of the code itself, which to this extent is adopted into the federal jurisprudence. The construction which a state may have put upon the enactment in question does not absolutely bind the federal courts. They constitute an independent judiciary system. It is not to be supposed that congress intended to place them, in each state, in reference to their own practice and procedure, upon the footing merely of subordinate local courts, required to look to the supreme court of the state for guidance. But this body of local law, thus adopted in the general, is construed by federal courts in the light of their own system of jurisprudence, as defined by the constitution of the United States and the acts of congress.[3] Nevertheless, federal courts incline to adopt the construction which is placed by a state court upon a provision

[1] Amy v. Watertown, 130 U. S., 301, 304 (1888); Lamaster v. Keeler, 123 U. S., 376, 388 (1887).

[2] Lewis v. Gould, 13 Blatch., 216 (1875).

[3] Erstein v. Rothschild, 22 Fed. Rep., 61, 64 (1884): "The act of Congress, at any rate, does not require the adoption with the local statutes of the local interpretation which may have been put upon them, or which may from time to time be enforced." Per Matthews, J. Cf. opinion of Sanborn, J., in O'Connell v. Reed, 56 Fed. Rep., 531, 535 (1893).

of its code,[1] when it does not run counter to the recognized limitations of the practice conformity act.

Limitations of the practice conformity act.

Sec. 179. These limitations are extensive and important. They are grounded on the far-reaching principle already referred to—that the federal courts constitute an independent judiciary system. Their judges do not derive their powers from the states, nor can the legislation of the states or the decisions of state courts determine the limits of these powers, or prescribe the duties which their exercise imposes. "One of the objects of the establishment of the federal courts, with jurisdiction to determine controversies between citizens of different states, was to provide a tribunal in each state where the rights of citizens of other states might be determined, unaffected by any possible influence that friendship for, or acquaintance with, a resident defendant might some times have in the local courts of his county. It was not the purpose of the act conforming the pleadings and practice of the federal courts to those of the state courts to prevent, or even to hinder, the accomplishment of this or any other object for which the federal courts were established. It was not the intention of congress to require, by the passage of this act of conformity, the adoption by the circuit courts of any rule of pleading, practice, or procedure enacted by state statute, or announced by the decision of a state court, which would enlarge or restrict the jurisdiction of the federal courts, or prevent the wise administration of the law in the light of their own system of jurisprudence, as defined by their own constitution, as tribunals, and the acts of congress upon that subject. On the other hand, that act expressly reserves to the judges of these courts the right, and, we think, imposes

[1] Rush v. Newman, 58 Fed. Rep., 158, 161 (1893); 7 C. C. A., 136.

upon them the duty, in the exercise of wise judicial discretion, to reject any statute, practice, or decision which would have such an effect.[1]

Construed in the light of these principles, and of its own terms, the practice conformity act evidently does not require a very high degree of conformity between federal and state procedure. Its limitations are of three kinds: (1) The conformity must not conflict with positive provisions of federal legislation; (2) even when there is no direct conflict, the conformity need be only "as near as may be," in the view of the general policy of the federal system; (3) the act itself does not purport to require conformity when the cause is of an equitable nature.

(1) *No conformity against positive enactments of congress.*

Sec. 180. It is a very well-settled rule of construction in the federal courts that, notwithstanding the practice conformity act, the provisions of a state statute and the usage which obtains in state courts will not be followed in the federal courts, either where they conflict with positive provisions of the federal statute, or where the latter prescribe the method in the given particular.[2]

So, generally, in the matter of the competency of witnesses, the mode of examination, the production and admissibility of evidence, the federal courts are not bound by the rules and usages that obtain in state courts;[3] for congress has legislated directly upon the mode of proof in

[1] Per Sanborn, J., in O'Connell v. Reed, 56 Fed. Rep., 531, 535–6; 5 C. C. A., 586, 591 (1893); and see note to this case in 5 C. C. A., pp. 594–608.

[2] Allnut v. Lancaster, 76 Fed. Rep., 131, 134 (1896); Chappell v. United States, 160 U. S., 499, 513 (1896); Seeley v. Kansas City Co., 71 Fed. Rep., 554 (1896); King v. Worthington, 104 U. S., 44, 50 (1881); Ex parte Fisk, 113 U. S., 713, 720 (1884); Randall v. Venable, 17 Fed. Rep., 162, 164 (1883); Amy v. Watertown, 130 U. S., 301, 304 (1888); Chamberlain v. Mensing, 47 Fed. Rep., 435, 436 (1891); Lancaster v. Keeler, 123 U. S., 376, 388 (1877); Citizens Bank v. Farwell, 56 Fed. Rep., 570, 573 (1893).

[3] Whitford v. Clark County, 119 U. S., 523, 525 (1886).

the trial of actions at law—it must be "by oral testimony and examination of witnesses in open court, except as hereinafter provided".[1] Accordingly, depositions taken for use in an action, afterwards discontinued, in a state court can not be used in an action thereafter begun, between the same parties and on the same cause, in a federal court, although the state practice allows depositions taken in a pending suit to be used in a renewed suit between the same parties on the same cause of action; and this because the federal statutes provide otherwise.[2]

(2) *Conformity "as near as may be"*.

Sec. 181. Less clearly defined but hardly less important is the second limitation referred to above. Even when there is no positive inhibition in the acts of congress, still the practice conformity act does not necessarily bring a state statute, in its entirety, into the federal system of jurisprudence. The act undertakes to conform the federal practice, pleadings, and forms and modes of proceeding in civil causes at law to the state model only "*as near as may be*"—not as near as *may be possible*, nor even as near *as may be practicable*.[3]

The vagueness of the act in this particular was appar-

[1] Rev. Stats., U. S., § 861; cf. Ib., § 863.

[2] Seeley v. Kansas City Co., 71 Fed. Rep., 554 (1896): "It was clearly not within the contemplation of the (federal) statute, as it was framed, taking sections 861 and 863 together, that depositions taken under a state statute for use in the state court could be admitted on a trial in the federal courts. While the manner of taking depositions in actions pending in the United States courts, both at law and in equity, in addition to the provisions and methods theretofore existing, has been extended by act of Congress (27 Stat., 7) so as to permit a party to take them 'in the mode prescribed by the law of the state in which the courts are held,' it goes only *to the mode of taking*, without in any degree touching or enlarging the limitations under which a deposition may be taken and used in the federal courts." Ib., p. 556, per Phillips, J.

[3] Indianapolis R. R. v. Horst, 93 U. S., 291, 301 (1876); Sherry v. Oceanic Steam Nav. Co., 72 Fed. Rep., 565, 566 (1895).

ently suggested for a purpose. In the view of the Supreme Court the words "imply that, in certain cases, it would not be practicable, without injustice or inconvenience, to conform literally to the entire practice prescribed for its own courts by a state in which federal courts might be sitting".[1] In effect the phrase leaves the federal courts some degree of discretion in conforming entirely to the state procedure. The qualification is not to be construed so as to subvert the command of the statute,[2] but it devolves upon a federal court affected by the statute a duty to construe and decide the local enactment in the light of the federal system. It gives federal judges the power to reject any *subordinate* provision in the state statute which, in their judgment, would unwisely encumber the administration of the law, or tend to defeat the ends of justice, as administered in federal tribunals.[3]

Illustrations of the limitation here.

Sec. 182. The exact nature of this limitation is not easy to define. In a general way, it is said that the conformity required by section 914 "applies to systems of judicial procedure as matters of separate study, and not to details of methods of doing the business of courts";[4] and that these details are left to be provided for by rules of court under section 918 of the Revised States.[5] But this

[1] Mexican Central Railway v. Pinkney, 149 U. S., 194, 207 (1893).

[2] Lewis v. Gould, 13 Blatch., 216 (1875).

[3] Indianapolis R. R. v. Horst, 93 U. S., 291, 301 (1876); Mexican Central Ry. v. Pinkney, 149 U. S., 194, 207 (1893); Mutual Accident Association v. Barry, 131 U. S., 100, 120 (1889); O'Connell v. Reed, 56 Fed. Rep., 531, 538 (1893); Sherry v. Oceanic Steam Navigation Co., 72 Fed. Rep., 565, (1895); cf. Jones v. Rowley, 73 Fed. Rep., 286 (1896); Ewing v. Burnham, 74 Fed. Rep., 384 (1896).

[4] Per Wheeler, J., in Ewing v. Burnham, 74 Fed. Rep., 384, 385 (1896).

[5] Which provides that "the several Circuit and District Courts may, from time to time, and in any manner not inconsistent with any law of the United States, or with any rule prescribed by the Supreme Court

does not greatly help the matter. The nature of the limitation is better shown by means of illustrations.

"Where a state law, in force when the act was passed," said Mr. Justice Swayne in 1876,[1] "has abolished the different forms of action, and the forms of pleading appropriate to them, and has substituted a simple petition or complaint setting forth the facts, and prescribed the subsequent proceedings of pleading or practice to raise the issues of law or fact in the case, such law is undoubtedly obligatory upon the courts of the United States in that locality. There may be other things, not necessary now to be specified, with respect to which also it is binding. But where it prescribes the manner in which the judge shall discharge his duty in charging the jury, or the papers which he shall permit to go to them in their retirement, as in Nudd v. Burrows,[2] or that he shall require the jury to answer special interrogatories in addition to their general verdict, as in this case, we hold that such provisions are not within the intent and meaning of the act of congress, and have no application to the courts of the United States."

Sec. 183. The same principle is illustrated in the recent case of Jones v. Rowley,[3] which was an action at law brought in the federal courts sitting in California. Defendant had filed what he called "a plea in abatement". Plaintiff moved to strike out this plea on the ground that

under the preceding section, make rules and orders directing the returning of writs and processes, the filing of pleadings, the taking of rules, the entering and making up of judgments by default, and other matters in vacation, and otherwise regulate their own practice as may be necessary or convenient for the advancement of justice and the prevention of delays in proceedings." But as § 918 is taken from old laws, long previous to the act of 1872, preserved in § 914, the latter, so far as it applies, should be construed to overrule the provisions of the former. Morrison v. Bernards Township, 35 Fed. Rep., 400, 401–2 (1888).

[1] Indianapolis R. R. v. Horst, 93 U. S., 291, 300 (1876).

[2] 91 U. S., 426 (1875).

[3] 73 Fed. Rep., 286 (1896).

it was not authorized by law. His argument was that, under certain provisions of the California code,[1] made applicable by section 914 of the federal Revised Statutes to the federal courts sitting in California, a *plea in abatement* was not authorized, but that the matters which, at common law, would be thus properly presented must, under section 914, be set forth by way of *answer*. This position, however, the learned court thought untenable. "That a defendant may plead to the jurisdiction of the court does not admit of question; and the fact that he calls his pleading *a plea in abatement* instead of an *answer*, as, perhaps, strictly speaking, would be the appropriate designation under the state practice of California, is no ground for striking out the pleading. Where objections are offered to the jurisdiction of the court, the better practice, for obvious reasons, is to determine such objections before the trial upon the merits, although, since the act of congress approved June 1, 1872,[2] carried into the Revised Statutes as section 914, objections to the jurisdiction of the court and matters in defense of the cause of action may be united in the same answer."[3]

So it has been held that a state statute which makes it the duty of the court, on a request of counsel, to require the jury to return, in writing, special findings upon particular questions of fact submitted to them, and also provides that if such special findings be inconsistent with a general verdict, the former shall control the latter, are not binding upon the federal courts and "are not within the meaning and intent of the act of congress adopting the practice of the state courts in suits at common law tried in the United States courts".[4] Likewise it has been held

[1] § 422 Cal. Code of Civ. Pro.

[2] 17 Stat., 197.

[3] Ib., per Wellborn, J., p. 287, 288.

[4] McElwee v. Metropolitan Lumber Co., 69 Fed. Rep., 302, 319 (1895); cf. also Lowry v. Mt. Adams Ry. Co., 68 Fed. Rep., 827, 829 (1895).

that the question of the finality of a decree, for purpose of appeal or otherwise, in the federal courts, is not affected by the procedure in the state courts, but must be governed by the statutes of the United States and the procedure and rules of decision in those courts.[1]

(3) *No conformity required in equity causes.*

Sec. 184. A more important restriction upon the adoption of code pleading into the federal system lies in this, that the practice conformity act has no application to equitable causes. They are excluded by the very terms of the statute. It is "the practice, pleadings, and forms and modes of proceeding in civil causes *other than equity and admiralty* causes, in the circuit and district courts" which must thus conform.[2] It is also provided affirmatively that "the forms and modes of proceeding *in suits of equity* and of admiralty and maritime jurisdiction in the circuit and district courts shall be according to the principles, rules, and usages which belong to courts of equity and of admiralty respectively".[3] Nor has any later legislation assimilated the federal procedure *in equity* with that prescribed by state codes.

Doctrine of the federal courts on the distinction between law and equity.

Sec. 185. These statutes but express a doctrine which has long prevailed in our federal courts. They have steadily recognized the distinction between law and equity as under the constitution matter of substance as well as of form and procedure. They persistently maintain the separ-

[1] Elder v. McClaskey, 17 C. C. A., 251, 254, 278 (1895); 70 Fed. Rep., 529; Kentucky Life Ins. Co. v. Hamilton, 11 C. C. A., 42, 47 (1894), 63 Fed. Rep., 93; In re Chateaugay Iron Co., 128 U. S., 544, 553 (1888)

[2] U. S. Rev. Stats., § 914.

[3] U. S. Rev. Stats., § 913.

ate administration of the two as necessary to the preservation of these essential distinctions between legal and equitable rights which are recognized in the federal constitution.

The cases in which these strictures are expressed have indeed commonly been those in which the resort was to equitable instead of to legal forms of relief, so that the defendant was deprived of his constitutional right of trial by jury; and a limitation of the doctrine when the resort is to legal forms of relief has been strongly urged upon the courts. Cases like Scott v. Neely [1] and Cates v. Allen,[2] which assert a more stringent rule are in truth—so it was contended—only to the effect that, when it is a question of jurisdiction on the chancery side of the federal courts, they are sedulous in observing a distinction between common law and equity, for the reason that the act of congress declares in express terms that the United States courts *sitting in equity* shall have jurisdiction in those cases only in which there is no plain, complete, and adequate remedy at law; but this practice conformity act, it was said, declares a more liberal rule with respect to common law jurisdiction.

The appeal here to the practice conformity act, and its rejection.

Sec. 186. In other words the contention was that, while congress had restricted the *equity* jurisdiction of the federal courts, it had enlarged, by a plastic and variable rule, the common law procedure so as to conform it to local practice in those courts which under that practice in the different states exercise common law powers.[3] But this proposed

[1] 140 U. S., 106 (1891).

[2] 149 U. S., 451 (1893).

[3] Cf. the argument in Davis v. Davis, in the Circuit Court of Appeals, 2 Fed. Rep., 81 (1896); 18 C. C. A., 438.

modification has been very positively rejected by the United States Supreme Court. The rule is asserted and enforced in its entirety, namely, that "the remedies in the courts of the United States are, at common law or in equity, not according to the practice of state courts, but according to the principles of common law and equity as distinguished and defined in that country from which we derive our knowledge of these principles, and, although the forms of proceedings and practice in the state courts shall have been adopted in the circuit courts of the United States, yet the adoption of the state practice must not be understood as confounding the principles of law and equity".[1]

The "fusion" of law and equity under a state system may be never so complete, but in the federal system the machinery of a court of law, in which the facts are found by the jury and the law is declared by the judge, can not be substituted for the usual and legitimate practice of a court of chancery; nor can the procedure for a court of chancery be substituted, in this system, for that of a court of law.[2] "In whatever form the subject has presented itself," said a federal judge in 1883, "whether as a matter of jurisdiction, pleading, or practice, as to methods of relief, defenses, or what not, the supreme and inferior federal courts have, with inexorable firmness, insisted upon preserving the *essential* distinctions between law and equity by administering them separately, as required by the constitution and laws of the United States. It is a distinction which inheres in the system by virtue of constitutional commands".[3] "The constitution of the United States,"

[1] Per Shiras, J., in Lindsay v. Shreveport Bank, 156 U. S., 485, 493 (1895).

[2] Lindsay v. Shreveport Bank, 156 U. S., 485, 493 (1895); Davis v. Davis, 72 Fed. Rep., 81 (1896); 18 C. C. A., 438; Scott v. Armstrong, 146 U. S., 499, 512 (1892).

[3] Per Hammond, J., in Whittenton Mfg. Co. v. Memphis Packet Co., 19 Fed. Rep., 273, 275 (1883).

said Taft, J., in the Circuit Court of Appeals, "requires that the distinction between common law and equity procedure shall be maintained, and the two jurisdictions can not be confused and mixed either by a state statute or rules of the federal court." [1]

The test of the equitable nature of a case under the practice conformity act.

Sec. 187. A suit in equity in a federal court follows the procedure of the English court of chancery, as modified by acts of congress and the rules of court made in pursuance of them.[2] When a question arises whether a particular cause requires legal or equitable relief, the doubt is to be settled "not according to the practice of the state courts, but according to the principles of common law and equity, as distinguished and defined in that country from which we derive our knowledge of those principles".[3] The rule as laid down by the Supreme Court in 1842 requires that in all cases where the rules prescribed by the Supreme Court or the Circuit Court do not apply, "the practice of the Circuit Court shall be regulated by the present practice of the High Court of Chancery in England, so far as the same may reasonably be applied consistently with the local circumstances and local conveniences of the district where

[1] United States v. Swan, 13 C. C. A., 77, 82 (1895).

[2] Bein v. Heath, 12 How., 168, 178 (1851): "The proceeding in a Circuit Court of the United States in equity is regulated by the laws of Congress, and the rules of this court made under the authority of an act of Congress. And the 90th rule declares that, when not otherwise directed, the practice of the High Court of Chancery in England shall be followed."—Per Taney, C. J. Hunton v. Equitable Life Assur., 45 Fed. Rep., 661, 662 (1891); Smith v. Burnham, 2 Summ., 612, 625 (1837); Gaines v. New Orleans, 27 Fed. Rep., 411 (1886); Grether v. Wright, 75 Fed. Rep., 742, 743-4 (1896); C. C. A.

[3] Sheffield Furnace Co. v. Witherow, 149 U. S., 574, 579 (1893), quoting Robinson v. Campbell, 3 Wheat., 212, 222 (1818).

the court is held, not as positive rules, but as furnishing just analogies to regulate the practice."[1]

This procedure is substantially uniform throughout the United States. In all essentials it is unaffected by state legislation in matters of equity jurisdiction.[2] Still there is some range of discretion. Although a state statute may not restrict or limit the equity powers of federal courts, "its provisions may justly be observed to the extent to which discretion can be exercised, within the general rules of equity jurisprudence".[3]

Sec. 188 If, on the other hand, the case is essentially an action at law, the equitable procedure will not be entertained by a federal court, although the state practice would have received it.[4] Hence, if a plaintiff in a state where the distinction between actions at law and suits in equity has been abolished chooses to set out a cause of action at law in a form which is peculiar to and characteristic of equity and not of common law pleading, a federal court may require him to replead.[5]

[1] Rule 90, Equity Rules.

[2] Ray v. Tatum, 18 C. C. A., 464, 466 (1896); U. S. v. Telephone Co., 20 Fed. Rep., 17, 32 (1886); Nickerson v. Atchison R. R., 30 Fed. Rep., 85 (1880); Hunton v. Equitable Life Assur., 45 Fed. Rep., 661, 662 (1891).

[3] Per Seaman, J., in Massachusetts Benefit Life Ass'n v. Lohmiller, 74 Fed. Rep., 23, 29 (1896.) See also Cowley v. Northern Pacific Railway, 159 U. S., 569, 582 (1895); Holland v. Challen, 110 U. S., 15, 25 (1883); Reynolds v. Crawfordsville Bank, 112 U. S., 405 (1884); Lanier v. Alison, 31 Fed. Rep., 100, 102 (1887); Southern Pacific Ry. v. Stanley, 49 Fed. Rep., 263, 265 (1892).

[4] Lindsay v. Shreveport Bank, 156 U. S., 485 (1895); Whitehead v. Shattuck, 138 U. S., 146, 151 (1891); Scott v. Neely, 140 U. S., 106, 109 (1891); Smyth v. N. O. Canal Co., 141 U. S., 656 (1891); Farmers Loan Co. v. Central R. R., 2 Fed. Rep., 656 (1880).

[5] Whittenton Mfg. Co. v. Memphis Packet Co., 19 Fed. Rep., 273, 281 (1883).

Application when a party blends legal and equitable claims.

Sec. 189. The rule has an important application when the plaintiff attempts to blend legal and equitable claims in one action. "The Ohio code of civil procedure," said Chief Justice Fuller, in Scott v. Armstrong,[1] "abolishes the distinction between actions at law and suits in equity, requires all actions (with some exceptions) to be brought in the name of the real party in interest, and permits all defenses, counterclaims, and setoffs, whether known as legal or equitable, to be set up therein. Section 914 of the Revised Statutes in providing that the practice, pleadings, and forms and modes of proceeding in civil causes, in the circuit and district courts, shall conform, as near as may be, to the practice, pleadings, and forms and modes of proceeding existing at the time in like causes in the courts of record of the state within which such circuit or district courts are held, in terms excludes equity causes therefrom, and the jurisprudence of the United States has always recognized the distinction between law and equity as under the constitution matter of substance, as well as of form and procedure; accordingly, legal and equitable claims can not be blended together in one suit in the circuit courts of the United States." If a blending of this sort has occurred and the case is removed into a federal court, there must be a repleading, although it require distinct proceedings in law and in equity.[2] Likewise, in these courts, legal defenses only can be interposed to legal actions. A defendant who has equitable grounds for relief against a plaintiff at law must seek to enforce them by a separate suit in

[1] 146 U. S., 499, 512 (1892). Cf. Myrick v. Heard, 31 Fed. Rep., 97 (1887); Hurt v. Hollingsworth, 100 U. S., 100, 103 (1879).

[2] Cf. Whittenton Mfg. Co. v. Memphis Packet Co., 19 Fed. Rep., 273 (1883).

equity, although, under the state code, the defendant in such a case may set up an equitable defense.[1]

When a new right of action is given by state legislation.

Sec. 190. For the most part, the general principle noticed above applies also when, as happens more and more frequently, one would assert in the federal courts a right of action which does not exist at common law and is not found in the federal statute book, but has been created by state legislation. If the case is otherwise a proper one for the federal courts, they will enforce this new right or privilege; but they will enforce it as a legal or as an equitable right, according as they view its nature.[2] If, for instance, the case as presented does not come under some of the heads of equitable jurisdiction of federal courts, it will be placed upon the law side, although the cause has been treated by a state court as equitable in its nature.[3] If the action is

[1] Davis v. Davis, 18 C. C. A., 438 (1896); S. C., 72 Fed. Rep., 81; Northern Pacif. R. R. v. Paine, 119 U. S., 561, 563 (1886); Church v. Spiegelburg, 31 Fed. Rep., 601 (1887).

[2] Cowley v. Northern Pacific Railroad, 159 U. S., 569, 582-3 (1895).

[3] Elliott v. Schuler, 50 Fed. Rep., 454, 457 (1892); Indianapolis Water Co. v. American Strawboard Co., 53 Fed. Rep., 970, 976 (1893). See also Gaines v. Fuentes, 92 U. S., 10 (1875), for the general principle, and compare Ellis v. Davis, 109 U. S., 485, 497 (1883): "It has often been decided by this court that the terms 'law' and 'equity,' as used in the constitution, although intended to mark and fix the distinction between the two systems of jurisprudence, as known and practiced at the time of its adoption, do not restrict the jurisprudence conferred by it to the very rights and remedies then recognized and employed, but embrace as well not only rights newly created by statutes of the states, as in cases of actions for the loss occasioned to survivors by the death of a person caused by the wrongful act, neglect, or default of another (Railway Co. v. Whitton, 13 Wall., 270, 287; Dennick v. Railroad Co., 103 U. S., 11), but new forms of remedies to be administered in the courts of the United States, according to the nature of the case, so as to save to suitors the right of trial by jury in cases in which they are entitled to it, according to the course and analogy of the common law."—Per Matthews, J.; and Scott v. Neely, 140 U. S., 106, 109 (1890): "The general

essentially for relief of an equitable nature, the equitable procedure of the federal courts is to be followed,[1] except when some special cause works a modification.

A moderating principle.

Sec. 191. But just here there is a moderating principle of considerable potentiality. It is a clearly recognized doctrine in the United States Supreme Court that a party, by going into a national court, does not lose any right or appropriate remedy of which he might have availed himself in the state courts of the same locality.[2]

The effect of this may be illustrated from Cowley v. Northern Pacific Railroad.[3] A special proceeding was commenced in a court of the State of Washington, under the statutes of that state, by filing a petition to set aside a judgment charged to have been obtained there through fraud and collusion between the attorney for the plaintiff and the attorney for the defendant, and against instructions from the plaintiff. On defendant's motion the proceeding was removed into the federal courts. After its removal, the case, said Mr. Justice Brown, delivering the opinion of the Supreme Court, "might properly be docketed and

proposition, as to the enforcement in the federal courts of new equitable rights created by the states, is undoubtedly correct, subject, however, to this qualification, that such enforcement does not impair any right conferred, or conflict with any inhibition imposed by the constitution or laws of the United States. Neither such right nor such inhibition can be in any way impaired, however fully the new equitable right may be enjoyed or enforced in the states by whose legislation it is created."—Per Field, J. Further illustrations appear in Goldsmith v. Gilliland, 22 Fed. Rep., 965, 966 (1885); Aspen Co. v. Rucker, 28 Fed. Rep., 220 (1886); Sprague Mfg. Co. v. Hoyt, 29 Fed. Rep., 421, 428 (1886); Borland v. Haven, 37 Fed. Rep., 394, 405-6 (1888).

[1] Bigelow v. Chatterton, C. C. A., 402, 406 (1892).

[2] Davis v. Gray, 16 Wall., 203, 231 (1872); Holland v. Challen, 110 U. S., 15, 25 (1883); Reynolds v. Crawfordsville Bk., 112 U. S., 405, 411 (1884); Cowley v. Northern Pacific Railroad, 159 U. S., 569, 583 (1895).

[3] 159 U. S., 569 (1895).

tried by the court as an equity suit, but it still remained, so far as the rights of the plaintiff were concerned, a special proceeding under the territorial statute; and the powers of the court in dealing with it *were gauged, not merely by its general equity jurisdiction, but by the special authority vested in its own courts by the statutes of the territory.* Had the case never been removed to the circuit court, it would have proceeded in the state court as a special proceeding under the territorial statute, and we are of opinion that, upon its removal to the circuit court, petitioner lost no right to which he would have been entitled had the case not been removed. Even if it were treated as in form a bill in equity, the right of the complainant would be gauged as well by the statute under which the bill was filed as by the general rules of equity jurisprudence. If any action or proceeding in a state court were subject to be defeated or impaired by one of the parties exercising his statutory right to remove it to a federal court, no one would be safe in instituting such a proceeding in any case wherein, by reason of diversity of citizenship or otherwise, it might be subject to removal. While the federal court may be compelled to deal with the case according to the forms and modes of proceeding of a court of equity, it remains in substance a proceeding under the statute, with the original rights of the parties unchanged.

"Although the statute of a state or territory may not restrict or limit the equitable jurisdiction of the federal courts, and may not directly enlarge such jurisdiction, it may establish new rights or privileges which the federal courts may enforce on their equity or admiralty side, precisely as they may enforce a new right of action given by statute upon their common law side".

A choice of remedies.

Sec. 192. On the other hand, the mere fact that state legislation has provided a legal form of procedure for an equitable right does not necessarily require that this procedure shall be followed when the right is sought to be enforced in the federal courts. "It may well be affirmed," said Mr. Justice Brewer in 1893,[1] "that a state, by prescribing an action at law to enforce even statutory rights, can not oust a federal court sitting in equity, of its jurisdiction to enforce such rights, provided they are of an equitable nature."

It follows that if a state statute creates a remedy at law for the enforcement of equitable rights, a litigant in the federal courts has a choice of remedies. He may avail himself of the new statutory legal remedy, if it be sufficient to meet the exigencies of the particular case, or he may proceed under the undoubted equitable jurisdiction which exists in the federal court, and which is not destroyed or limited in any degree by the creation of a legal remedy by state legislation. But whatever course he takes in the federal courts must be clearly defined in his pleading.[2]

[1] Sheffield Furnace Co. v. Witherow, 149 U. S., 574, 579 (1893).

[2] First Nat. Bank v. Peavey, 69 Fed. Rep., 455, 459 (1895). "The case having been removed from the state court by the defendant, it is open to the plaintiff to determine whether, in this court, he will proceed at law or in equity. He has the right to reform his pleadings, and to select either the law or the equity side of the court as the forum of litigation. The present order will therefore be that the demurrer is overruled, and that the plaintiff be required to reform the petition, and, in doing so, to determine whether the case shall be proceeded with at law or in equity, and, in either event, that the pleading be made clear and specific."—Ib., per Shiras, Dist. J., p. 459, 460.

When state legislation creates a right and prescribes an exclusive remedy.

Sec. 193. The foregoing doctrine, although broadly stated, is not to be taken without qualification, at least, not as implying that if state legislation in creating a right of an equitable nature prescribes also a certain remedy at law as the exclusive remedy for its enforcement, the federal courts may separate the new statutory right from its remedy. For the supreme court has also asserted very positively the general principle that when a liability and a remedy are *created* by the same statute the remedy provided is exclusive of all others. "A general liability created by statute without a remedy," said the court in 1874, "may be enforced by an appropriate common law action. But where the provision for the liability is coupled with a provision for a special remedy, that remedy, and that alone, must be employed."[1] In other words, if a state statute *creates* a right and *provides a remedy* for its enforcement, this remedy, whether at law or in equity, must be adopted, regardless of the tribunal in which the proceedings are had. If, however, the state statute does not create the right sought to be enforced, but only redeclares it, so that it would exist in the absence of the state statute, then it exists as a provision of the general or common law, and when its enforcement is sought in the federal courts, the form of remedy is determined by the principles which differentiate legal and equitable jurisdiction in these courts.[2]

Sec. 194. What constitutes an exclusive remedy is not an easy question. The opinion last referred to, like the opinion in Pollard v. Bailey,[3] would seem to assume that,

[1] Pollard v. Bailey, 20 Wall., 520, 527 (1874), per Waite, C. J.

[2] Per Shiras, J., in First Nat. Bank v. Peavey, 69 Fed. Rep., 455, 457 (1895), citing decisions.

[3] 20 Wall., 520, 527 (1874).

if the act which creates the liability provides also a certain remedy, it *thereby* becomes exclusive. Such a test is no less arbitrary than convenient. In many, possibly in most instances, a remedy thus provided would naturally be exclusive; but the principle involved should hardly be reduced to an arbitrary rule of technical construction. It should rest not so much on the language of the statute as on the intent of the legislature which creates the right. If the statute expressly declares that a certain remedy is exclusive of all others, this should settle the matter. But, if the language of the statute does not unquestionably declare that the remedy provided is exclusive, there may, it would seem, be a rational question whether the mere *mention* of a remedy in the creating statute is to have this effect. The general nature of the new statutory liability is to be regarded. There may be special reasons why a certain remedy should be provided and yet not be exclusive. But if, all things considered, the state legislation which creates a right does provide a certain remedy for its enforcement *as an exclusive* remedy, the rule applies. When federal courts undertake to enforce such a right, they will conform to the remedy.[1]

[1] Cf. Whitehead v. Entwhistle, 27 Fed. Rep., 778, 780 (1886).

CHAPTER VI.

Codes of the British Empire in their Relation to Codes of the United States.

Section I. The English code.

1. Its enactment and leading features.
    1. The state of the reform movement in England about 1848.
    2. Actual legislation.
        1. Its general character.
        2. Its distinct series of statutes.
            1. Common law procedure acts.
            2. Chancery reform acts.
            3. Judicature acts.
                1. The chief characteristic of this stage.
                2. Passage of the judicature acts.
                3. Their historical bearings.
                4. Their threefold purpose.
                5. Rules of court instead of direct legislation.
2. The suggestive resemblance between English and American code pleading.
    1. In general.
    2. Their cardinal points of agreement.
        1. Single civil action.
        2. Proper party plaintiff.
        3. Joinder of parties.
        4. Joinder of causes of action.
        5. Matter to be stated in a pleading.
        6. Limited series of pleadings.
        7. Production of an issue.
            1. The common law and the statutory issue.
            2. The salient points of comparison between the two statutory issues.
        8. Amendment of pleadings.

SECTION II. OTHER CODES IN THE BRITISH EMPIRE.

1. GENERAL CHARACTER OF THE ENGLISH REFORM MOVEMENT IN THE PROVINCES.
2. EARLY EXPERIMENTAL CODIFICATION IN INDIA.
3. THE INFLUENCE OF THE ENGLISH JUDICATURE ACTS AND RULES.
    1. THEIR GENERAL RESULT.
    2. CHARACTERISTIC EXAMPLES OF THE BRITISH CODES IN IRELAND, ONTARIO, NEW ZEALAND, VICTORIA, NOVA SCOTIA.
    3. THEIR VALUE TO AMERICAN CODE PLEADERS AND THE CAUSE OF REFORM.

State of the reform movement in England about 1848.

Sec. 195. Before the change considered in the foregoing pages—this change from common law to code pleading in the state and the federal courts of most of the American commonwealths—had run its course, a similar yet greater revolution had occurred in the ancestral home of the common law. The movements towards this end had taken definite form in England at a somewhat earlier day than with us; the year 1832 promised much for the cause of law reform on the other side of the Atlantic. But the chief immediate results in actual legislation were some partial reforms in the chancery, and the halting rules of Hilary Term of 1834. As things stood in the first year of Victoria's reign, English law was entering upon another lease of youth, and thinking lawyers felt the new influence. "The flood-tide of 1832 had not yet ebbed. In letters, in science, in trade and industry, there was on all hands consciousness of fresh vigor and expectation of great results. As it must needs fall out, men's expectation was in some things beyond the mark, in some, wide of it, in many, far short of it."[1] But, in matters of procedure, the enactment of the New York code of 1848 found the English legislators

[1] See article by Sir Frederick Pollock, 3 Law Quart. Rev., 344 (1887).

still standing in doubt over the weightier questions of reform.

Influence of the first American codes.

Sec. 196. The startling character of this New York legislation, however, its radical and extensive aims, going far beyond the boldest designs then entertained in England, had a notable effect there. The practical workings of the new system were watched by English reformers with care. Its comparative success stimulated them to new efforts. "While all people," said an English law writer of that day,[1] "are agreed that reform is needed, and while the new common law commission are issuing suggestions, halting and faltering, willing, perhaps, but unable, to free their minds from that peculiar tone which long and successful practice under our present system inevitably induces—a practical people in the western hemisphere have appointed a commission, and, quietly, expeditiously, and cheaply, and out of laws similar to our own and derived from us, have created a simple, single, and intelligible judicial system, which has hitherto worked well in the state (New York) by which it was first sanctioned, and has in consequence been adopted by several other states of the American Union. And let us not forget that it is not among a poor, homely, uneducated, and simple people that this great experiment in legislation is being tried, but among a people who are our rivals in commerce, equal to us at least in intelligence, wealth, and luxury, with all the wants of a high taste of civilization, and whose laws to be successful must embrace nearly as wide a field as our own. The boldness of the attempt, and the righteousness of the motives which led to it should at least command our respect and sympathy. We venture to express a hope that the example may not be entirely lost upon ourselves, but

[1] 14 Law Magazine, N. S. (London), 1, 2, 17, 18 (1851).

that it will stimulate our law reformers to raise their minds at once to the contemplation of a radical and efficient reform; for they now have before them a proof that it is possible to sweep away all preexisting laws without rushing into chaos."

The actual legislation on the subject.

Sec. 197. Whatever the inducing causes, actual reformatory legislation on the English procedure began anew, and more vigorously than before, shortly after the year 1848. But the movement was still a cautious one. As it turned out, the English reformers were to go further than the American reform has ventured to go, but they were still resolved that a venerable system should not be overturned, as in America, at a single blow. They felt their way slowly. The enactment of their leading reformatory statutes, which began in 1852, extended through twenty years.[1]

Sec. 198. The more notable changes were at first by distinct series of statutes, relating respectively to the courts of law and the court of chancery; afterwards the whole system of English courts and their pleading, at law and in equity, were recast in one series of statutes. These reform-

[1] A good illustration of this conservative temper is found in 12 Solicitors' Journal and Reporter (London), 643, 645 (1868). A leading article on pleading advocates "the giving up of the whole theory of the science of pleading," as it then existed in England, for a system in which "the plaintiff should state in concise and simple language the facts upon which his claim arises," and the defendant should state his defense in a like simple manner; but at the same time it is declared to be unnecessary to make "any sudden or violent change" in order to introduce these radical alterations. "New common law procedure acts," says the writer, "might be passed modifying the procedure by degrees. It is now eight years since the last act upon this subject was passed, and it is full time that another step was taken along the path which has been already so successfully commenced." It may be, however, that a course less bold than that which was taken by the New York reformers in 1848, would have been fatal to the reform in America.

atory enactments are accordingly divided into three distinct groups: (1) a series of statutes establishing a reformed system of pleading at law—the "Common Law Procedure Acts," so called, whose course of enactment extended through eight years from 1852;[1] (2) a series of statutes establishing a reformed system of equity pleading, enacted under different titles during the course of ten years from 1852;[2] and (3) the judicature acts, whose beginning was in 1873, whose amendments have run through many years, 1875, 1877, 1879, 1881, 1884, 1890, 1891, and 1894,[3] and whose end is not yet.

(1) *Common law procedure acts.*

Sec. 199. The first of these statutes became a law in June, 1852, and went into operation in the following October.[4] It was a right extensive enactment, running to two hundred and thirty-six sections, and including two schedules of forms—a short *code of procedure*, as it were, for courts of law. It was followed within two years by an amending and enlarging statute of more than one hundred sections,[5] which in turn was followed, six years later, by another enlarging and moderating statute, the common law procedure act of 1860.[6]

These statutes, destined although they were to a short life in England, were no sudden growth. They were based in the main upon the reports of distinguished law commissioners whose labors had begun and produced some positive

[1] 15 & 16 Vict., c. 76; 17 & 18 Vict., c. 125; 23 & 24 Vict., c. 126.

[2] 15 & 16 Vict., c. 86; 15 & 16 Vict., c. 87; 21 & 22 Vict., c. 26; 25 & 26 Vict., c. 42.

[3] 36 & 37 Vict., c. 66; 38 & 39 Vict., c. 77; cf. 39 & 40 Vict., c. 59; 40 & 41 Vict., c. 9; 42 & 43 Vict., c. 78; 44 & 45 Vict., c. 68; 47 & 48 Vict., c. 61; 53 & 54 Vict., c. 44; 54 & 55 Vict., c. 53; 57 & 58 Vict., c. 16.

[4] 15 & 16 Vict., c. 76, "The Common Law Procedure Act, 1852."

[5] 17 & 18 Vict., c. 125, "The Common Law Procedure Act, 1854."

[6] 23 & 24 Vict., c. 126.

results as early as 1831. In other words, parliament was some twenty years preparing for the partial reform effected by the common law procedure acts.

Their effect in England.

Sec. 200. Their direct effect was in large part negative; they pruned away the faults of the older pleading at law. Still they wrought great and positive changes for the better, a few of which may be noticed here.

"Causes of action of whatever kind," it was provided, "may be joined in the same suit, provided they be by and against the same parties."[1]

Much of the old verbiage was abolished. "All statements which need not be proved, such as the statement of time, quality, quantity and value, when these are not material; the statement of losing and finding, and bailment, in actions for goods or their value; the statement of acts of trespass having been committed with force and arms, and against the peace of our Lady the Queen; the statement of promises which need not be proved, as promises in indebitatus counts, and mutual promises to perform agreements, *and all statements of a like kind, shall be omitted.*"[2] Special demurrers also are abolished, with all the frivolous learning which they rendered necessary.[3] And, still more significant, the reform breaks down part of the wall of separation between the administration of law and the administration of equity; for, under the act of 1854, several equitable defenses were permitted.[4]

[1] 15 & 16 Vict., c. 76, § 41. But the section did not extend to replevin or ejectment, and a court or judge had "power to prevent the trial of different causes of action together, if such trial would be inexpedient."

[2] 15 & 16 Vict., c. 76, § 49.

[3] Cf. 15 & 16 Vict., c. 76, § 51.

[4] Cf. 17 & 18 Vict., c. 126, §§ 83, 84.

Their influence in America.

Sec. 201. The influence of these changes was quickly felt in America. Such notable alterations in common law procedure, deliberately made at its ancestral home, where its virtues stood in the clearest light, came at an opportune moment in some of our states, which were hesitating over the problems of reform. The commissioners who framed the Iowa code of 1860 left it on record that they were "most largely indebted" to the English common law procedure acts of 1852 and 1854.[1] The Maryland act of 1856, "to simplify the rules and forms of pleadings and practice in the courts of law," was in the main a close copy from the same statutes. Other states, also, although, like Maryland, unwilling to enter upon the new and untried way of the codes, found themselves able to follow this reform by English legislation. But, curiously enough, some of these same states were not able to follow the statutory reforms which were presently to come in England; so that, while the common law procedure acts already belong to ancient history in England, they have today a present interest in more than one community on this side of the Atlantic. For in several of our states the movement towards a simplification of the law has gone but little, if any, beyond the point reached by these statutes.

Their short life in England.

Sec. 202. But in England they were, as I have said, only a temporary expedient, soon to give place to far more extensive and radical legislation.

They left the reform incomplete in at least two points of vital importance. The great principle that a pleading should be a plain and concise statement of the material facts alone had not yet been established — it was still

[1] Report on Civil Code of Iowa, 1860.

possible for substance to be sacrificed to form;[1] and the wall of separation between legal and equitable procedure was still retained. The drift, however, was setting very strongly towards a simple, harmonious, and systematic procedure in which substantial justice should prevail over formal justice, so strongly that the common law procedure acts make a short chapter in the history of English law. Within twenty-five years they had given place to the very comprehensive scheme for reform prescribed in the judicature acts.

(2) *Chancery reform acts.*

Sec. 203. Meanwhile a similar movement was making important changes in the administration of equity. In the year 1852, the year of the first common law procedure act, parliament passed also two statutes, one "to amend the practice and course of proceeding in the High Court of Chancery,"[2] and one "for the relief of suitors of the High Court of Chancery".[3] They were followed in six years by the short but important chancery amendment act of 1858.[4] Four years later came a "Chancery Regulation Act, 1862,"

[1] "Here was a case where all the necessary facts were before the court, and were sufficiently stated in the declaration, but the case could not be heard because these facts were not pleaded in the proper way. Because the plaintiff complained on those facts of a wrong done him independent of contract, he was not entitled to argue that there appeared upon the declaration a wrong done him by a breach of contract. If the arrangement of the words had been a littte altered, and the plaintiff's charge had been for breach of contract instead of for negligence, no difficulty would have occurred. If the plaintiff's cause of action had been stated in plain and ordinary language instead of in a technical form, this difficulty would not have arisen." 12 Solicitors' Journ. and Rep., 643, 644 (1868), referring to the pleadings in Readhead v. Midland Ry., Q. B., 15 W. R., 831. The difficulties alluded to were finally avoided by the parties agreeing to take the judgment of the exchequer chamber on a special case without pleadings; cf. Law Rep., 4 Q. B., 379, 380 (1869).

[2] 15 & 16 Vict., c. 86.

[3] 15 & 16 Vict., c. 87.

[4] 21 & 22 Vict., c. 26.

scarcely a page in length, but very significant in its requirements.[1]

The drift towards fusion.

Sec. 204. It is plain to see, in these enactments, that the court of chancery and the courts of law in England were now drifting rapidly towards the idea of "fusion," which had been given effect in the American codes not long before. The act of 1852 permits chancery to require the oral examination of witnesses before itself.[2] The act of 1858 confers on Chancery power to award damages in some cases, and permits it to impanel a jury for the purpose of assessing damages or trying questions of fact "before the court itself". Upon every such trial, "the Court of Chancery," declares the statute, "shall have the same powers, jurisdiction, and authority as belong to any judge of any of the said superior courts sitting at nisi prius".[3] The short act of 1862 goes further into the fundamentals. It required that chancery should no longer refuse or postpone the application of remedies within its jurisdiction until questions of law and fact on which the title to such remedies depended had been determined or ascertained by courts of law, but that the court of chancery must determine every question of law and fact incident to the relief sought, "whether the title to such relief or remedy be or be not incident to or dependent upon a legal right". There was a proviso, however, quite in harmony with the principle—when questions of fact before a court of chancery could be more conveniently tried by a jury at the assizes, it was declared lawful for chancery to direct such a trial.

But these statutes, like the common law procedure acts, were tentative measures; they failed to satisfy the demand of their day. The reformed system of equity pleading

[1] 25 & 26 Vict., c. 42.
[2] 15 & 16 Vict., c. 86, § 39.
[3] 21 & 22 Vict., c. 27, §§ 2, 3, 4.

which they created flourished for twenty years and then was merged, with the reformed common law pleading, in the greater system created by the judicature acts.

(3) *Judicature acts. Chief characteristic of this stage.*

Sec. 205. The most characteristic thing about this stage of the movement was its "fusion" of law and equity. The mischief which arose from their separation was early recognized. Before the passage of the first common law procedure act, indeed, a commission on law reform had reported that "a consolidation of the elements of a complete remedy in the same court was obviously, not to say imperatively, necessary to the establishment of a consistent and rational system of procedure". About the time of the third common law procedure act, 1860, three law judges publicly declared that the existence of two conflicting systems of law recognizing inconsistent and incompatible rights, administered by two tribunals, each refusing to give effect to rights which would be enforced by the other, was not only an anomaly in jurisprudence, but had been found to be attended by practical inconvenience and mischief of the most serious character. In 1869, also, a judicature commission reported that "the first step towards meeting and surmounting the evils complained of would be the consolidation of all the courts of law and equity into one court, in which should be vested all the jurisdiction exercisable by each and all the courts so consolidated". In the following year a bill constructed in conformity with this plan was introduced into parliament, but it failed of passage.

Passage of the judicature acts.

Sec. 206. The hour, however, was now almost ripe for the revolution. A similar measure, introduced by Lord Chancellor Selborne, was carried in 1873, the first and most important of the judicature acts.[1] It was followed in 1875 by an amendatory and supplemental act,[2] and both came into operation at the same time, November 1, 1875.[3] This was in the Chancellorship of Lord Cairns, whose name and that of Lord Selborne will, therefore, says an English writer, "forever remain associated with the greatest and probably most useful change in the way of law reform which has taken place in this country for centuries".[4] But the movement which resulted in the judicature acts had been promoted by all the recent chancellors and by most of the leading judges.

The historical bearings of the judicature acts.

Sec. 207. The general effect of the judicature act of 1873 was to sweep away the English system of common law pleading even more completely than our codes have swept it away. And yet, as with us, the practitioner in England can not afford to forget the old procedure entirely.

Both the radical nature of this latest phase of the English reform and its historical bearings may be illustrated from the remarks of Mr. Montague Crackanthrope, of the English bar, before the American Bar Association in 1896.[5]

"The English system of common law pleading," said he "was finally swept away by the English judicature act of 1873. It had been encumbered with obsolete learning, and had been terribly abused by the ingenuity of pleaders during centuries of adroit manipulation. The abuses were not, I think, original, and much had been done to remedy them; but the system had fallen into discredit, and had

[1] 36 & 37 Vict., c. 66, "Supreme Court of Judicature Acts, 1873."

[2] 38 & 39 Vict., c. 77, "Supreme Court of Judicature Act, 1875."

[3] Cf. 37 & 38 Vict., c. 83, extending the time of the act of 1873.

[4] 12 Ir. Law Times, 528, (1878).

[5] The paper referred to, on "The Uses of Legal History," appears in full in 54 Alb. Law Journ., 136, (Aug. 29, 1896).

become the scapegoat for the sins of the profession. It was determined that it should no longer be necessary to plead formal causes of action, but that each party should tell his plain tale unfettered by technicalities, or, as the rules expressed it, that his pleading should contain, and contain only, a summary statement of the material facts on which he proposed to rely.

The change was of enormous historical importance. The old system had been the mould upon which the whole common law had been gradually formed. All legal conceptions had been defined, analyzed, and formulated through the operation of that elaborate machinery. It provided a natural classification of the law, saving it from absolute chaos, so that students learned their principles as they went along, by mastering their procedure. Declarations, pleas, and demurrers have now become matters of antiquarian interest, as far as actual practice is concerned. But, until the whole system of English law shall be recast and codified, the old learning respecting them will be indispensable to all who wish to be sound common lawyers. Without it a great deal of quite recent authority will remain obscure, and the old books in great measure unintelligible. Even in so simple a matter as an action of contract, it is necessary to know the peculiar and not unromantic history of the action of assumpsit. In an action for injuries against a carrier we must still be familiar with the distinction between the breach of a duty to carry safely and a breach of a contract to carry, though we are no longer put to a choice between the one and the other form of action. And so long as written pleadings remain, the best masters of the art will be they who can inform the apparent license of the new system with that spirit of exactness and self-restraint which flows from a knowledge of the old."

The threefold purpose of the judicature acts.
(a) Consolidation of the courts.

Sec. 208. The chief aim of the judicature acts was to create and establish a simple, uniform law of procedure for all the superior courts of England. To this end three things were provided for: a consolidation of the courts, a unification of the law to be administered, and a simplification of the pleadings.

In the first place, the great and historically independent tribunals, the High Court of Chancery of England, the Court of Queen's Bench, the Court of Common Pleas at Westminster, the Court of Exchequer, the High Court of Admiralty, the Court of Probate, the Court for Divorce and Matrimonial Causes, were "united and consolidated together" into one Supreme Court of Judicature.[1]

Historical aspect of this consolidation.

Sec. 209. It is natural and proper enough to regard this consolidated supreme court as the first of its kind in the history of English law. The Court of Queen's Bench, the Court of Common Pleas at Westminster, the Court of Exchequer, the Court of Chancery could each claim some six centuries of existence as distinct and separate tribunals when they were thus united in one court in 1875. But it will hardly escape the curious that this result may fairly be regarded as in the nature of a reunion rather than a union of the English courts. The provisions of the judicature acts have this interesting aspect: in the "Supreme Court of Judicature" they restore in its integrity for the most part, but in a modernized form and under a new name, that ancient supreme court of judicature which stands at the threshold of modern English law — the

[1] 36 & 37 Vict., c. 66, § 3.

"Court of our Lord the King," the *Curia Regis*. The history of its gradual rise to supremacy by absorbing the jurisdiction of the popular courts of the English, of its gradual separation, along the lines of more or less technical distinctions, into seemingly distinct and conflicting tribunals, and of its coalescence in our own day, is the history of English procedure for more than six centuries.

Sec. 210. It is not to be understood, however, that the Supreme Court of Judicature comprises every judicial tribunal in the English system. The House of Lords is the true supreme court of the English system. It dominates the "Supreme Court," so called, and receives appeals from its Court of Appeal. The Judicial Committee of the Privy Council also is a court of great dignity and power, which stands still further apart from the Supreme Court of Judicature. It belongs rather to the judicial system of the British Empire than to that of England. As the House of Lords is the supreme court of appeal for Great Britain and Ireland, so is the Judicial Committee the supreme court of appeal for India, the Colonies, the Channel Islands, and other portions of the British Empire.

There may be also special tribunals of a subordinate character in the English system, for special kinds of work. The Railway and Canal Commission is a notable instance. The ancient jurisdiction of the Lord Chancellor in lunacy cases is expressly excepted by the judicature act from the jurisdictions transferred to the High Court of Justice.[1] And the new county courts, themselves tribunals of important and growing jurisdiction, are not directly included in this consolidation of English courts.

[1] 36 & 37 Vict., c. 66, § 17.

The new county courts and their experiment in a simplified procedure.

Sec. 211. The familiar name of "County Courts" recalls the most ancient days of our law; but the present English County Courts are ancient only in name. They have arisen through statutory enactment within the half century. Starting with a small beginning in 1846, in an act "for the more easy recovery of small debts and demands in England,"[1] they have steadily grown in the character and extent of their jurisdiction,[2] until they now afford a partial realization in England of Bentham's idea of local, "single-seated" tribunals with so wide a range of jurisdiction that every man could find an adequate court of justice sitting at his market-place.

Sec. 212. They are found in every county of England; and some of the more populous centers have county courts established in specially divided districts. Their jurisdiction is local, confined to such matters as arise within the district of the trial court. It is restricted also with respect to the amount involved in the action; but there is an evident tendency to draw the line of this restriction at a considerable sum. It was £20 when the court was created; it is now £500 in a large number of causes, chiefly equitable; while in some causes the pecuniary limit is withdrawn entirely if both parties consent in writing to try their case in a county court.[3]

[1] 9 & 10 Vict., c. 95.

[2] The list of statutes evidencing this growth is a long one. Especially significant was the act of 1865 (28 & 29 Vict., c. 99), conferring certain equity powers, and the act of 1868 (31 & 32 Vict., c. 71), giving the county courts some powers in admiralty. The present cardinal enactment is the elaborate act of 1888 (51 & 52 Vict., c. 43), "to consolidate and amend the county courts acts."

[3] But in other cases the old idea of the county court reappears in a very narrow pecuniary limit—£50 if the action is founded on contract (except for breach of promise of marriage), or on tort (except libel, slander, and seduction), unless the written consent of both parties is had.

In other respects the jurisdiction of these tribunals has acquired a wide range. With some restriction here and there, they may now act in common law, equity, probate, administration, and admiralty matters. And, by the judicature act of 1873, a county court has power to grant, and must grant, in any proceeding before it, every relief, redress, or remedy, or combination of remedies, either absolute or conditional, and must give effect to every ground of defense or counterclaim, equitable or legal (within the limits of its jurisdiction), "in as full and ample a manner as might and ought to be done in the like case by the High Court of Justice".[1]

But, however wide this jurisdiction, it is carefully subordinated to that of the High Court of Justice. With certain exceptions, an appeal lies to this court "if any party in any action or matter in a county court shall be dissatisfied with the determination or direction of the judge, in point of law or equity, or upon the admission or rejection of any evidence".[2] And the workings of the court are largely under the direction and control of the Lord Chancellor.

Sec. 213. With so extensive and varied a jurisdiction, running parallel, to a considerable extent, with the more important jurisdiction of the High Court of Justice, and of the trial courts under our codes, the procedure of these statutory county courts should naturally have considerable significance. It is all the more significant from the fact that with their widening powers, they have retained the extreme simplicity of procedure which marked their origin in 1846 as a poor man's court. Their jurisdiction then was far below that usually granted by our legislatures to a justice of the peace; their procedure was framed accordingly. It was as simple as possible. An action was begun on the plaintiff's oral application to a clerk of the court,

[1] 36 & 37 Vict., c. 66, § 89.

[2] County Court Act, 1888, 51 & 52 Vict., c. 43, § 124.

who was required thereupon "to enter in a book to be kept for this purpose in his office a plaint in writing, stating the names and the last known places of abode of the parties, and the substance of the action intended to be brought". The plaint being entered, "a summons, stating the substance of the action and bearing the number of the plaint on the margin thereof, shall be issued under the seal of the court according to such form, and be served on the defendant so many days before the day on which the court shall be holden at which the cause is to be tried, as shall be directed by the rules made for regulating the practice of the court, as hereinafter provided".[1] On the day appointed the judge tries the case in a summary way. The parties may appear by counsel, but this is a luxury, hardly to be expected. Very often the judge is the advocate of both parties.

Sec. 214. This rudimentary procedure, well enough suited to the business of the court as first organized, has been retained for the complicated questions which may now arise under its enlarged powers.[2] The experiment is an interesting one, but apparently its success is open to question.[3] It carries simplicity in procedure further than the complexities of the business now put upon these courts appear to permit; and in this respect their history is not without significance in America. But apart from these features of rudimentary simplicity, the procedure of the county courts is generally assimilated to that of the High Court of Justice. The basic principles are the same as those of the judicature acts, which alone will require attention in our further consideration of the British codes.

[1] 9 & 10 Vict., c. 95, § 59.

[2] 51 & 52 Vict., c. 43, § 73.

[3] Cf. the articles in 7 Law Quar. Rev., 346 (1891); 5 Ib., 1 (1889); 5 Ib., 134 (1889); 3 Ib., 1 (1887).

"Divisions" of the consolidated court.

Sec. 215. To its consolidated court, the judicature act of 1873 gave two "permanent" divisions—a "High Court of Justice" and a "Court of Appeal".[1] The High Court of Justice was nominally divided, for the sake of convenience, into five divisional courts, known respectively as the Chancery Division, the Queen's Bench Division, the Common Pleas Division, the Exchequer Division, and the Probate, Divorce, and Admiralty Division.[2] Each divisional court was to consist of a certain number of judges—"but not so as to prevent any judge from sitting whenever required in any divisional court, or for any judge of a different division than his own".[3]

A classification of business under the names of formerly distinct tribunals.

Sec. 216. Although preserving the names once borne by ancient tribunals, each of a limited and partly distinct jurisdiction, these divisional courts do not exercise a partial jurisdiction. The name of the Queen's Bench Division recalls, indeed, a venerable common law jurisdiction destitute of equity powers; but under the judicature acts every kind of equitable relief may be claimed in an action in the Queen's Bench; and every kind of legal relief valid under the principles of equity may be claimed in the Chancery Division.

Nor are these divisional courts "permanent," like the divisions of the supreme court into a High Court of Justice

[1] 36 & 37 Vict., c. 66, § 4. Cf. § 16, transferring to and vesting in the High Court of Justice the jurisdiction which at the commencement of this act was "vested in or capable of being exercised by all or any" of eleven courts, including those mentioned in the text, and certain others. Cf. Ib., §§ 17, 18 et seq.; cf. 38 & 39 Vict., c. 77, § 9.

[2] 36 & 37 Vict., c. 66, § 31.

[3] 36 & 37 Vict., c. 66, § 31.

and a Court of Appeal. They were created, as the statute itself declared, "for the more convenient dispatch of business". They afford an easy method of classifying the business of the court. Their number may be changed as occasion requires. And, in fact, their number has been reduced to three—a Chancery Division, a Queen's Bench Division, and a Probate, Divorce, and Admiralty Division.[1]

Effect on current law reports.

Sec. 217. This classification of the business of the High Court of Justice is reflected in the English series of law reports. Cases determined by the Chancery Division and on appeal therefrom in the Court of Appeal are reported in volumes of the "Chancery Division," and cited, according to the year of the report and the serial volume in the year, under the abbreviation "Ch." Thus, "[1894] 3 Ch. 1" denotes a decision reported on the first page of the third volume of the Chancery Division Reports for the year 1894; and the addition of "C. A." to the citation would indicate that this decision was by the Court of Appeal.[2]

So cases decided by the Queen's Bench Division, and by the Court of Appeal on appeal therefrom, appear in volumes cited in like fashion under the abbreviation "Q. B." For instance, "[1896] 1 Q. B. 198" denotes a decision reported on page 198 of the first volume of the reports of the Queen's Bench Division for the year 1896.[3] Likewise, cases in the Probate, Divorce, and Admiralty Division, and on appeal therefrom in the Court of Appeal, are reported in the " Probate Division," and cited under the

[1] The Exchequer and Common Pleas Divisions being consolidated with the Queen's Bench Division. See Order in Council, Dec. 16, 1880.

[2] The volume may include also decisions in lunacy cases.

[3] The volume may include also decisions on "Crown Cases Reserved," and decisions of the " Railway and Canal Commission."

abbreviation "P." Thus, "[1895] P. 87" indicates a decision of this divisional court, or on an appeal from it, reported on page 87 of the first and only volume of reports for the Probate, Divorce, and Admiralty Division of the High Court of Justice for the year 1895.[1]

But, as the Supreme Court of Judicature does not include the House of Lords or the Judicial Committee of the Privy Council, there are also the "Appeal Cases," one volume a year as a rule, which contain the decisions by these tribunals. The mode of citation is as in other cases; "[1895] A. C. 117" is a decision reported on page 117 of the first and only volume of appeal cases for 1895.

(*b*) *Unification of the substantive law.*

Sec. 218. In the second place the judicature acts aimed to effect a unification of the substantive law. Every division of the consolidated court was enabled and required to administer all such remedies as any party might be entitled to, whether at law or in equity, in every cause, action, or dispute which was properly before it. "The High Court of Justice and the Court of Appeal respectively," so runs the statute, "in the exercise of the jurisdiction vested in them by this act in every cause or matter pending before them, respectively, shall have power to grant, and shall grant, either absolutely or on such reasonable terms and conditions as to them shall seem just, all such remedies whatsoever as any of the parties thereto may appear to be entitled to in respect of any and every legal or equitable claim properly brought forward by them respectively in such cause or matter; so that, as far as possible, all matters so in controversy between the said parties respectively may be completely and finally determined, and all multiplicity of legal proceedings concerning

[1] The volume includes also decisions in the Ecclesiastical Courts.

any of such matters avoided''.[1] And, since there was an actual conflict in some states of fact between the doctrine of law and the doctrine of equity, it was further enacted generally that in all matters "in which there is any conflict or variance between the rules of equity and the rules of the common law with reference to the same matter, the rules of equity shall prevail''.[2]

(*c*) *Simplification of the pleading.*

Sec. 219. In the third place the pleading was greatly simplified. It ceased to be technical. The old forms of distinct actions were in effect abolished. "A proceeding to be called an action," took the place of "all *actions* which have hitherto been commenced by writ in the Superior Courts of Common Law at Westminster, or in the Court of Common Pleas at Lancaster, or in the Court of Pleas at Durham," and of all *suits* which have hitherto been commenced by bill or information in the High Court of Chancery, or by a cause in rem or in personam in the High Court of Admiralty, or by citation or otherwise in the Court of Probate''.[3] Nor was it otherwise necessary for a plaintiff to define in his pleading in what particular legal relation he claimed to stand towards the defendant. As under the American codes, it became the duty of a party pleading to state all the material facts of his claim and nothing more; the form which his legal rights might take should be determined by the court from the facts averred on either side.[4] The ancient names of the pleadings

[1] 36 & 37 Vict., c. 66, § 24, subsect. 7; cf. Wright v. Redgrave, 11 Ch. D. (C. A.) 24, 34 (1879); Salt v. Cooper, 16 Ch. D. 544, 549 (1880), for the construction of this section of the act.

[2] 36 & 37 Vict., c. 66, § 25 (11). A similar provision is occasionally found in the American codes.

[3] 36 & 37 Vict., c. 66, Schedule, Rule 1.

[4] Hanmer v. Flight, 24 W. R., 346 (1876); Metropolitan Ry. v. Defries, 2 Q. B. D., 189 (1877).

vanished with their forms. A "statement of claim" was substituted for the declaration and the bill in equity; a defense, for the plea and the answer; a reply, for the replication. After the reply there could be no pleading, without leave of court, except a joinder of issue.

Rules of court instead of direct legislation.

Sec. 220. Their general purpose and main results considered, the English and the American system of pleading are in remarkable accord, as will presently appear;[1] but they have one very salient point of divergence in the way in which they were framed. In the American codes almost all the principles and rules of judicial procedure were framed *for but not by* the judicial power. They were the direct work of the legislature. They exist in the forms of inexorable law. In the English system, on the other hand, almost all these principles and rules are framed *for and by* the judicial power, but under a delegated authority from the legislature. Excepting a few general provisions, the principles and rules of procedure in the English code exist not directly as statutes, but as rules of court. In other words, the courts themselves were permitted and required to build the complicated machinery which they must operate, and they may modify it as their experience suggests, without resorting to direct legislation. Parliament, however, was careful to retain a veto power upon proposed changes in procedure. By the terms of the act of 1873,[2] all rules of court made in pursuance of the statute were to be laid before each house of Parliament within forty days next after the same were made, if Parliament was then sitting, or, if not, within forty days after the then next meeting of Parliament, and thereupon Parliament, by means of an address presented to the Crown within forty

[1] Infra, §§ 225 et seq.

[2] 36 & 37 Vict., c. 66, § 68.

days, might cause any of these rules to become void and of no effect, "but without prejudice to the validity of any proceedings which may in the meantime have been taken under the same".

Scope of the rules of court in the English code.

Sec. 221. The principle that the rules of judicial procedure may be framed in the first instance by judges of the superior courts is, of course, no novelty in either American or English law. It is hardly less familiar to the profession than rational. Every code state has its rules of court. Still better known are the equity rules of the federal system, framed by the Supreme Court of the United States under authority of the act of 1792—a partial code of procedure which has been before the country since 1822.[1] Nor is it a strange doctrine with us that courts may, on their own motion and without direct resort to the legislature, repeal, amend, or add to the established rules of judicial procedure as experience or changing conditions require from time to time.[2] The difference between the English code and our own in this respect is therefore in degree rather than in kind.

How far the rules of court extend in the English code may be illustrated from the judicature acts of 1873 and 1875. Under the terms of the act,[3] rules of court might be made, at any time after the passage and before the com-

[1] When the rules, then thirty-three in number, were promulgated in 7 Wheaton, pp. x–xiii.; cf. Act of May 8, 1792, c. 37, s. 2.

[2] Here also the federal equity rules afford a line of illustrations. The thirty-three rules of 1822 give place to a code of ninety-two rules framed by the Supreme Court in 1842 (see appendix to 17 Pet., pp. lxi–lxxvii). And the latter have been amended or added to on several occasions since. The facility with which this code is adapted to new conditions is illustrated in 1 Wall., v (1864); 7 Otto, viii (1878), 14 Ottc, ix (1882); 144 U. S., 689–691 (1892); 149 U. S., 793 (1893); 152 U. S., 709-710 (1894).

[3] Cf. 38 & 39 Vict., c. 77, s. 17.

mencement of the act, by order in council on the recommendation of certain judges for any of the following topics:

(1) For regulating the sittings of the High Court of Justice and the Court of Appeal, and of any Divisional or other court thereof respectively, and of the judges of the said High Court sitting in chambers; and,

(2) For regulating the pleading, practice, and procedure in the High Court of Justice and Court of Appeal; and,

(3) Generally for regulating any matters relating to the practice and procedure of the said courts respectively, or to the duties of the officers thereof, or of the Supreme Court, or the costs of proceedings therein.

From and after the commencement of the act, the Supreme Court was authorized "at any time, with the concurrence of the majority of the judges thereof present at any meeting for that purpose held (of which the Lord Chancellor shall be one) to alter and annul any rules of court for the time being in force, and to have and exercise" the power of making new rules on the subjects specified.

Sec. 222. The statute proper [1] numbers but one hundred sections, and the great majority of these relate to the constitution of the consolidated court, its jurisdiction, the powers of its different judges, its officers and offices. Rules of pleading are scarcely touched upon. But the statute as amended in 1875, when it went into effect, is followed by a schedule of "rules of court," numbering sixty-three "orders" with an aggregate of four hundred and fifty-three sections, and dealing with the familiar topics of pleading which appear in the direct *enactment* of our codes.

It may be added that the power of the judges to alter, annul, or add to these rules has been somewhat freely exercised, notably in 1883, when a new code superseded

[1] 36 & 37 Vict., c. 66.

the rules of 1873 and 1875. In 1893 there was another revision affecting a considerable number of the rules. They are sometimes referred to as the new rules of 1893.

The advantage of rules of court.

Sec. 223. There is, of course, much to commend this manner of framing the English code. A hurried legislative committee is hardly the body to define the rules of judicial procedure; it is naturally a task for the judges.

But, apart from this, the English codifiers appear to have had two other things in mind—(1) the certainty that use would presently reveal in the new pleadings errors and defects which should have a readier cure than direct legislation could afford; and, (2) the danger that however fully the rules of a statutory procedure might be in touch with the current needs of the day, the system would fossilize (as common law pleading has fossilized, as some of our codes tend to fossilize) unless the courts themselves were authorized and empowerd to adapt their procedure readily to new conditions. The English code gives better heed than our own code to Lord Coke's aphorism, Nihil simul inventum est et perfectum;[1] and it is more nearly in line with the wise suggestion made by Austin about 1832. "No code," said he, "can be perfect; there should, therefore, be a perpetual provision for its amendment on suggestions from the judges who are engaged in applying it, and who are in the best of all situations for observing its defects. By this means the growth of judiciary law, explanatory of and supplementary to the code can not indeed be prevented altogether, but it may be kept within a moderate bulk by being wrought into the code itself from time to time."[2]

But, while American lawyers commend the plan which has been adopted for framing the English code, it is well

[1] Co. Lit., § 372.

[2] Austin, Juris., p. 697.

to bear in mind that a similar plan, if adopted by the New York reformers in 1848, would probably have stopped short of any radical change. The rules of Hilary term or some equally faltering reform would have been the main result. The legal mind was then, far more than now, timid of changes in the law, fearful of plunging into chaos if it left the trodden path. Crude as the reform of 1848 was in many respects, it was yet bold and stimulating. It enabled even lawyers to contemplate a radical departure from an established system of law as not necessarily fatal. It has been largely instrumental in bringing on the more radical, even if more cautious, reforms of the English code, whose later development can now offer in return many valuable suggestions.

Sec. 224. It does not follow, however, that the special feature which is under consideration—the use of rules of court instead of direct legislation for declaring and amending the principles of procedure—is entirely suited, in its length and breadth, to our conditions. The arrangement does indeed give the procedure much more elasticity than is possible when direct legislation must be invoked for every alteration which the experience of practitioners shows to be desirable. But so great a power of change may prove not an unmixed blessing. Its success presupposes not only a high degree of learning and prudence in the judiciary, but stability in the office of judge. A procedure which might change with the fancy of five-year judges would bring a host of evils in its train. Ever fruitful of contention and delay, a changeable procedure is a grievous burden to the community, which must pay the price of interpreting all new regulations of procedure, whether by rules of court or direct enactments.[1] The safer

[1] The price which has to be paid for alterations is indicated by the fact that between 1875 and 1890 the English courts handed down four thousand decisions on the judicature rules, and the principles intended to be worked out by them. See 34 Solic. Journ. and Rep., 244 (1890).

principle is that alterations in the law should be made only when shown to be necessary; and other things being equal, that is the better system which tends to prevent unnecessary change.

The suggestive resemblance between English and American code pleading.

Sec. 225. The timid conservatism which marked the earlier history of the reform in England, and for years kept it in the rear of the similar movement on this side of the Atlantic, had evidently passed when the judicature acts and rules appeared. A new influence was abroad. The judicial spirit itself suffered a change. Technicality after technicality was brushed away with a rapidity which only those recognized who watched the process closely. Rules which a few years before had been deemed of essential importance were swept aside as worse than useless subtleties. The tide of ridicule turned back upon the common law itself. It was a Lord Chief Justice of England who suggested, in 1883, the formation of a *museum* of common law procedure. As the Yellowstone Park was intended to preserve "the strange and eccentric forms which natural objects sometimes assume," he would have a kind of *pleading park*, in which the glories of the negative pregnant, absque hoc, replication de injuria, rebutter, and surrebutter, and all the other weird and fanciful creations of the pleader's brain might be preserved for future ages, to gratify the respectful curiosity of our descendants, and "where our good old English judges, if ever they revisit the glimpses of the moon, may have some place in which their weary souls can still find the form preferred to the substance, the statement to the thing stated".[1]

[1] Lord Coleridge, address at a reception by the New York Bar Association in 1883.

The common purpose of both systems.

Sec. 226. Quite as many of the old landmarks in pleading have been swept away by this recent English legislation as by the American codes. In many instances, indeed, the comprehensive provisions of the judicature acts and rules carry the change not only as far as the codes of civil procedure have gone, but considerably beyond the point at which American legislatures have deemed it prudent to stop. The framers of the English system appear to have thought that the most direct course to the end which both systems have in view—a complete and final determination of a controversy in its entirety, and according to its essential facts—was to put the least possible restraint upon the discretion of the court in dealing with a case; on the other hand, our codes have kept closer to the common law theory that judges should be required to exercise no more discretion than is absolutely necessary. Where the provisions of the American system are imperative, the corresponding rules in the English system are often subordinated to the discretion of its judges, who may make such modification as is just, with a view to the convenient "determination of the real matter in dispute". But the underlying principle of both systems is the same. They are in more than substantial agreement as to what they overturn and as to what they establish. One purpose runs through the changes in both—to establish a simple and uniform procedure in all civil causes, to open one broad and straight highway into a complete court of justice for every violated civil right. In each system the theory of the pleading has the same fundamental purpose, that of enabling the court to render substantial justice in one proceeding as to the whole controversy. The rules of *practice*, which point out the particular steps to be taken in the disposition of a case, do indeed differ under the two systems in many respects, but the rules of *pleading* under the judicature acts and rules are in remarkable accord with those of the American codes.[1]

Sec. 227. Without attempting any very minute comparison, it will be worth our while to notice some of the more important points of this agreement, not so much for the sake of the parallelism itself as for the light which the later and further development of the English rules may throw upon the principles of our own codes. Various things indicate that the reform movement has not yet run its course in America. Our system is not yet as flexible as it should be. We may well profit from the efforts of the English reformers, dealing with a problem very like our own, as they have profited from our earlier efforts.

Cardinal points of agreement between English and American code pleading.

(1) *As to the single civil action.*

Sec. 228. Both systems abolish the old forms of action and create a single civil action to take the place of the suit in equity and the different actions at law. The civil action of the English system, indeed, has a wider scope than the civil action of our codes in that it applies also to suits in admiralty.[2]

[1] For a brief comparison by Mr. David Dudley Field see 25 Am. Law Rev., 515, 525 (1891). The London Law Magazine and Review for 1879, Vol. 5 (4th Series), 59, 62, begins a somewhat elaborate comparison between the New York Code of 1848 and the Judicature Acts and Rules; but the writer concludes "that it is unnecessary to continue the comparison; anyone who has any knowledge of the two systems knows how closely the latter system follows the former (the New York Code) in theory, nomenclature, and substance." But this may be a little misleading. The Judicature Acts and Rules, while in accord with the New York Code of 1848, do not copy its provisions.

[2] Ante, § 219.

(2) *As to the proper party plaintiff.*

Sec. 229. Both systems provide also for bringing the action in the name of the real party in interest; and both permit a modification of convenience in allowing an executor, an administrator, or a trustee to sue without joining the beneficiary.[1]

(3) *As to the joinder of parties.*

Sec. 230. Both systems, again, provide liberally for the joinder of parties; but here the English rules go beyond the codes. Thus the rules of 1883 declared that "all persons may be joined as plaintiffs in whom the right to any relief claimed is alleged to exist, *whether jointly, severally, or in the alternative.* And judgment may be given for such one or more of the plaintiffs as may be found to be entitled to relief, for such relief as he or they may be entitled to, without any amendment".[2] And so of the defendants. All persons may be joined as defendants "against whom the right to any relief is alleged to exist, whether jointly, severally, or in the alternative. And judgment may be given against such one or more of the defendants as may be found to be liable, according to their respective liabilities, without any amendment. It

[1] Trustees, executors, and administrators may sue and be sued on behalf of, or as representing the property or estate of which they are trustees or representatives, without joining any of the persons beneficially interested in the trust or estate, and shall be considered as representing such persons; but the court or a judge may, at any stage of the proceedings, order any of such persons to be made parties either in addition to or in lieu of the previously existing parties." Rules of 1883, Order XVI, r. 8.

[2] Rules of 1883, Order XVI, r. 1. "But, the defendant, though unsuccessful, shall be entitled to his costs occasioned by his so joining any person who shall not be found entitled to relief unless the court or a judge in disposing of the costs shall otherwise direct." On the beneficial effect of this rule see remarks of Kekewich, J., in Kirke v. North (1895), 2 Ch., 747, 749.

shall not be necessary that every defendant shall be interested as to all the relief prayed for, or as to every cause of action included in any proceeding against him; but the court or a judge may make such order as may appear just to prevent any defendant from being embarrassed or put to expense by being required to attend any proceeding in which he may have no interest." [1]

Sec. 231. The rules also expressly declare that "no cause shall be defeated by reason of the misjoinder or non-joinder of parties"; that in every cause "the court may deal with the matter in controversy so far as regards the rights and interests of the parties actually before it"; and that, at every stage of the proceedings, the court or judge "may order that the names of any parties, whether plaintiffs or defendants, who ought to have been joined, or whose presence before the court may be necessary in order to enable the court *effectually and completely to adjudicate upon and settle all the questions involved in the cause or matter*, be added".

(4) *As to the joinder of causes of action.*

Sec. 232. No less radical are the changes introduced by the judicature acts as to the joinder of causes of action. The restrictions which the American codes still insist upon in this relation do not appear. The English rules are almost startlingly liberal; they go far towards removing all restrictions upon joining causes of action, provided the court approves. In general, "the plaintiff may unite in the same action several causes of action, but if it appear to the court or a judge that any such causes of action can not be conveniently tried or disposed of together, the court or judge may order separate trials of any such causes of action to be had, or may make such other order as may be neces-

[1] Rules of 1883, Order XVI, rr. 4, 5.

[2] Rules of 1883, Order XVI, r. 11.

sary or expedient for the separate disposal thereof".[1] The ancient fundamental doctrine that legal and equitable causes of action can not be joined has been abrogated; so has the old rule that tort and contract must not be joined. Nor does the joint or the several character of the claim affect the matter. Claims by plaintiffs jointly may be joined with claims by them or any of them separately against the same defendant. Claims by or against a husband and wife may be joined with claims by or against either of them separately. With three exceptions, in which the right to join is affected by the subject matter of the action, the plaintiff under the rules of 1883 might unite in his statement of claim any number of causes of action which existed at the date of his writ of summons,[2] subject to the power of the court to exclude such causes of action as convenience or justice requires should be disposed of separately. If the plaintiff wishes to recover damages with respect to a cause of action which has vested in him since the date of his writ of summons, he may issue a second writ and then apply for a consolidation of the actions.

The only limitations here.

Sec. 233. But, as has been said, the rules of 1883 recognized three exceptions to the plaintiff's presumptive right to join all causes of action existing in his favor against the defendant. If the action is for the recovery of land, the plaintiff can not on his own motion join with it any cause of action "except claims in respect of mesne profits or arrears of rent or double value in respect of the premises claimed, or any part thereof, and damages for breach of any contract under which the same or any part

[1] Rules of 1883, Order XVIII, r. 1.

[2] It will be remembered that in the English practice the action is commenced by a writ of summons, which, as in several of our code states, may precede the "statement of claim."

thereof are held or for any wrong or injury to the premises claimed''; but a different joinder may be permitted by the court or a judge.[1] So claims by a trustee in bankruptcy as such may not, unless by leave of the court or a judge, be joined with a claim in any other capacity.[2] And claims by or against an executor or administrator as such may be joined with claims by or against him personally only in case the "last mentioned claims are alleged to arise with reference to the estate with respect to which the plaintiff or defendant sues or is sued as executor or administrator''.[3]

Practical object of the main rule.

Sec. 234. The nature of these exceptions, it will be observed, rather emphasizes the comprehensive character of the change and its practical object. They are exceptions of convenience only. The rules retain no trace of the technical and arbitrary distinctions which marked the common law on this point and still appear in the rules found in most of our codes; but the test is directly the question of practical convenience in the trial of the action. "Any defendant,'' say the rules of 1883, "alleging that the plaintiff has united in the same action several causes of action which can not be conveniently disposed of together, may at any time apply to the court or a judge for an order confining the action to such of the causes of action as may be conveniently disposed of together. If, on the hearing of such application as in the last preceding rule mentioned, it shall appear to the court or a judge that the causes of action are such as can not all be conveniently disposed of together, the court or judge may order any of such causes of action to be excluded, and consequential

[1] Rules of 1883, Order XVIII, r. 2.

[2] Ib., r. 3.

[3] Ib., r. 5.

amendments to be made and may make such order as to costs as may be just."[1]

(5) As to the matter to be stated in a pleading.
(a) Agreement of the two systems on the cardinal principle.

Sec. 235. On the question, what shall be expressed in a pleading? the cardinal principle of the judicature acts and rules is essentially the same as that of our codes. A statement of claim, like a petition, or complaint, must be simply a plain and concise statement of the substantive facts of a cause of action between the plaintiff and the defendant; and the other pleadings of fact come under a similar doctrine. "Every pleading," declare the rules of 1883, "shall contain, and contain only, a statement in a summary form of the material facts on which the party pleading relies for his claim or defense, but not the evidence by which they are to be proved."[2]

Value of English decisions in this respect.

Sec. 236. In this respect the English decisions often prove of value to our code pleaders. The substantive law of England and the substantive law of America are for the most part the same; and in both England and the code states of America the vital question as to the sufficiency of a civil pleading now depends upon a question of substantive law: What are the facts which the substantive law declares necessary to constitute a cause of action in favor of the plaintiff against the defendant? In both systems these facts of a cause of action — its "substantive," its "material" facts—are to be plainly and concisely stated. If they are not stated, or can not be reasonably inferred from what is stated, the action fails, however formally the pleading is drawn up. If they are stated, the pleading

[1] Ib., rr. 8, 9.
[2] Rules of 1883, Order XIX, r. 4.

will stand, even when it has been framed upon an erroneous theory as to the relief which these facts warrant.[1] The form which the plaintiff's right should take is no part of the substantive facts of the cause; rather it is a conclusion of law—a conclusion which is to be drawn by the court from the facts stated, and not by the plaintiff. His business is merely to state the facts. In both England and America the primary question in pleading is no longer whether the facts stated are sufficient for some particular form of action, but simply whether they constitute any cause of action within the court's jurisdiction.

The practical importance of this is well indicated by the scope of a negative decision as to what constitutes a cause of action. At common law, a court would not decide that no action lay on a given state of facts, but only that no action of such a form lay on the state of facts under examination. But now a negative decision goes to this extent, in England and in America, that on the facts stated *no* action lies on behalf of the plaintiff against the defendant.

Old principles in new aspects.

Sec. 237. Among a progressive people it is hardly possible, as the history of common law pleading itself shows, to frame a final answer to the question, What facts constitute the different causes of action? There are always new developments and new aspects. The principle remains the same, but it comes in a new guise, and must be questioned. Onr own day bears witness to the questions of legal obligation which grow out of the use of electricity or of the bicycle, out of the growth of the office-building or the flat-building, out of the spread of labor organizations, out of the organized application of the boycott. Even the modern wire fence has tested the limits of a very ancient

[1] This should be qualified to some extent if judgment is by default.

legal principle. Into these and other dark corners of the law the decisions of the High Court of Justice and the Court of Appeal often throw a light which is hardly less useful to American than to English practitioners. When it happens, as it does often happen, that an English decision discusses the essential facts of a case which stands upon the border line of liability under the principles of the substantive common law or the bearings of some monumental statute which has been copied on this side of the Atlantic, pleaders in our code states have a precedent of very persuasive authority.

(*b*) *Advanced position of the English code as to brevity and expedition.*

Sec. 238. But, while the cardinal principle as to what a pleading should express is the same in both systems, there are very important particulars in which the later English rules with respect to the contents of a pleading go further than the American system. Their provisions in behalf of brevity are more stringent. They contain also some special provisions, unlike anything we have as yet, which seek to induce not only brevity, but a high degree of expedition in pleading.

Rules requiring brevity.

Sec. 239. A general rule is laid down for the statement of claim, the defense, with its setoff, or counterclaim, and the reply. They "shall be as brief as the nature of the case will admit".[1] The statement of facts in every pleading is to be "in a summary form".[2] Moreover, certain brief forms of pleading are given, in appendices to the rules, and it is provided that these forms must be used when applicable; that when they were not applicable

[1] Rules of 1883, Order XIX, r. 2.

[2] Rules of 1883, Order XIX, r. 4.

"forms of the like character, as near as may be," shall be used; and that when the forms given "are applicable and sufficient, any longer forms shall be deemed prolix, and the costs occasioned by such prolixity shall be disallowed to or borne by the party so using the same, as the case may be".[1] In short, the English rules make it very clear that one of the first duties of a pleader is to follow brevity in all his statements—to follow it closely but, of course, only so far as brevity is consistent with the plain statement of every material fact upon which he relies. Brevity, it is said, is the soul of good pleading. And a practical effect is given this principle by a further provision that in adjusting the costs of an action, the taxing officer "shall at the instance of any party, or may without any request, inquire into any unnecessary prolixity, and order the costs occasioned by such prolixity to be borne by the party chargeable with the same".[2]

Provisions to induce expedition.

Sec. 240. No less notable, and suggestive for the American reformer, are the efforts of the later rules under the judicature act to secure expedition as well as brevity in pleading. These take the form of permissive enactments; the plaintiff may adopt them or not, as he thinks best. They relate primarily to the very beginning of the action, the writ of summons and its indorsement. Their general effect will be the clearer for a preliminary word or two concerning the usual procedure with respect to the summons under the English practice.

[1] Rules of 1883, Order XIX, r. 5.

[2] Rules of 1883, Order XIX, r. 2. There was a similar provision in the rules of 1875, but it appears to have failed of its intended effect, because the taxing officer had no express power of his own motion to visit the party chargeable with prolixity with the costs occasioned by it.

The usual procedure under the English code.

Sec. 241. An action in the High Court of Justice is begun, not as in many of the code states, by filing in court the "first pleading on the part of the plaintiff" and *then* issuing a summons for the defendant, but by issuing the writ of summons first and serving the statement of claim after the defendant has appeared. The summons, as with us, is a formal document commanding the defendant to "enter an appearance" within a designated number of days, if he wishes to dispute the plaintiff's claim; otherwise, judgment will be taken against him. A statement of claim need not be delivered[1] until a considerable time after the defendant's formal entry of appearance. If the plaintiff chooses he may have five weeks or more after the commencement of his action before he is required to set forth his precise ground of complaint in a statement of claim. In order, however, that a defendant may know at once why he is sued, the plaintiff is required, on taking out his writ of summons, to make upon it an "indorsement of claim"[2]—a short statement of the nature of his claim, or of the relief required in the action. This may and should be in the briefest form. A long protracted litigation can be properly heralded by such indorsements as the following:

[1] As in New York, and several other states, the formal pleadings in the High Court of Justice are not filed in the first instance with the court (which is the practice in a number of our states), but are delivered between the parties according to certain regulations. The solicitor of one party delivers his pleading to the solicitor of the other party, or to the party himself, if he does not appear by solicitor. This goes on until the pleading is "closed." The case is then entered for trial, and two copies of the complete pleadings are made out and lodged with the court. The copy, which is marked with a stamp, denoting the fee paid on entry, is deemed the record.

[2] "The indorsement of claim shall be made on every writ of summons before it is issued." Rules of 1883, Order III, r. 1.

"The plaintiff's claim is for damages for fraudulent misstatements contained in a prospectus issued by the defendant as director of the South African Diamond Company, Limited."

"The plaintiff's claim is against the defendants as executors of M. W., deceased, for damages for a trespass upon the land of the plaintiff committed by said M. W. within six months before his death."

"The plaintiff's claim is for damages for a libel contained in the ——— Intelligencer for Thursday, September 17, 1896."

In fine, a general indorsement is a mere index to the action, and not unlike the indorsements which lawyers in code states whose actions begin with the filing of a petition in court are accustomed to insert in their precipes for summons.[1] In the natural course of things the general indorsement is to be followed by a complete statement of claim.

Special devices for greater expedition.

Sec. 242. But, for the sake of greater expedition in pleading, the later English rules permit certain departures from this course. In some cases a "special indorsement" or "an indorsement for an account" enables the plaintiff to dispense with a more elaborate statement of claim; in certain conditions "an indorsement for trial without pleadings" enables him to dispense with a statement of claim altogether, and hasten into a trial without formal pleadings.

Novel as any one of these three devices would be in a court of record with us, they are in full harmony with the chief end of code pleading. They tend to a simplification of procedure in the interests of speedy and substantial justice. They are in line also with the probable development of our American system. Their adoption, or the adoption of something like them, with us would aid in meeting a

[1] Cf. Ohio Rev. Stats., §§ 5036, 5037.

demand which our codes have not yet satisfied—the demand for greater simplicity, more rapidity, and less technicality in legal procedure. For the sake, then, of their suggestiveness as to this felt want in our own case, if for no other reason, it will be worth while to notice each of these devices with a little more particularity. And first of the Special Indorsement.

Pleading by way of special indorsement.

Sec. 243. In certain cases the rules permit a plaintiff to dispense with the usual statements of his case and to expedite its hearing by indorsing his writ specially, it being provided that in these cases "the indorsement of the writ shall be deemed to be the Statement of Claim".[1] This special indorsement is in effect a Statement of Claim written upon the summons. Naturally it must be very brief, but it must give such particulars as are needed to inform the defendant specifically concerning the nature and extent of the claim made against him. The defendant is entitled to have sufficient particulars to enable him to satisfy his mind whether he ought to pay or resist.[2] No other Statement of Claim can be delivered, except as distinctively an amended Statement under the rules governing amendments. The form of the special indorsement is therefore considerably longer than that of "general indorsements". Nevertheless, it is often very short, considering the length to which a petition or complaint framed under like conditions of fact might extend with us.

Illustrations of its use.

Sec. 244. The following will serve as illustrations of pleading by way of Special Indorsement, the causes them-

[1] Rules of 1883, Order XX, r. 1.

[2] Walker v. Hicks, 3 Q. B. D., 8, 9 (1877); Smith v. Wilson, C. A., 5 C. P. D., 25, 26 (1879); Odgers, Principles of Pleading, 22.

selves, it will be observed, being such as might induce considerable prolixity.

If the action is on a negotiable instrument, the special indorsement may be such as this:

"The plaintiffs' claim is 20*l.* 17*s.* 8*d.* principal, noting and interest on the defendant's dishonored acceptance.

Particulars:		£	s.	d.
1891. November 21st	To amount of bill of exchange, dated June 18th, 1891, due this day, accepted by the defendant in favor of Smith Brothers, and by them indorsed to the plaintiffs for full value and consideration	20	10	0
	To noting and interest thereon to date	0	7	8
	Total	20	17	8

The plaintiffs also claim interest on 20*l.* 10*s.* of the above sum at 5*l.* percent from date hereof until payment."[1]

Sec. 245. If the action is on a trust, the special indorsement may be in the following form—and the reader will notice how a similar state of facts would tempt a pleader under our codes to go into a voluminous petition or complaint:[2]

"The plaintiff's claim is, as the present trustee of a trust legacy of 2,750*l.*, bequeathed by the will of John Brogden, deceased, to the defendants, and one Samuel Budgett, upon trust in favor of the testator's daughter, Mary Jane Billing, and her children, to have the legacy, which has remained unpaid by reason of a breach of trust on the part of the defendants, and which is now due from them upon a trust, paid by the defendants, together with interest thereon from the 12th day of April, 1885 [payment of such interest being directed by the testator in his will at the rate of four percent per annum]. The defendants have admitted that assets have come to their hands sufficient to answer the said legacy and interest.

[1] Lawrence v. Willcocks (1892), 1 Q. B., 696; cf. Dando v. Boden (1893), 1 Q. B., 318; London Bank v. Clancarty (1892), 1 Q. B., 689.

[2] Cf. Odgers, Principles of Pleading, 21; Hamilton v. Brogden, 60 L. J. Ch., 88 (1890).

Particulars:	£	s.	d.
1885, April 12. Principal of Legacy	2,750	0	0
1890, March 18. Interest thereon from 12th April, 1885, to this day at four percent less income tax,	526	12	9
	3,276	12	9

Sec. 246. If the action is to recover land after the expiration of a term, the special indorsement might be like this:

"The plaintiff's claim is to recover possession of a lot of land situate at ——— in the county of ——— and described as follows ———, which lot was demised by plaintiff to defendant by an agreement in writing bearing date September 15, 1895, for a term which expired on July 31, 1896. Plaintiff also claims mesne profits from said 31st day of July, 1896, until the possession of the said land is delivered to him."

Advantages from pleading by special indorsement.

Sec. 247. Several advantages accrue from indorsing a writ specially:

1. If the defendant does not appear, the plaintiff may at once, without leave, take final judgment for the full amount claimed, upon filing an affidavit that the writ of summons was properly served.

2. If the defendant does appear, the plaintiff may, on an affidavit verifying his cause of action and stating that in his belief there is no defense to the action, "apply to a judge for liberty to enter final judgment for the amount so indorsed, together with interest, if any, or for the recovery of the land (with or without rent or mesne profits) as the case may be, and costs. The judge may, thereupon, unless the defendant, by affidavit, *by his own viva voce evidence*, or otherwise, shall satisfy him that he has a good defense to the action on the merits, or disclose such facts as may be deemed sufficient to entitle him to defend, make an order empowering the plaintiff to enter judgment accord-

ingly".[1] Or, in case the defendant shows only a very weak or shadowy defense, he may be ordered to pay a sum of money into court within so many days, as proof of his *bona fides*; otherwise judgment will be given against him.

3. If no attempt is made to obtain this speedy judgment, or if the defendant, satisfying the court that he has a good defense, obtains leave to make it, still he must plead at once to the special indorsement. No further Statement of Claim is to be delivered, unless, of course, there is an amended Statement as such.

Limitations on pleading by special indorsement.

Sec. 248. This expeditious procedure is not open to every cause. The rules limit it—somewhat arbitrarily, perhaps—to six kinds of actions coming under one general head, namely, "when the plaintiff seeks only to recover a debt or liquidated demand in money payable by the defendant, with or without interest, arising:

(a) Upon a contract express or implied (as, for instance, on a bill of exchange, promissory note, or cheque, or other simple contract debt).

(b) On a bond or contract under seal for payment of a liquidated amount of money.

(c) On a statute where the sum sought to be recovered is a fixed sum of money, or in the nature of a debt, other than a penalty.

(d) On a guaranty, whether under seal or not, where the claim against the principal debtor is in respect of a debt or liquidated demand only.

(e) On a trust.

(f) In actions for the recovery of land (with or without

[1] Rules of 1893, Order XIV, r. 1. This application is to be made by a summons to the defendant "returnable not less than four clear days after service accompanied by a copy of the affidavit and exhibits referred to therein." Ib., r. 2.

a claim for rent or mesne profits) by a landlord against a tenant whose term has expired or has been duly determined by a notice to quit, or against persons claiming under such tenant."[1]

The scope of these classes, however, is very considerable. It is generally understood to include every liquidated demand payable in money, although it may not be a "debt" in the strictest sense of that word. "Whenever the amount to which the plaintiff is entitled," says a recent English commentator on the rule, "can be ascertained by calculation or fixed by any scale of charges, or any other positive *data*, it is said to be *liquidated* or 'made clear'; and then the writ can be specially endorsed."[2]

Pleading by way of indorsement for an account.

Sec. 249. Another provision designed to induce expedition, under the English system, relates to those cases in which the plaintiff can not claim a specific sum because he does not know how much a trustee or agent has, in

[1] Rules of 1883, Order III, r. 6.

[2] Odgers, Principles of Pleading, 16. "Where the price of goods sold and delivered is expressly agreed beforehand, or where the amount to be paid for a certain piece of work is fixed by a contract in writing, here there is a debt which is clearly within the rule. But supposing no price was fixed, and the plaintiff is to be paid whatever is usual in the trade, or such sum as the jury should think fair and reasonable ('*quantum meruit*,' 'such sum as he has earned,' or, '*quantum valebant*,' 'such sum as the goods were worth'), still the case is within the rule. (Stephenson v. Weir, 4 L. R. Ir., 369; Whelan v. Kelly, 14 L. R. Ir., 387.) This is clear from the very first precedent of a special indorsement given in Appendix C, section IV, an action on a butcher's bill, where it is improbable that the exact price to be paid for each joint was expressly fixed at the time it was ordered. But what is excluded by these words from the operation of the rule is an action for unliquidated damages, that is to say, an action in which the amount to be recovered depends on all the circumstances of the case and on the conduct of the parties, and is fixed by opinion or conjecture. In such cases one can not say positively, beforehand, whether the jury will award the plaintiff a farthing, or forty shillings, or a hundred pounds." Ib., pp. 15, 16.

fact, received on his behalf. In such cases the plaintiff is not bound to await the usual course of pleading in an action, but may indorse his writ with a claim that such account be taken.[1] The principle extends to all cases of ordinary account—to accounts of a partnership, for instance, to an executor's account, to ordinary trust accounts. The indorsement may be in a very summary form, like the following:

"The plaintiff's claim is as trustee in bankruptcy of one James Smith for 640*l.* 1*s.* 10½*d.*, money payable by the defendant to the plaintiff for goods sold and delivered by the said J. S. to the defendant, and for money received by the defendant to the use of the said J. S., and for an account of all mutual dealings between the defendant and the said J. S. from May 3, 1887, up to the present time, and of all moneys received by the defendant from the said J. S. between those dates, and that the defendant may be ordered to pay to the plaintiff the amount found due to him on taking such account."[2]

Advantages from its use.

Sec. 250. If, in a proper case, such an indorsement is made and the defendant fails to appear, an order for the account claimed will be made at once as of course. If the defendant does appear, the order will still be made, unless the defendant shows that there is some preliminary question to be tried.[3] The application for the order can be at any time after the appearance day for the defendant. And if the order is made on such an application, the account may be taken, by a special or by an official referee, in whatever method will best advance the ends of justice.[4]

[1] Rules of 1883, Order III, r. 8.
[2] Odgers, Principles of Pleading, p. 27.
[3] Order XV, r. 1.
[4] Cf. Turpin v. Pain, 44 Ch. D., 128, 136-7 (1890).

Procedure by indorsement for trial without pleadings.

Sec. 251. Still more brief and expeditious is that later device of the English rules which goes under the name of "indorsement for trial without pleadings". It was introduced by the Rules of November, 1893, declaring that "a plaintiff may without pleadings proceed to trial subject to the following rules".[1] Of these rules the first is in these terms: The indorsement of the writ of summons shall contain a statement sufficient to give notice of the nature of his claim or of the relief or remedy required in the action, and shall state that if the defendant appears the plaintiff intends to proceed to trial without pleadings.

Purpose and application of this device.

Sec. 252. This indorsement, it will be observed, while applicable generally, is not intended as a pleading; the plaintiff is to be permitted to go to trial without any pleading. Apparently the aim of the rule is to secure a statement which will be more precise than a general indorsement, but will not give the details usual in a "special indorsement," which, as we have seen, is really a pleading indorsed on the summons.

Yet the defendant is entitled to a statement sufficient to inform him of the extent of the plaintiff's claim; and, as the object of the new device is expedition, it may be well for the plaintiff to anticipate a possible dilatory application by the defendant for particulars, and state in the indorsement as much as the defendant can reasonably require to know.

[1] Rules of November, 1893, Order XVIII, A. See 38 Solic. Journ. and Rep., 73.

Its working illustrated.—The indorsements.

Sec. 253. The following forms are suggested by a leading English text writer as sufficient indorsements in their respective causes:[1]

ACTIONS TO RECOVER DAMAGES FOR BREACH OF CONTRACT.

Non-repair.

The plaintiff's claim is for damages for the defendant's breaches of covenant in not repairing and in not yielding up in proper repair, the house No. 401, Piccadilly, W., which the plaintiff demised to the defendant by an indenture dated January 8th, 1886, which contains the covenants sued on.

Particulars of dilapidations were left at the house for the defendant on January 11th, 1893; they exceed three folios.[2]

If the defendant appears, the plaintiff intends to proceed to trial without pleadings.

Money had and received.

The plaintiff's claim is, as executor of J. S., deceased, for 172*l* 10*s*., money received by the defendant for the use of J. S.

Particulars:

1892.	£	*s.*	*d.*
January 3d—To amount of rents of No. 5 South Street, collected by the defendant	72	10	0
February 5th—To deposit on intended sale of Elm Villa	100	0	0
	172	10	0

And for interest thereon at the rate of five per centum per annum till payment or judgment.

[1] Odgers, Principles of Pleading, pp. 7, et passim.

[2] This refers to a proviso in Order XIX, r. 6, that "if the particulars be of debt, expenses, or damages, and exceed three folios, the fact must be so stated, with a reference to full particulars already delivered or to be delivered with the pleading".

If the defendant appears, the plaintiff intends to proceed to trial without pleadings.

Breach of promise of marriage.

On December 27th, 1892, the defendant verbally promised to marry the plaintiff. On August 3d, 1893, he married another lady. And the plaintiff claims 1,000*l.* damages.

If the defendant appears, the plaintiff intends to proceed to trial without pleadings.

Wrongful dismissal.

The plaintiff's claim is for damages for wrongful dismissal. On December 21st, 1892, the defendant engaged the plaintiff as an electrical engineer for one year certain, beginning January 1st, 1893, at a salary of 300*l.* per annum, payable quarterly. On February 19th, 1893, he discharged the plaintiff from his employment.

The plaintiff also claims salary at the rate of 300*l.* from January 1st to February 19th, 1893.

If the defendant appears, the plaintiff intends to proceed to trial without pleadings.

ACTIONS IN TORT.

Railway accident.

The plaintiff's claim is for 100*l.* damages for personal injuries sustained by him in a collision near Box on May 9th, 1893, when he was traveling on the defendants' railway as a passenger from London to Bristol. Such injuries were caused by the defendants' negligence.

Particulars:	£	*s.*	*d*
Loss of 15 weeks' salary as clerk, at 2*l.* per week .	30	0	0
Medical attendance	10	10	0
Nurse for six weeks	3	0	0
Extra nourishment	2	10	0
	46	0	0

If the defendants appear, the plaintiff intends to proceed to trial without pleadings.

Seduction.

The plaintiff claims damages for the defendant's seduction of the plaintiff's servant, his daughter Agnes.

Particulars:

June 15, 1892, carnal intercourse. March 23, 1893, child born.

If the defendant appears, the plaintiff intends to proceed to trial without pleadings.

Wrongful death.

(Lord Campbell's Act, 9 & 10 Vict. c. 93.)

The plaintiff, as executor of C. D., deceased, brings this action for the benefit and on behalf of Eliza, the widow, and William, Margaret, and Mary, the children of C. D., who have suffered damage from the defendant's negligence in carrying the said C. D. by omnibus, whereby the said C. D. was killed in Cornhill on the 15th of January, 1893.

And the plaintiff claims 500*l.* damages.

If the defendant appears, the plaintiff intends to proceed to trial without pleadings.

ACTIONS FOR RECOVERY OF LAND.

Reversioner v. Persons claiming under tenant for life.

The plaintiff's claim is to recover possession of the house known as 182, Piccadilly, W., of which the Rev. John Roberts was seised in fee at the date of his death (April 17th, 1863). By his will dated February 3d, 1863, he devised the said house to his daughter, Anne Roberts, for life, with remainder to the plaintiff in fee. Anne Roberts died on October 3d, 1893.

And for mesne profits.

And for an injunction.[1]

If the defendants appear, the plaintiff intends to proceed to trial without pleadings.

[1] See Reed v. Wotton (1893), 2 Ch., 171, holding that an interlocutory injunction being only a substitute for damages between the issue of the writ, and the trial was not inconsistent with the rule against the joinder of causes of action in general with a cause of action for the recovery of land.

Eviction for non-repair.

The plaintiff's claim is to recover possession of a house known as No. 45, Gaisford Street, Kentish Town, N. W., which the plaintiff demised to the defendant for a term of twenty-one years by a lease dated May 3d, 1881, which contained the repairing covenants usual in leases for such a term, and a proviso for reentry on breach. The defendant has broken all the said covenants.

The plaintiff also claims £—— damages.

If the defendant appears, the plaintiff intends to proceed to trial without pleadings.

Its working illustrated.—Steps subsequent to the indorsement.

Sec. 254. When the writ of summons, thus indorsed, has been served upon the defendant, he must enter his appearance in the usual way; and thereupon, "within ten days after appearance, the plaintiff shall serve twenty-one days' notice of trial without pleadings".[1]

Discretion of the court.

Sec. 255. It is not an absolute rule, however, that if these steps be taken, there can be no pleading in the case. But, the action being thus begun, no pleadings can be required or delivered except by order of the court, and then only in case the defendant, within ten days after appearance, applies by summons for the delivery of a Statement of Claim. On such summons the judge may order: (1) that a Statement of Claim shall be delivered, in which case the action shall proceed in the usual manner; or (2)

[1] Rules of November, 1893, Order XVIIIA, r. (2). For the sake of greater certainty this notice is required to be in the form following, "with such variations as circumstances may require": *Notice of trial without pleadings* (Order XVIIIA). Take notice of trial of this cause without pleadings in Leicester (or as the case may be) for the — day of —— next. X. Y., plaintiff's solicitor (*or as the case may be*). Dated, ——. To Z, defendant's solicitor (*or as the case may be*).

that the action shall proceed to trial without pleadings, in which case it may be further ordered, if the judge shall think fit, that either party shall deliver particulars of his action or defense''.[1]

Whether or not there shall be pleadings rests, it will be observed, with the defendant, subject to the discretion of the court. The plaintiff's election to proceed to trial without pleadings appears in his indorsement on the writ and is irrevocable. The rules are express that when a summons has been thus indorsed, no pleadings shall be required or delivered ''except by order of the judge made under rule 3 of this order''.[2]

Defenses available in such proceeding.

Sec. 256. When the judge orders that the action shall proceed to trial without pleadings, and makes no order as to particulars, all defenses are open at the trial to the defendant. Where particulars are ordered to be delivered, the parties are bound by such particulars, so far as regards the matters in respect of which the order for particulars was made.[3]

If the defendant does not take out a summons for a Statement of Claim in actions thus begun, he ''is not allowed to rely on a setoff or counterclaim, or on the defense of infancy, coverture, fraud, statute of limitations, or discharge under the bankruptcy act, unless he has given

[1] Rules of 1893, Order XVIIIA, r. (3); cf. r. (6).

[2] Rules of 1893, Order XVIIIA, r. (6); for rule (3) see ante.

[3] Order XVIIIA, r. 4. " Hence, a defendant should always ask for particulars of the special damage, if any, sustained by the plaintiff, as the plaintiff is not bound to state such damage in an indorsement on a writ. And if any plaintiff has ventured to dispense with pleadings in an action of libel or slander, he should, on the defendant's summons, ask for particulars of the facts, if any, on which the defendant proposes to rely at the trial to prove the truth of his words."

(within ten days after appearance) notice to the plaintiff, stating the grounds and particulars upon which he relies.[1]

Caution as to using this method.

Sec. 257. But, however expeditious this new method may be, and however anxious the plaintiff may be for a speedy judgment, it is not always wise for him to dispense with pleadings. Discussing the rules of 1893, a Queen's Counsel has thought it prudent to sound this note of caution, which, indeed, touches one of the prime reasons for permitting pleading at all: "The great advantage of having pleadings is that the plaintiff can by their aid obtain an outline of his opponent's case; he can discover what

[1] Rules of 1893, Order XVIIIA, r. 5. The notices here referred to may be as follows (cf. Odgers, Principles of Pleading, pp. 37, 38):

In case of setoff or counterclaim

Take notice that the defendant intends at the hearing of this action to give in evidence and rely upon the following ground of defense:

1.

The defendant was an infant within the age of twenty-one years when the alleged contract (or promise) was made. He was born at ——, in the county of ——, on ——.

2.

The defendant is now (*or*, she was at the time when the supposed claim arose, *or* the supposed contract or agreement was made) the wife of ——, of ——. She was married to him at ——, in the county of ——, on the — day of ——. He resides at ——, in the county of ——.

3.

The defendant was induced to make the alleged promise (*or* agreement, *or* to accept, *or* indorse the said bill of exchange, *or* to make the said promissory note, *or* to execute the alleged deed, *or* to contract the alleged debt) by the fraud of the plaintiff, of which the following are the particulars: (Here add particulars of the alleged fraud.)

4.

The plaintiff's claim is barred by the Statute of Limitations (21 Jac. I., c. 16); [*or, if a specialty debt*, 3 & 4 Wm. IV., c. 42; *or, in an action* for the *recovery of land*, by the Real Property Limitation Act, 1874.]

facts the defendant is prepared to admit, how much he denies, and what is the line of defense he proposes to adopt at the trial. It may be that the plaintiff knows, or thinks he knows, this already; it may be that he has the evidence necessary for his case either ready or easily available, and does not therefore require to obtain any admissions from his opponent. If so, he may indorse his writ with a statement that he intends to proceed to trial without pleadings. But, if the plaintiff is not ready with the evidence necessary for his case, or if he is in the dark as to the nature of the defense which will be set up at the trial, then I should advise him to proceed in the usual way and to deliver a Statement of Claim."[1]

(6) *As to limited series of pleadings.*

Sec. 258. The English system, like the American, imposes a restriction upon the number of stages through which pleading may continue. Here again, the inflexible logic of the common law theory gives way to practical convenience.

Common law pleading, it will be remembered, sought to lead plaintiff and defendant, through their alternate formal allegations, to a single, definite, and material issue of law or of fact. The aim was to reach a single point affirmed on one side and denied on the other. With this in view, the

5.

The defendant is a discharged bankrupt. He obtained his order of discharge from the (*name the court*) on the — day of ———.

Or,

The defendant was discharged by composition or scheme of arrangement pursuant to sect. 18 of the Bankruptcy Act, 1883, on the — day of ———.

Dated the —— of ———, 189—.

A. B., Defendant's Solicitor.

To the Plaintiff, or Messrs. X. & Y., his Solicitors.

[1] Odgers, Principles of Pleading, 2.

forensic altercation of the parties might be carried, at least in theory, to an almost unlimited extent—through declaration, plea, replication, rejoinder, surrejoinder, rebutter, surrebutter, and other stages still, if need be, until the desired issue was produced. In point of fact, however, the pleading seldom went beyond the replication. Nor was the issue always as single, certain, and definite as the theory seemed to promise.

The arbitrary rule of most of our codes.

Sec. 259. The American codes, as we have seen, commonly cut the pleading off at the reply or a demurrer thereto; and some do not permit a reply.[1] In either case the rule is peremptory in nearly every code. Apparently the great majority of our codes approve the view taken by the commissioners who framed the New York Act of 1848. "We conceive," say they, "that, taking the cases together, it is better to stop with the reply. There would scarcely ever happen a case where it would be of any use to go further, were the parties at liberty to do so. By the time the reply is made, the facts will have been so developed as to leave no doubt of the precise point in dispute. *If the right to go further, however, were given, it would be liable to abuse and frequently cause delays.*[2]

Flexibility of the English system herein.

Sec. 260. Under the English system the limitation is not thus inflexible; it is left to the discretion of the court. There are four pleadings as of right—the Statement of Claim, the Defense, with or without counterclaim, the Reply, and the Joinder of Issue. But after the reply "no pleading other than a joinder of issue shall be pleaded without leave of the court or a judge, and then shall be

[1] Ante, § 128n.

[2] Report of February 29, 1848, p. 142.

pleaded only upon such terms as the court or judge shall think fit".[1] And still further to avoid a possible abuse of justice through a protracted pleading, it is also provided that subject to this rule "every pleading subsequent to the reply shall be delivered *within four days* after the delivery of the previous pleading, unless the time shall be extended by the court or a judge".[2]

General accord of both systems in practice.

Sec. 261. In practice, however, there appear to be seldom more than three pleadings in the High Court of Justice;[3] and some cases require but two actual pleadings. For the rules provide that "if the plaintiff does not deliver a reply, or any party does not deliver any subsequent pleading within the period allowed for that purpose, the pleadings shall be deemed to be closed at the expiration of that period, and all the material statements of fact in the pleading last delivered shall be deemed to have been denied and put in issue";[4] and that "as soon as any party has joined issue upon the preceding pleading of the opposite party simply without adding any further or other pleading thereto, or has made default as mentioned in Order XXVII, rule 13, the pleadings as between such parties shall be deemed to be closed".[5]

Exclusion of the demurrer from the series of English pleadings.

Sec. 262. The demurrer, it will be noticed, does not appear in the English series of pleadings mentioned above. This is due to a recent change in the rules. Special de-

[1] Rules of 1883, Order XXIII, r. 2.
[2] Rules of 1883, Order XXIII, r. 3.
[3] Cunningham & Mattinson, Prec. Pl., 22.
[4] Rules of 1883, Order XXVII, r. 13.
[5] Rules of 1883, Order XXIII, r. 5.

murrers were abolished, as has been seen, as early as 1852,[1] but general demurrers, going to the substance of the pleading, were permitted until 1883. In that year, however, all demurrers, at least in name, were abolished in the English system. The rules prescribe as follows:

1. No demurrer shall be allowed.

2. Any party shall be entitled to raise by his pleading any point of law, and any point so raised shall be disposed of by the judge who tries the cause at or after the trial, provided that by consent of the parties, or by order of the court or a judge on the application of either party, the same may be set down for hearing and disposed of at any time before the trial.

3. If, in the opinion of the court or a judge, the decision of such point of law substantially disposes of the whole action, or of any distinct cause of action, ground of defense, setoff, counterclaim, or reply therein, the court or judge may thereupon dismiss the action or make such other order therein as may be just.

4. The court or a judge may order any pleading to be struck out, on the ground that it discloses no reasonable cause of action or answer, and in any such case or in case of the action or defense being shown by the pleadings to be frivolous or vexatious, the court or a judge may order the action to be stayed or dismissed, or judgment to be entered accordingly, as may be just."[2]

[1] Com. Law Proc. Act, 1852, Ss. 50–53, 89.

[2] Rules of 1883, Order XXV, rules 1–4. With reference to these rules Bullen and Leake remark: "Hence, if a party seeks to raise by his pleading any objection in point of law, as distinguished from any ground of defense or reply, etc., upon the facts, he may do so by pleading such objection in his defense or reply, etc., stating it in a succinct form (as required elsewhere by the orders).

"An objection in point of law may be pleaded together with grounds of defense or of reply upon the facts, without it being necessary to obtain any leave for that purpose, and in such cases the objection in point of law does not require any separate heading, but should be stated in a

Essence of demurring retained.

Sec. 263. The effect of this is evidently not to destroy the essence of a demurrer, although its name and distinctive form disappear from the system of pleading. The old name, it would seem, might have been retained; at least, the new name, "an objection in point of law," expresses exactly what a demurrer was, and still is with us. And the principle holds under the English system as with us, that "every objection in point of law asserts or implies that the pleading objected to is insufficient on the face of it; hence it admits for the moment that the allegations contained in it are true".[1]

(7) *On the production of an issue.*

Sec. 264. Neither the English nor the American system of pleading, as we have seen, attempts to reach the nicety which characterized the common law issue; still the ancient theory of the *issue* reappears in the provisions of both these statutory systems. It is more than a theory or a name with them. Both retain in a material degree the peculiarity of the common law, that the questions to be decided must be

separate paragraph, which should follow the paragraphs containing the statement of the party's case upon the facts, and be numbered consecutively with them.

"The date, title, and description of a defense or reply, etc., containing an objection in point of law is the same as that of an ordinary defense or reply, etc., upon the facts, and it must be delivered in the same manner and within the same time as such defense or reply, etc.

"A party who pleads an objection in point of law must distinctly state in his pleading the ground of objection relied upon, and if several different grounds of objection are relied upon, they should be distinctly stated in separate paragraphs. The mode of stating objections in point of law and the extent to which the statement of them is required to be specific, will, of course, vary according to the subject matter of the action or defense, etc., in respect of which the objection is pleaded. In some cases the objection may be allowed to be stated in general terms." (Bidder v. McLean, 20 Ch. D., 512); 2 B & L. Prec., 82 (1888).

[1] Odgers, Principles of Pleading, p. 106.

evolved, not by the court from the litigants' statements at large, but by the litigants themselves through their mutual altercation under the rules of pleading. Both systems seek, through stringent provisions framed in much the same way, to have the pleadings narrow the controversy to one or more matters maintained by one party, denied by the other, and accepted by both as the question or questions to be decided. These controverted matters, of law or of fact, retain in both systems, and are fairly entitled to, the ancient name of *issues*, itself one of the oldest words in our jurisprudence.[1]

There are, however, material differences between the common law and the statutory issue. The mode of procedure towards the latter is more flexible, in both England and America, than the common law deemed proper; and the issue itself, in both systems, is at once less precise yet often more material than was the issue of the old pleading.

Salient points of comparison between the statutory issues.

Sec. 265. As between themselves, the two statutory systems have a number of suggestive points of difference, as well as of resemblance; and some of these are worth noticing here. They group themselves under the following heads: (a) The Rules of Elimination for securing an issue speedily; (b) The Singleness of the Issue; (c) The Certainty in the Issue.

(*a*) *Rules of elimination—Under the American codes.*

Sec. 266. Under the American codes, a party must, as at common law, demur *or* plead at each stage of the pleading. If he demurs, he raises at once an issue of law. If

[1] The word is found at the very beginning of the Year Books; and the distinction which our codes make in terms between the "issue of law" and the "issue of fact" is the survival of an ancient distinction between the "issue en ley" and the "issue en fet." See Year Book, 3 Edw. II., 59.

he pleads, he must either admit or deny the truth of the material allegations made by the adverse pleading. If he expressly denies the truth of all these allegations, an issue of fact arises at once. But it is possible that the direct response is to some only of the allegations; or the defendant may confess that the claim asserted against him is true as far as the facts stated by the plaintiff are concerned, but assert that there are other facts which avoid its prima facie effect as against himself—that is, he may plead by way of confession and avoidance. In the former case, the codes seek to expedite the production of the issue by requiring that allegations not responded to shall be deemed to be admitted; the issue is narrowed to the facts denied. In the case of a plea by confession and avoidance, the forming of the issue is naturally postponed one stage at least. The facts alleged by the defendant in avoidance of the plaintiff's claim may themselves be open to a response in confession and avoidance. But, at this point, a number of the codes, departing from the common law, as we have seen, and from the general theory of the issue, cut the pleading off abruptly, and compel an arbitrary issue. They require that new matter in the answer shall be deemed to be controverted.

Other codes, however, provide for a *reply* in such cases,[1] and subject it to the same rule of elimination which governs the answer, and to one other—both designed with a view to hastening the issue:

(1) The reply must admit or deny the new matter alleged in the answer; and what is not denied is deemed to be admitted, if material;

(2) The reply must not "depart" from the petition or complaint; that is, the plaintiff's allegations of fact in his

[1] Some codes, which permit a reply, require it only in response to a counterclaim; other codes require a reply to all allegations of new matter in the answer.

two pleadings must be consistent parts of one case. He must not set up a new cause of action in his reply.

Their arbitrary issue.

Sec. 267. The reply, however, may allege new matter in avoidance of an answer which has been by way of confession and avoidance on the part of the defendant. And theoretically the pleading might continue in this way for a considerable number of stages before an issue of fact is evolved; but, with an exception or two, all the codes which permit a reply require that the pleading of fact shall go no further. They force an issue at once by the provision that if there is no demurrer the allegations of new matter in the reply shall be deemed to be controverted by the defendant "as upon a direct denial or avoidance". The theoretical awkwardness of this is apparent in its phraseology. It implies what, of course is true, that the reply may be met with matter in confession and avoidance; in other words, the issue may possibly be diverted after it is supposed to have been reached.

Under the English code.

Sec. 268. Under the recent English rules, a party may both demur *and* plead to the same matter in the same pleading. But in such a case, the demurrer—the "objection in point of law"—is passed upon, like a demurrer with us, before the answer to the facts is tried; and if the court or a judge is of opinion that the decision on this point of law "substantially disposes of the whole action, or of any distinct cause of action therein, the court or judge may thereupon dismiss the action or make such other order therein as may be just".[1]

If the Statement of Defense goes to the facts or if the

[1] Order XXV, r. 3.

plaintiff Replies to the facts, these pleadings must in turn either admit or deny the facts alleged in the last preceding pleading. Every allegation of fact, "if not denied specifically or by necessary implication, or stated to be not admitted in the pleading of the opposite party, shall be taken to be admitted".[1]

Departures.

Sec. 269. And the English rules, like most of our codes, are express in forbidding a "departure" in the reply, which, of course, is the first stage where it can occur, or in any subsequent pleading. No pleading "shall, except by way of amendment, raise any new ground of claim or contain any allegation of fact inconsistent with the previous pleadings of the party pleading the same".[2] A *departure* is a fault of one and the same kind in either system; and the following remarks of an English text writer explaining it are no less applicable under the American pleading. "A departure takes place when in any pleading the party deserts the ground that he took up in his preceding pleading, and resorts to another and a different ground; or, to give Lord Coke's definition, 'A departure in pleading is said to be when the second plea containeth matter not pursuant to his former, and which fortifieth not the same; and therefore it is called *decessus*, because he departeth from his former plea'.[3] This is clearly embarrassing; a Reply is not the proper place in which to raise new claims; *to permit this would tend to spin out the pleadings to an intolerable length.*"[4]

[1] Rules of 1883, Order XIX, r. 13. "Except as against an infant, lunatic, or person of unsound mind, not so found by inquisition." Ib.

[2] Order XIX, r. 16.

[3] Co. Litt.. 304 a.

[4] Odgers, Principles, 214.

Encouragement of a natural issue.

Sec. 270. But the English rules do not insist that the pleading must stop in every case with the answer, or, at the furthest, with the reply. The altercation may run through later stages—a *rejoinder*, a *surrejoinder*, a *rebutter*, a *surrebutter*, for the old names are preserved, as under the code of Kentucky—until an issue is evolved in fact. It would seem, however, that this is due to the apprehension of a possible need in exceptional cases rather than to a felt want. "The cases will be rare where it is either necessary or desirable to do more than join issue upon a reply, though no doubt they will from time to time arise in practice."[1]

When the English code forces an issue.

Sec. 271. Such a postponement is treated by the rules themselves as an exception which should not be encouraged; they are express in providing that with the exception of a formal joinder of issue there can be no pleading subsequent to the reply save by leave, and then only upon such terms as the court shall think fit.[2] Nor is a formal issue insisted upon. "If the plaintiff does not deliver a reply, or any party does not deliver any subsequent pleading within the period allowed for that purpose, the pleadings shall be deemed to be closed at the expiration of that period, and all the material statements of fact in the pleading last delivered shall be deemed to have been denied and put in issue."[3]

The results of this, in the ordinary run of cases, would appear to be very close to those of the provisions in our codes which cut the pleading off at the answer or the reply. But there is this difference here as in a number of other

[1] Cunningham & Mattinson's Precdts., 91, 92.
[2] Order XXIII, r. 2.
[3] Order XXVII, r. 13.

instances: the English rules are less arbitrary than our own. They manifest a higher regard for the unusual case.

This same elasticity is shown in their provisions as to the "Joinder of Issue" and the "Settling of the Issues" under the direction of the court. Both are of secondary importance, but they may serve a useful purpose in producing clear-cut issues.

Further elasticity of the English system. Its Joinder of Issue.

Sec. 272. The "joinder of issue" is simply a compendious traverse which may be used in the Reply if the answer has set up no counterclaim, and in the subsequent pleadings without restriction. "Such joinder of issue shall operate as a denial of every material allegation of facts in the pleading upon which issue is joined, but it may except any facts which the party may be willing to admit, and shall then operate as a denial of the facts not so admitted." [1] The effect of thus joining issue, it will be observed, is merely to contradict the facts last pleaded by the adverse party. It does not confess and avoid; it does not raise an objection in point of law. Nor is it a necessary pleading even when the purpose of the pleader is merely to deny. He may omit any further pleading and thus raise a "general issue" as to the facts alleged in the answer or other subsequent pleading. But the "joinder of issue," it would seem, may be of considerable practical utility in defining and classifying the questions of fact to be decided.

Its operation illustrated.

Sec. 273. Its operation in this respect, and in connection with a rule whereby the pleading may run a natural course, beyond the answer or reply, until the issues are

[1] Rules of 1883, Order XIX, r. 18.

really evolved, is best explained by the following series of precedents,[1] which will serve to illustrate also two or three other features referred to above:

The plaintiff delivered a Statement of Claim, indorsed on his writ, as follows:

1. The defendant agreed that if the plaintiff would supply goods to C. D., he would see the plaintiff paid therefor.

2. On the faith of this guarantee, the plaintiff supplied C. D. with the following goods, the price of which is 213*l.* 8*s.* 11*d.*

(Particulars.)

3. Yet the defendant has not paid the plaintiff the said price or any part thereof.

And the plaintiff claims 213*l.* 8*s.* 11*d.*

The Defense was in five paragraphs, the first traversing, the others confessing and avoiding, thus:

1. The defendant never agreed as alleged.

2. There is no memorandum in writing of the alleged agreement sufficient to satisfy the Statute of Frauds.

3. The plaintiff discharged the defendant from all liability by giving time to the principal debtor, the said C. D.

4. By a deed dated January 13th, 1891, made between the plaintiff and the defendant, the plaintiff released the cause of action on which he now sues.

5. Such cause of action, if any, did not accrue within six years, and the defendant will rely on the Statute of Limitations (21 Jac. I. c. 16).

The Reply was drawn in these terms:

1. The plaintiff joins issue with the defendant upon paragraphs 1, 2, and 3 of the Defense.

2. The plaintiff was induced to execute the said release by the fraud of the defendant. Particulars of such fraud are as follows: (*stating them*).

[1] I take these precedents from Odgers, Principles, pp. 107, 108.

3. On May 15th, 1893, the defendant wrote and signed an acknowledgment that the debt now sued for remained unpaid and due to the plaintiff.[1]

To this there was a Rejoinder, as follows:

The defendant joins issue with the plaintiff on paragraphs 2 and 3 of his Reply.[2]

At this point it will be noticed the Reply and the Rejoinder together have marked out the issues with great precision. But it may be that these issues although thus clearly designated by the parties are in themselves roving and uncertain. Here, then, the other rule to which I had reference above, the power of the court to "settle the issues," comes into useful operation.

Settling the Issues.

Sec. 274. For the rules provide that "where in any cause or matter it appears to the court or a judge that the issues of fact in dispute *are not sufficiently defined*, the parties may be directed to prepare issues, and such issues will, if the parties differ, be settled by the court.[3]

Illustration.

Sec. 275. A good illustration of the application of this is found in West v. White,[4] which was an action commenced in the Chancery Division for the purpose of restraining, and obtaining damages in respect of, an alleged nuisance of smoke and vapors from the defendants' cement-works.

The defendants applied for a special jury, and the court

[1] Paragraphs 2 and 3 respectively confess and avoid paragraphs 4 and 5 of the Defense.

[2] He does not join issue on paragraph 1, because that is itself a joinder of issue.

[3] Rules, 1883, Order XXXIII.

[4] 4 Ch. D., 631 (1877).

directed that issues should be prepared and settled. The defendants insisted that the following issue should be included among those agreed upon: "Whether the business of the defendants is conducted in a proper manner and in a place reasonably fit for the same." But the parties were unable to agree. The court refused to insert the proposed issue. "It is too wide, too roving, and too speculative in its nature," said Bacon, V. C, "to deserve the name of an issue." Finally this order was entered: "Let the following questions of fact be tried at Maidstone in the County of Kent, before a special jury of the said County of Kent, at the next Spring Assizes:

1. Whether the defendants have carried on their works at S. in such a manner as to occasion a nuisance to the plaintiffs?

2. Whether the new works of the defendants, now in course of erection, will cause a nuisance to the plaintiffs?

3. Whether the nuisance, if any, to the plaintiffs, occasioned by the works of the defendants, existed in the same degree twenty years ago, or has been materially increased during the last twenty years?

4. What, if any, damage has been occasioned to the plaintiffs, or any of them, by the nuisances, if any, committed by the defendants.[1]

(*b*) *The singleness of the issue.*

Sec. 270. It will be observed that there are three general ways in which a party who intends to contest an action, may deal with each subject of claim asserted against him.

1. He may take the position that, even if the statements of fact made concerning it are true, they are still insufficient in law to constitute a cause of action or a defense against him in the action.

[1] Cf. 2 Brett's Com., 749.

2. He may assert that these statements or a certain essential portion of them are not true in fact.

3. He may contend that, while the statements are true in fact, as far as they go, they are only half the truth, that there are other facts, as between himself and his opponent, which quite change the complexion of the case; and, pleading these facts, he may seek to avoid the liability which otherwise he confesses would arise against him. In other words, to return to the older nomenclature, he may (1) *demur*, or (2) *plead* by way of *traverse*, or (3) *plead* by way of *confession and avoidance*.

These three positions are evidently quite distinct in themselves. Does it follow that when all three are available in a given case they must appear each in a separate and distinct pleading? Moreover, these positions are not only distinct in their nature, but they occasion two very different kinds of issues—the issue in law and the issue in fact. Does it follow that these issues must be raised, if at all, through separate pleadings? On such questions our codes are in some respects, not in all, more liberal than the common law; and the English rules, as recently developed, are more liberal than our codes, but suggestive of possible changes in them.

The common law's devotion to singleness of issue.

Sec. 277. The common law, which steadily converted its theoretical differentiation into inflexible rules of procedure, answered the first of these questions very positively in the affirmative. Above everything else an issue must be "single"; and to this end the common law asserted as a steadfast principle that "duplicity" of allegation must be avoided at every stage of the action. The *plea* could set forth but one matter of defense to each count in the declaration; the *replication*, but one answer to a *plea*. Not only did the rule thus forbid the production of more than one matter of defense to each subject of claim, but every defense produced must be simple, entire, connected, and confined to one point. It must not present a variety of distinct, independent answers to the same matter, for this would destroy the singleness of the contemplated issue, and greatly embarrass the jury and the court in disposing of it. A litigant, therefore, could not both demur and plead to the same matter, "lest an issue in fact and an issue in law, in respect of a single subject, should be produced". If both ways appeared to be open to him, he must make his election and demur *or* plead.[1] In like manner a party was required to elect between a plea by way of traverse and a plea by way of confession and avoidance to the same claim. For "a pleading will be double that contains several answers, whatever be the class or quality of the answer".[2]

The half-way doctrine of our codes.

Sec. 278. These restrictions of the common law have had a partial but remarkable survival in some accepted doctrines of code pleading. The express enactments found in the earlier and repeated in almost all the succeeding codes were not as clear on the point as might be. They left an opportunity for the rise of ancient scruples; nor was the opportunity permitted to go unused. Pleaders in almost all the code states have long been instructed that a party can not demur *and* plead at the same time to the

[1] Stephen, Pl., 267. The rule, however, only prohibited the pleading and demurring *to the same matter*. It did not forbid this course as applicable to *distinct statements*. Thus, a man might plead to one count, or one plea, and demur to another. Ib.

[2] Stephen, Pl., 247. But as the object of the principle was to enforce a single issue upon a single subject of claim, admitting of several issues, the rule did not apply when the claims were distinct in the theory of the common law. And the reader will remember that the common law's elaborate theory of *several counts* gave an opportunity for issues of different aspects, even to the same state of facts.

same matter. It is true that the reason commonly assigned for this sounds like an echo from the old law reports, "wary and wise" in logical technicality; yet it has been repeated for upwards of half a century. "By his demurrer," says an able text-writer as late as 1891, "a party insists that he is not bound to answer; but if he answer, he overrules his own demurrer, unless he elect to waive his answer."[1] "The filing of a demurrer *and* answer," remarked the Supreme Court of Ohio in 1856, "and tendering an issue of law and of fact at the same time, and in the same paper, when the petition contains but one cause of action, is certainly a strange practice, and one more honored in the breach than in the observance. The defendants ought to have been compelled to elect between the two incongruous issues they sought to present, and the paper to have been reformed or stricken from the files."[2] If one does demur and answer to the same matter in one pleading, and his duplex pleading is not stricken from the files, the common doctrine is that the answer must be deemed a waiver of the demurrer, or the pleader must withdraw his answer. The two, it is said, can not stand together.[3]

[1] Bryant, Code Plead., 222.

[2] Davis v. Hines. 6 O. S. 473, 477 (1856). Yet the court was also of the opinion that "as no motion for that purpose seems to have been made, we do not know that the court was obliged to act in the premises on its own motion." Ib., p. 478.

[3] Spellman v. Weider, 5 How. Pr. (N. Y.), 5 (1850); Howard v. Michigan R. R., 5 How. Pr. (N. Y.), 206 (1850); Munn v. Barnum, 12 How. Pr., 563 564 (1855); Fisher v. Scholte, 30 Iowa, 221, 222 (1870), where the court follows professedly "a well-settled rule in the English chancery practice, that if any part of the matter covered by the demurrer was also covered by a plea or answer, the whole demurrer was waived or overruled by the plea or answer." Ludlow v. Ludlow, 109 Ind., 199, 201 (1886); Moore v. Glover, 115 Ind., 367, 372 (1888): A demurrer to a complaint will be deemed to be abandoned when the defendant files an answer without first requiring a decision on the demurrer, and such party will be precluded from thereafter making any question upon it.

Our rejection of the common law in part.

Sec. 279. But, while our codes thus keep to the ancient common law theory when the question concerns demurring and answering, they depart very far from the common law when the question relates to different kinds of answers. A pleader is no longer required to choose between a traverse and a confession and avoidance if both grounds of defense exist as against the same claim. He must, it is true, present them as distinct grounds, but subject to this he may set them up in one and the same answer. He may plead as many defenses in fact, with as many counterclaims, or setoffs, as he has, "whether they are such as have been heretofore denominated legal or equitable, or both". Nor need they be consistent in their legal aspects, provided they can be truthfully sworn to in fact. "Certainly," said Welch, C. J., in a comparatively recent decision on the Ohio code,[1] "it is not consistent with the spirit and intention of the code that a party having one or the other of two good defenses, without the means of knowing otherwise than from the developments to be made upon the trial which of the two, in fact or in law, is his true defense, shall, at his peril, be compelled to elect in advance on which he will rely, to the exclusion of the other. When, from the nature of the case, it is rendered uncertain which of two grounds of defense is the true and proper one, it is competent for the defendant in his answer to set them both up, provided they will admit of being stated in such form that the answer can be sworn to without falsehood, and in good faith."

Cf. Phillips Code Pl., § 306; Bryant's Code Pl., § 222; Kinkead's Code Pl., 108. On the Massachusetts doctrine see Hobson v. Satterlee, 163 Mass., 402, 403 (1895).

[1] Citizens Bank v. Closson, 29 O. S., 78, 81 (1875); in connection with the principle of this case the student will bear in mind the doctrine of the same court in Davis v. Hines, 6 O. S., 473, 477 (1856).

Accordingly, when the inconsistency arises by implication of law, from the new matter being in the nature of a plea in confession and avoidance, and not from statements directly contradictory in fact, both defenses may appear in the same pleading.[1]

In short, most of our codes violate the theory of the common law in that they permit more than one answer in fact to be made in one pleading to the same claim, but they hold to the theory of the common law in forbidding a party to set up in one pleading both an answer in law and an answer in fact to the same claim.

Antiquated nature of the distinction made by our codes here.

Sec. 280. There are two facts, curious and significant, which are worth a passing notice in this connection. They belong to a somewhat numerous class, crude frag-

[1] Mott v. Burnett, 2 E. D. Smith (N. Y.), 50, 52 (1852); Bell v. Brown, 22 Cal., 671, 678 (1863); Willson v. Cleaveland, 30 Cal. 192, 200 (1866); Booth v. Sherwood, 12 Minn., 426, 428 (1867); Conway v. Wharton, 13 Minn., 158 (1868): To a complaint alleging five causes of action upon contract, the answer set up seven separate defenses. The sixth was a plea of the statute of limitations. The seventh set up an accounting between the parties within six years, resulting in an agreement that defendant should deliver to plaintiff a wagon, in full settlement and satisfaction of all claims of plaintiff against defendant, and a delivery of the wagon in pursuance thereof. Upon a motion to strike out the sixth defense, as sham, and the entire answer for duplicity in pleading the sixth and seventh defenses, the trial court ordered that the sixth defense be stricken out for inconsistency. *Held*, that the facts averred in the seventh defense did not show that the sixth defense was false, and that the order was erroneous.

See also Shed v. Augustine, 14 Kan., 282, 285–6 (1875); Bruce v. Burr, 67 N. Y., 237 (1876); Witte v. Lockwood, 39 O. S., 141, 143 (1883); McKinster v. Hitchcock, 19 Neb., 100, 105 (1886); Judy v. Louderman, 48 O. S., 562, 571 (1891); Lawrence v. Peck, 3 S. D., 645, 648 (1893); Koll v. Bush, Col., 40 Pac. Rep., 579 (1895).

On the limitations of the principle, see Wright v. Bachellor, 14 Kan., 259, 267 (1876); and cf. Pomeroy, Code Rem., § 722; Bryant, Code Pl., § 184.

ments of the older procedure, taken in the very shape in which they were found and hurriedly built into the system of code pleading with little regard to its symmetry and harmonious effect. (1) The distinction by which a code pleader may not both demur *and* plead to the same matter, yet may plead both by way of traverse and also by way of confession and avoidance, springs not from the period of the codes themselves, but from an act of parliament passed one hundred and forty years before the earliest of our codes —from the statute of 4 Anne.[1] (2) In retaining this distinction, the codes are more conservative, even more technical, than some of the most steadfast upholders of common law pleading have deemed it well to be in modern times.

This statute of 4 Anne provided that "it shall and may be lawful for any defendant or tenant in any action or suit, or for any plaintiff in replevin, in any court of record, with the leave of the same court, to plead as many several matters thereto as he shall think necessary for his defense". Relating in terms to *pleas*, the statute, it was held, gave no authority for *demurring* and pleading at the same time to the same matter;[2] on that question the common law remained as it was, both in England and America.

But the curious thing is that this distinction, thus created in the older procedure through an incomplete statutory reform of Queen Anne's reign, remains imbedded in our theory of code pleading long after its disappearance from some systems which in general are more conservative than the codes. As early as 1788, for instance, the Virginia legislature provided that the defendant in any action "may plead as many several matters, *whether of law or fact*, as he shall think necessary for his defense".[3] For many years the learned author of Minor's Commentaries, than

[1] Chap. 16, § 4 (1705).
[2] Stephen, Pl., 267.
[3] Hening's Stats. at Large (Va.), Anno 1788, ch. 67, § 40.

whom the common law has had no more steadfast admirer amid the changes of recent times, appears to have questioned the wisdom of the restriction at any stage. "It is worth observing," says he, "that to allow one to plead and to demur at the same time is likely to lead to far less confusion and inconvenience than the pleading of several matters of fact, the issues upon which must be tried by a jury. Indeed, the issue of law arising upon a demurrer, tried as it is by the court, would never occasion any embarrassment at all, nor necessarily any delay. There seems, therefore, no reason of sound policy why the privilege of demurring and pleading to the same matter at the same time should not be extended to every stage of the altercation."[1] And under the provisions of the Massachusetts Act of 1852, namely, that "to raise an issue in law, the *answer* shall contain a statement that the defendant *demurs* to the declaration or to some one or more counts therein, as the case may be,"[2] it has become a frequent practice in Massachusetts to insert demurrers in answers to the merits.[3]

Liberality of the English code as to singleness of issue.

Sec. 281. This tendency, thus appearing in isolated instances in America, to permit a party to raise at once all the issues, in law and in fact, concerning any one claim, is given full effect by the later English rules. The demurrer, as a distinct and separate pleading, has indeed been abolished by them; but its principle is preserved in the "objection in point of law". Under the English rules a party, in his defense, may in effect demur to the opposing pleading, or traverse it, or confess and avoid it; or he may

[1] 4 Minor's Insts., 951–2. The question, as Stephen points out, is one of expediency. Cf. Stephen, Pl., 152, 153.

[2] Mass. Stats., 1852, § 17; Publ. Stats., c. 167, § 25.

[3] Cf. Hobson v. Satterlee, 163 Mass., 402, 403 (1895).

set up at once any two of these methods against one and the same claim; or he may at once demur, *and* traverse, *and* confess and avoid the same allegation. But, while appearing at once and the same time, these three distinct things—the demurrer, the traverse, and the confession and avoidance—must be kept clear and distinct in the pleading. There should be no ambiguity about the point of the defense. "A plea which may be either a traverse or an objection is embarrassing and will be struck out." There is also this practical limitation upon multiplying the issues. "Where the court or a judge," say the Rules of 1883, "shall be of opinion that any allegations of fact denied or not admitted by the defense ought to have been admitted, the court or judge may make such order as shall be just with respect to any extra costs occasioned by their having been denied or not admitted."[1] Moreover, "any party may, by notice in writing, at any time not later than nine days before the day for which notice for trial has been given, call on any other party to admit for the purposes of the cause, matter, or issue only, any specific fact or facts mentioned in such notice. And in case of refusal or neglect to admit the same within six days after service of such notice, or within such further time as may be allowed by the court or a judge, the costs of proving such fact or facts shall be paid by the party so neglecting or refusing, whatever the result of the cause, matter, or issue may be, unless at the trial or hearing the court or a judge certify that the refusal to admit was reasonable, or unless the court or a judge shall at any time otherwise order or direct."[2] "It

[1] Rules of 1883, Order XXI, r. 9.

[2] Rules of 1883, Order XXXII, r. 4. "Provided that any admission made in pursuance of such notice is to be deemed to be made only for the purposes of the particular cause, matter, or issue, and not as an admission to be used against the party on any other occasion, or in favor of any person other than the party giving the notice; provided, also, that the court or a judge may at any time allow any party to amend or

is foolish," says an English commentator on the judicature acts and rules, "to multiply the issues needlessly, as your client will probably have to pay the costs of those which he fails to prove, even though he has succeeded in the main issue."[1]

(c) Certainty in the issue.

Sec. 282. Several of the rules referred to above show the difference between Singleness of the Issue and Certainty in the Issue. When there is more than one issue in respect to one subject of suit, there is no singleness of issue, but that *duplicity* of issue which the common law abhorred; yet every such issue may have the requisite degree of *certainty*. On the other hand, an issue, though never so *single*, may be most deficient in *certainty*. Very often, indeed, the common law issue was thus deficient, because of its doctrine of the "general issue". And any examination of the principle of code pleading, in America or England, respecting the Singleness of Issue will naturally center about this old-time doctrine. Let us notice it with reference (i) to the common law, (ii) to the American codes, (iii) to the English code.

(i) *The General Issue at common law.*

Sec. 283. The "general issue" was a notable and important feature in common law pleading. It was of frequent occurrence; it could be raised at a word in most of the usual actions, it was admirably suited to the convenience of the pleader. It was invoked through certain formulae of answer, or *plea*, fixed by ancient usage as a proper method of traversing the declaration when the defendant meant to deny the whole or the principal part of

withdraw any admission so made on such terms as may be just." Ib. Cf. Cunningham & Mattinson, Precedents, p. 56 (1884).

[1] Odgers, Principles, 106.

its allegations—through the plea of *non est factum* in some cases, of *nil debet* in others, of *non detinet*, of *not guilty*, or as the case might be.

Its nature.

Sec. 284. The characteristic thing about the general issue was that it gave no certainty of fact to the issue. Instead of directly denying some particular fact or group of facts asserted by the plaintiff, it denied the *legal aspect* of his claim. For instance, if the action was for goods sold and delivered, the defendant need not deny in his pleading that he had ordered the goods, or that they were delivered to him, or that they were not of the quality stipulated for, or that his time of payment had expired, or that there was a memorandum of the contract in writing sufficient to satisfy the statute of frauds. But he would plead the general issue of *nil debet*—that he "*does not owe* the sum of money". He directly denies, therefore, only the conclusion of law upon which the plaintiff's claim rests.

Its extent.

Sec. 285. Theoretically the issue thus raised was as wide as the legal aspect of the plaintiff's claim; the range of testimony which the defendant might introduce under it included whatever state of fact nullified the conclusion of law upon which the plaintiff had grounded his case. And within limits which varied somewhat with the different actions, this theoretical scope of the general issue was realized in practice, at least in the later development of the common law. Thus, in the supposed case of an action to recover the price of goods sold and delivered, a declaration alleging that the defendant "is indebted" to the plaintiff in a certain sum for goods sold and delivered, is met by the plea of *nil debet*, that the defendant "does not owe" the sum of money thus claimed of him; and learned common law judges reasoned as follows: The defendant *does not owe* this sum if any one of the following facts be true:

(1) That he never ordered the goods.

(2) That they were never delivered to him.

(3) That they were not of the quality ordered.

(4) That they were sold on a credit which has not expired.

(5) That the sale though made is void or voidable at the defendant's option, through infancy, lunacy, or otherwise.

(6) That there has been a payment according to the defendant's promise.

(7) That there has been an arbitrament, an accord and satisfaction, or some other matter ex post facto by which the defendant's obligation has been discharged. Accordingly, the plea of *nil debet* was held to leave it open for the defendant to show at the trial any one of the foregoing facts. There was, indeed, hardly any matter of defense in an action of debt to which the plea of *nil debet* might not be applied, and this because the issue was taken upon a conclusion of law only. "For almost all defenses in an action of this sort," says Stephen, "resolve themselves into a denial *of the debt*".[1]

With some variations in degree, the same vagueness characterized several other of the general issues. Under the plea of *non assumpsit*, as it was gradually developed, a defendant was permitted, in any action of assumpsit, not only to contend that no promise was made, or to show facts impeaching the validity of the promise, but (with some few exceptions) to prove any matter of defense whatever which tended to deny his debt or liability.[2] Under

[1] Stephen, Pl., 173. "Bankruptcy, tender, and the Statute of Limitations appear to have been the only defences which could not be proved under the plea of *nil debet*, and they were excepted 'because they do not contest that the debt *is owing*, but insist only that no action can be maintained for it.'" 4 Minor's Insts., 641, and authorities there cited.

[2] Stephen, Pl., 176.

the plea of *not guilty* in trespass on the case in general, the defendant might not only contest the truth of the declaration, but, with certain exceptions, to prove any matter of defense that tended to show that the plaintiff had no right of action, though such matters were in confession and avoidance; as, for example, a release given or satisfaction made.[1]

The mischief of it.

Sec. 286. Evidently such issues are issues in name only. They set at naught a fundamental purpose of every true issue. They do not tend to develop the merits of the controversy. They give neither the court nor the plaintiff any definite information as to the real character of the defense which will be made at the trial. They encourage surprise, confusion, and miscarriage of justice. They are grossly unfit for trial by a jury. Of all such issues in general it may be said, in the words of a life-long upholder of the common law, that they have in truth "no advantage but to save trouble and thought to lawyers, and to cover up the delinquencies of the incompetent".[2]

Its strong vitality.

Sec. 287. The practical mischief of the General Issues was early recognized in the reform movement in England. The Rules of Hilary Term, halting as they were in some respects, made here several important changes for the better. Many defenses which had been held admissible under the general issue at common law were required to be pleaded specially. But these restrictions appear to have met with less approval on this side of the Atlantic. The General Issue with us remained very much as it had been; and its common law extent was still, for the most part, unrestricted when the codes came on.

[1] Stephen, Pl., 177.
[2] 4 Minor's Insts., 642.

Its antagonism to the theory of code pleading.

Sec. 288. It is sometimes said that the codes have abolished the General Issue. Certainly their fundamental principle is antagonistic to it, for the codes are fundamentally a *fact* system. Their general purpose is to avoid the pleading, whether in affirmative statement or in denial, of mere conclusions of law, and to compel concise statements or denials of material facts, such as the parties can truthfully affirm or deny on oath; but the General Issue, as we have seen, denies a mere conclusion of law. It presents no direct issue of fact. No oath can support it except by indirection. Accordingly, the courts of code states have intimated, now and then, that a pleading equivalent to the General Issue should not be tolerated under the codes.[1]

A similar view appears to have been taken by those who framed our earliest code. The New York enactments of 1848 were express in requiring that "the answer of the defendant shall contain in respect of each allegation of the

[1] Leightner v. Menzel, 35 Cal., 452, 460 (1868): The complaint averred the sale and delivery to defendant of certain quantities of meat and their value; the answer denied the indebtedness in general terms only. The jury found for the plaintiff in the amount claimed. "It is true," said the court, "that the answer in general terms denies the indebtedness, but not the delivery or amount of the meats—*it does not deny the allegations of fact constituting the cause of action*, but only the legal conclusion resulting from the facts. The plaintiff, so far as this issue is concerned, *would have been entitled to judgment for the precise amount of the verdict upon the pleadings without any evidence.*" Knox County Bank v. Lloyd, 18 O. S., 353, 365 (1868): "To tolerate and give effect to this form of allegation as a pleading, would defeat one of the beneficial objects of the code, which aims to narrow issues of fact to such matters as the parties, on their oaths, can deny."—Per White, J. Hauser v. Metzger, 1 Cinti. Sup. Ct. Rep., 164, 165 (1871): "We think that the answer was what would be regarded, before the code, as *the general issue*, and it was a principle of the code to do away with mere traverses, and compel the defendant to set out in his answer, *in a substantial way*, his whole defence."—Per Storer, J. See also Taylor v. Purcell, 60 Ark., 606 (1895), 31 S. W. Rep., 567.

complaint controverted by the defendant, *a specific denial thereof*, or. of any knowledge thereof sufficient to form a belief".[1]

Practical convenience of the general issue.

Sec. 289. But the General Issue was not so easily disposed of. Like the common counts, it had several elements of popularity. However incongruous its retention may appear in any philosophic or liberal view of the science of pleading, its temporary convenience in particular cases was plain. It often chimed in harmony with the practitioner's present need. The fact that it rendered a discriminating knowledge ot the case unnecessary at the time of answering but still left a wide door open to all sorts of defenses and various neat surprises, appealed to such degree of procrastination, to such measure of timid caution, as can be laid to the charge of lawyers.

(ii) *The General Denial in our codes.*

Sec. 290. And so it came about that the enactment of 1848 was presently amended. The New York code of 1849 required that the answer should contain, "in respect of each allegation of the complaint controverted by the defendant, a *general or specific* denial thereof".[2] With a little vacillation, this retrograde enactment has since been the rule in New York,[3] and has found its way into nearly every succeeding code. We have, therefore, no "General Issue" *eo nomine;* but in its stead we have the "General Denial".

[1] N. Y. Code of 1848, § 128.

[2] N. Y. Code of 1849, § 149.

[3] The New York Code of 1851 returned to the earlier position and allowed a specific denial only. The Code of 1852 reestablished the "*general or specific denial;*" and such is still the law in New York.

Difference between the General Denial and the General Issue—in form.

Sec. 291. The two are not the same thing with only a slight variation in name. They differ in form, they differ also in substantial effect. The General Denial follows none of the old formulae of the general traverse. A code pleader who would briefly deny the whole claim asserted against him does not answer, in case the action is on a bond, that "the said supposed writing obligatory is not his deed"; or, if the action is in assumpsit, that "he did not undertake or promise, in manner or form as the plaintiff has complained"; or, if the action is in debt on simple contract, that "he does not owe the said sum of money above demanded, or any part thereof, in manner and form as the said plaintiff hath complained"; or, if the action is for a tort, that "he is not guilty of the premises above laid to his charge in manner and form as the said plaintiff hath complained." But instead of these forms of denial, designed, it will be observed, for the distinct forms of action at common law, the codes are held to permit one general form, adapted to any kind of action and substantially as follows: "The defendant, answering the complaint of the plaintiff herein, denies each and every allegation thereof."

In other respects—range of testimony.

Sec. 292. Apart from this difference in form, the General Denial differs from the General Issue in two other notable respects. It permits a less extensive range of testimony; on the other hand, it has a less certain application in particular instances. Thus, the General Denial puts in issue all the material allegations of the petition or complaint; the plaintiff must prove every issuable fact alleged by him; the defendant may introduce whatever facts contradict the case thus made by the plaintiff. But, as commonly understood by the courts, the General Denial does not permit the introduction of a distinctively affirmative defense. All such facts as payment in whole or in part, release, arbitrament, accord and satisfaction, and whatever else is in confession and avoidance of the plaintiff's case must be pleaded specially,[1] under the codes. The General Issue, however, at least in its later development at common law, and especially when there was a plea of *nil debet*, *non assumpsit*, or *not guilty* in trespass on the case, often permitted a defendant not only to contradict the facts alleged by the plaintiff, but to prove any matter of defense which tended to show that the plaintiff had no such right of action as he asserted against the defendant, although this matter was in confession and avoidance of the declaration.

Certainty of application to particulars.

Sec. 293. But, while more restricted in its range than the old-time General Issue, our General Denial is less certain in its application to particulars; its operation and effect are less clearly fixed and determined beforehand. The plea being named—*non est factum*, *non assumpsit*, *nil debet*, or as the case might be—the plaintiff at common law could be sure that such and such matters of defense and none others were admissible. However wide the scope of the issue, it always went to certain things found in the declaration, and to these things alone. Its range was wide and often embarrassing, but its application was predetermined with great exactness. Under the codes, no precise application can be assigned in advance to a General Denial.

[1] McKyring v. Bull, 16 N. Y., 297, 309 (1857), is the leading case.

It is as varied as the statements in a petition or complaint—almost as varied as the idiosyncrasies of pleaders. It may differ materially in actions of substantially the same kind. And the reason for this lies in the fact that a General Denial looks directly to the allegations in the petition or complaint; but under the rules of code pleading there is no necessary or exact uniformity in these allegations even in actions brought on substantially the same material facts and seeking the same kind of relief.

A curious and instructive result follows: in some actions —an action on a bond, for instance—the General Denial may admit testimony as to facts which would not have been included in the corresponding General Issue of the common law. For instance, in *debt* on specialty or in *covenant*, the plea of *non est factum* merely denied that the deed mentioned in the declaration was the deed of the defendant. If his case consisted of anything but a denial of the execution of such a deed as alleged, or of some fact showing its absolute invalidity at common law, the plea of *non est factum* was improper.[1] But if, in such a case under the code, the plaintiff has seen fit to aver other facts in his petition or complaint, the General Denial will admit evidence to contradict them although no such evidence would have been allowed under the General Issue. The General Denial, in short, is as variable as that most variable of pleadings, the petition or complaint.

And in general.

Sec. 294. Compared, then, with the old-time General Issues, and regarded somewhat at large, the General Denial is narrower in its scope than most of them, wider, possibly, than a few, and less certain in its application to particulars than any. Nevertheless, it is plain that the General Issue and the General Denial have very much in common.

[1] Stephen, Pl., 171; 1 Chit. Pl., 489.

The language of the codes was once thought to admit the use of the old formulae, and their adoption by code pleaders was recommended from the bench and in textbooks.[1] After almost half a century, we may still find here and there a learned judge in a code state, who speaks of the General Denial as if the several general issues had in fact survived in it. And it is unfortunately still true of the General Denial, as of the General Issue, that its chief merit is "in saving trouble and thought to lawyers and covering up the delinquencies of the incompetent". It is liable to grave abuses and is often abused. The result may, indeed, be an interesting lesson in pleading for the opposite party, but it involves, in too many cases, a needless clogging of the administration of justice.

A contemporary instance of its pitfalls.

Sec. 295. Of this, and of the kind of pitfall which the General Denial often conceals from the unwary, a single illustration may be given here. In a recent case before one of the Ohio Circuit Courts,[2] themselves tribunals of intermediate appeal from the Common Pleas, it appeared that the petition below had averred, along with the other facts of the cause of action, that the plaintiff was a corpora-

[1] "The wit of man," said a New York judge in 1853, construing the code of that state, "has never yet devised, and it may well be doubted whether the present generation, with all its labors, will ever bring forth any *formula* equal to the old general issue for the purposes of a general denial. It united the great elements of all good pleading, brevity, simplicity, and comprehensiveness. And if the principle of a general denial is to be reinstated, of which we have all the encouragement derivable, from the fact that it has stood firmly as the law of the land since the sixth day of May last, notwithstanding its previous unsteadiness, I see no reason why the courts should not sanction the old form of pleading, the general issue, and thus put an end to this vexatious and useless course of litigation." Barculo, J., in Salinger v. Lusk, 7 How. Pr. Rep., 430, 432. The same view was urged upon Ohio practitioners in 1856. See Nash, Pl. & Pr. 63, 64.

[2] Memphis Packet Co. v. Fogarty, 2 Ohio Dec., 706 (1895).

tion under the laws of Kentucky. The answer denied "each and all the allegations of the petition". There was, apparently, no rational question as to the plaintiff's being a corporation as alleged, but the General Denial put this fact, as well as the really disputed facts of the case, in issue. At the trial the plaintiff was caught unprepared with the best evidence of its incorporation and the defendant excepted to the evidence offered on this point. On appeal, the circuit court reversed the judgment below for other reasons, but took occasion to condemn the use which the defendant had made of the General Denial. "We speak of it," said Smith, J., "only to express our disapprobation of a method of pleading too much resorted to in practice, that is, the interposition of a general denial to each and every allegation of the adversary's pleading, and having it sworn to, when it is manifest, and shown to be so at the trial, that, as to many of such allegations so denied under oath, the person making such affirmation actually knew, or had good reason to know, at the time that they were really true. This, we think, is a manifest evasion, or a direct violation of the letter and spirit of our statute, which is intended to prevent the raising of sham issues, and not to throw upon the party making an allegation the burden of proving it when, if a proper answer were filed, the fact alleged would be in terms admitted, or admitted by the failure to deny the same. We think that there should be a reform in this respect, and that our courts should assist in bringing it about."

Place of the General Denial in our legal theory.

Sec. 296. Such are the leading characteristics of the General Denial which is permitted by most of the codes and used in multitudes of cases. It is not a general issue, but near akin to it. It was not part of the progressive movement of code pleading, nor found in the earliest code, but a reaction from it. Historically considered, it leaves the doctrine of code pleading on this point about where the Rules of Hilary Term left common law pleading in England fourteen years before our first code of procedure was enacted.

(iii) *Abrogation of the General Issue by the English code.*

Sec. 297. The English Rules of 1883 appear to be nearer the position taken by the New York code of 1848 than are the present rules of our own codes. The latter, as we have seen, retain the General Issue in part; the former abolish it not only as it had come to be at common law, but also as it had been left by the Rules of Hilary Term in 1834. The enactments which bear upon the point are specific and imperative. They render it very clear that if a defendant intends to deny the whole claim made against him, he should not make a merely general denial or traverse merely the legal aspect of the claim, but he must respond to it in its matters of fact, must take it matter by matter, and must traverse each matter separately.[1]

Its rules requiring certainty in the issue.

Sec. 298. "It shall not be sufficient," say the rules, "for a defendant in his Statement of Defense to deny generally the grounds alleged by the Statement of Claim, but each party must deal specifically with each allegation of fact of which he does not admit the truth except damages."[2] That there may be no question as to the result, implied in the foregoing provision, when there is a failure to deny specifically, it is further provided that every allegation of

[1] Byrd v. Nunn, 7 Ch. D., 284, 287 (1876): Benbow v. Low, 13 Ch. D., 553 (1880); Burdette v. Hemphage, 92 Law Times L. J., 294 (1892); but see Adkins v. North Metropolitan Tramways Co., 63 L. J., Q. B., 361 (1893).

[2] Order XIX, r. 17.

fact in the pleading "if not denied specifically or by necessary implication, or stated to be not admitted in the pleading of the opposite party, shall be taken to be admitted, except as against an infant, lunatic, or person of unsound mind not so found by inquisition".[1]

The principle that a denial must go directly to matters of fact and not to legal aspects of the plaintiff's claim, is enforced both by general provisions and by examples. "When a party in any pleading denies an allegation of fact in the previous pleading of the opposite party, he must not do so evasively, but answer the point of substance. Thus, if it be alleged that he received a certain sum of money, it shall not be sufficient to deny that he received that particular amount, but he must deny that he received that sum or any part thereof, or else set out how much he received. And if an allegation is made with divers circumstances, it shall not be sufficient to deny it along with those circumstances."[2] If it happen that a contract, promise, or agreement alleged in a pleading is met by a bare denial, this denial, it is provided, "shall be construed only as a denial in fact of the express contract, promise, or agreement alleged, or of the matters of fact from which the same may be implied by law, and not as a denial of the legality or sufficiency in law of such contract, promise, or agreement, whether with reference to the Statute of Frauds or otherwise.[3]

Examples.

Sec. 299. Various examples, designed to show the practical bearing of these principles, are embodied in the rules, substantially as follows:

(1) When the action is for a debt or liquidated demand in money payable by the defendant upon a contract express

[1] Order XIX, r. 13.
[2] Order XIX, r. 19.
[3] Order XIX, r. 20.

or implied, or in other cases in which the plaintiff's writ may be specially indorsed, "a mere denial of the debt shall be inadmissible".[1]

(2) "In actions upon bills of exchange, promissory notes, or cheques, a defense in denial must deny some matter of fact; e. g., the drawing, making, indorsing, accepting, presenting, or notice of dishonor of the bill or note."[2]

(3) When the action seeks only to recover a debt or liquidated demand in money payable by the defendant, with or without interest, arising (a) upon a contract express or implied (as, for instance, on a bill of exchange, promissory note, or cheque, or other simple contract debt); or (b) on a bond or contract under seal for payment of a liquidated amount of money, the rules further provide that "a defense in denial must deny such matters of fact, from which the liability of the defendant is alleged to arise, as are disputed; e. g., in actions for goods bargained and sold or sold and delivered, the defense must deny the order or contract, the delivery, or the amount claimed; in an action for money had and received, it must deny the receipt of the money, or the existence of those facts which are alleged to make such receipt by the defendant a receipt to the use of the plaintiff".[3]

[1] Order XXI, r. 1. This rule, it will be observed, corresponds to the doctrine laid down by our courts in a large number of cases. Cf. Haggard v. Hay's Admr., 13 B. Mon. (Ky.), 175 (1852); Larimore v. Wells, 29 O. S., 13 (1875); Emery v. Baltz, 94 N. Y., 408, 412 (1884); Callanan v. Williams, 71 Iowa, 363 (1887); Gale v. James, 11 Colo., 540, 543 (1888); Lake v. Steinbach, 5 Wash. St., 659, 663 (1893). For a modification of this doctrine in some states see Quin v. Lloyd, 41 N. Y., 349, 352 (1869); McLaughlin v. Wheeler, 1 S. Dak., 497, 505 (1891).

[2] Order XXI, r. 2.

[3] Order XXI, r. 3.

The only general denial permitted by the English code.

Sec. 300. To this rule of the English procedure, that a defendant must deal specifically with every allegation of fact in the Statement of Claim which he does not admit, there appear to be but two exceptions—both relics of the old practice. (1) "No denial or defense shall be necessary as to damages claimed or their amount; but they shall be deemed to be put in issue in all cases, unless expressly admitted."[1] (2) If the action is for the recovery of land, the plaintiff must set out his title in full, stating each separate link, but the defendant, if a tenant in possession, is not as a rule required to admit or deny specifically the different averments in the claim asserted against him. "It shall be sufficient," say the rules, "to state by way of defense that he is so in possession, and it shall be taken to be implied in such statement that he denies, or does not admit, the allegations of fact contained in the plaintiff's statement of claim. He may, nevertheless, rely upon any ground of defense which he can prove except "as hereinbefore mentioned."[2]

The principle in the English courts.

Sec. 301. The General Denial permitted by most of our codes would seem to have no ground to stand upon in the English system, so explicit and imperative are its provisions forbidding a general and requiring a specific denial of every allegation of fact which the defendant does not admit.[3] But the principle of the General Denial appears to have

[1] Order XXI, r. 4.

[2] Order XXI, r. 21. Cf. Odgers, Principles, 183. There was another exception, of twenty years' duration. Certain public bodies and functionaries were entitled to plead "Not guilty by statute." But this right was abolished January 1, 1894, by Stat. 56 & 57 Vict., c. 61, s. 2, at least wherever it had been conferred by any public General Act.

[3] Note especially Order XIX, r. 17, ante.

taken deep root in the nature of the English, as of the American, lawyer, whether on the bench or at the bar. He will go far to find some excuse for it; nor does he find it difficult to show that on logical grounds a general denial—a denial of "*each and all*" the allegations of the opposing pleading—amounts to the same thing as a specific denial.

Notwithstanding the explicit and imperative rules noticed above, a recent decision of the Queen's Bench appears to have admitted, under no very clear restrictions, a general denial of the same form and bearing as that which in the course of half a century has so often clogged the administration of justice in America. While the decision is perhaps not to be taken too seriously—for the learned court appears to have regarded the question involved as being a question not of principle but of costs—its reasoning is very suggestive.

The familiar denial of "each and all."

Sec. 302. The case was Adkins v. North Metropolitan Tramways Company.[1] Here the plaintiff had set out in his statement of claim several allegations of fact to support a claim for personal injuries against the defendants because of their alleged negligence. The defendants in their Defense merely stated that they "denied *each and all* the several statements and allegations set out in paragraph 2 of the Statement of Claim," and repeated the same form of denial to paragraph 3 of the Claim.[2] The plaintiff

[1] 63 L. J., Q. B., 361 (1893); 10 Times Law Rep., 173.

[2] The phrase, it will be noticed, is a favorite form of the "General Denial" with us. And see Lewis v. Coulter, 10 O. S., 451, 452 (1859): "Where the denial is general it should be not simply of '*all*,' but of '*each and all*,' or, '*each and every*' of the allegations referred to." Werk v. Christie, 2 Ohio Dec., 552, 554 (1895); "The first defense which may be claimed to be a *general* denial is not such in reality. It does not deny each and every allegation of the petition." Per Smith, J.

applied to strike out or amend such a statement of Defense, and appealed from the refusal of both the master and the judge at chambers to allow his application. *Held*, that the appeal must be dismissed on the ground that, while the Defense did not comply strictly with the rule[1] requiring a specific traverse of each allegation denied, yet it was intended to, and did in effect, specifically deny each and every allegation of the Statement of Claim; that it was not embarrassing; and that it could be amended by repeating the denial specifically to each allegation if that were really required by the plaintiff."

A denial so given, say the court, "is a long way off the old plea of the general issue, which no one alleges to be now sustainable". But on the line of reasoning followed by the learned judges, it would seem to be no difficult matter to restore the general issue, in effect, for some at least of its most objectionable uses. The similar General Denial in America, always convenient for the defendant, is not always embarrassing to the court or to the plaintiff; but, on the other hand, it may be very embarrassing to both, and has often proved a cause of needless confusion in the trial and of a temporary miscarriage of justice. It should be said, however, that certain specific rules in the English code would probably prevent its use in a number of important instances where we still retain it.

(8) *Amendment of pleadings.—Liberality of the later common law here.*

Sec. 303. The later doctrine of the common law was liberal with respect to amendments in civil pleading. Their use was favored as "an antidote" to some of the mischiefs whose presence in the common law system could not be entirely disguised.[2] Their general principle was

[1] Order XIX, r. 17, ante.

[2] Steph. Pl., 393; 4 Minor's Insts., 1083–84.

that so long as the form of action was not changed and the court could see that the identity of the cause of action was preserved, the particular allegations of a declaration might be changed and others superadded, "in order to cure imperfections and mistakes in the manner of stating the plaintiff's case".[1]

With so laudable an end in view, this doctrine was carried far. Now and then a writer on the common law raised a voice of protest against the license of amendment. Occasionally, indeed, an amendment, by leave of court, might go even to a change of form in the action, although as a rule, the courts insisted upon preserving the boundaries between the different actions at law as of great and substantial importance.[2] Equity also allowed amendments right freely, up to the point of changing the character of the bill or answer.[3]

The greater liberality of the codes.

Sec. 304. The tradition, then, with which the framers of the codes had to do, was favorable to a very liberal policy respecting amendments. But the codes went further than this tradition. They were, it was said, more than liberal. Their provision with respect to amendments by leave of court, "in the furtherance of justice," was declared to "create a perfectly irresponsible despotism in the court". In the view of old-time pleaders it was "the law of the Autocrat of Russia".[4]

The principle and almost the only limitation imposed by the codes upon a court's power to permit amendments is in brief that the amendment shall not bring in a new

[1] Stevenson v. Mudgett, 10 N. H., 338 (1839).

[2] 1 Chit. Pl., 220; cf. Little v. Morgan, 31 N. H., 499 (1855), for the limitation here.

[3] Walden v. Bodley, 14 Pet., 156, 160 (1840).

[4] Cf. Nash Pl. and Prac., 109 (1856).

cause of action. In terms, this corresponds somewhat closely to the limitation fixed in the older procedure, whether at law or in equity; but in fact there is a material and characteristic difference. Under the older pleading, the application of the principle was greatly hampered by the distinction between legal and equitable procedure, and by the various distinctions between the forms of action at law. A change in the form of action was apt to be a change in the *nature* of a common law action. Under the codes, however, the principle is quite unhampered by such restrictions.

Illustration of the characteristic difference between the old pleading and the new in this respect.

Sec. 305. The bearings of this, itself the chief difference here between the old pleading and the new, will be clear from an illustration. In Little v. Morgan,[1] decided as the codes were coming into use, the plaintiff had sued in assumpsit to recover the amount of an award by referees, upon a submission of the parties. At the trial it appeared that the submission *was under seal.* After the defendant had argued the case, he moved for a non-suit, on the ground that the action should have been *debt* or *covenant*, on account of the seal. The plaintiff then moved to amend the declaration into the form of a declaration in *debt.* The trial court refused to permit this, and the refusal met with unanimous approval in the appellate court. "A declaration in assumpsit," said Woods, C. J., "is inconsistent with the nature of a declaration in debt. Debt will lie, in many cases, for a cause of action where assumpsit will not lie. To adopt debt by way of amendment for assumpsit, *in a case where assumpsit will not lie*, is, in effect, to introduce into a declaration, and make effective, and to allow a recovery for, a cause of action not before legitimately intro-

[1] 31 N. H., 499 (1855).

duced into the declaration. The grounds of the action requiring the amendment, of course, constituted no cause for which such a form of action as was supposed would afford a remedy. The various forms of action have always been regarded as substantial and material. A uniform practice has treated them as being so." The result was to throw the case out although the amendment would not have affected the material facts of the controversy but only the legal aspect of the claim.

Relics of bygone distinctions in some American codes.

Sec. 306. All this suggests the technicality of a bygone age. Certainly such a doctrine has no natural place in the reformed procedure of America or England. Unfortunately, however, this technical rule of the older pleading can not be regarded as a mere curiosity. Nicely logical in a way, its influence on the mental habitudes of lawyers was very great, so great that in part, at least, it has survived the rise of the codes. It appears to be responsible for the doctrine, still echoed here and there in code states by text-writers and courts, that "an action upon a contract can not be changed to one in tort, or from tort to contract";[1] and for the doctrine that an amendment changing a legal to an equitable cause of action can not be made, either as of

[1] Cf. Supervisors v. Decker, 34 Wis., 378 (1874). Here the original complaint stated a cause of action for the wrongful conversion of money; the amended complaint was like the original, except that its words "and converted the same to his own use," etc., were omitted. The summons was unchanged; the substantial cause of action was unchanged. But, said the court, it so happens that the words thus omitted "give character to the action, and show it to be one in tort;" and it was held that the amendment was not proper. Link v. Jarvis, 33 P., 206, decided by the Supreme Court of California in 1893, is sometimes cited as a recent case to the same effect. But here the doctrine is the merest dictum.

course or by leave, "not even when the facts stated would sustain either action".[1]

But these relics of the older theory are not so common as to affect very seriously the truth of the proposition that the restriction imposed by the codes in forbidding an amendment which would "change substantially the claim or defense" does not refer to the *form* of the remedy, but to the general identity of the transaction constituting the cause of complaint.[2]

Accord of the American and English systems as to the general principle.

Sec. 307. In both America and England the rules of the new pleading are evidently designed to confer upon courts the amplest power to correct mistakes in process, pleading, and other respects, so long as *the substantial rights* of the parties are not affected. The dominant theory of both systems is that a case must not go off upon a technicality or a mere legal abstraction. Both enjoin a liberal policy, in order that litigants, while in court, may have their differences settled and determined. Both systems make it the duty rather than the mere privilege of a court to allow amendments at all stages of the case in furtherance of

[1] Carmichael v. Argard, 52 Wis., 607, 609 (1881); Fischer v. Laack, 76 Wis., 313, 321 (1890).

[2] Spice v. Steinruck, 14 O. S., 213, 216 (1863); Culp v. Steere, 47 Kan., 746, 751 (1892); Hopf v. U. S. Baking Co., 21 N. Y. Sup., 589 (1892), where it was contended that an amendment "which changes the nature of the action from one of tort to contract," is not authorized by the code. The court ruled otherwise, and is careful to point out that cases which hold that if the *claim* is in contract, the *recovery* must be in contract, do not hold that a *claim* in tort may not be amended into a *claim* in contract. Such amendment, indeed, may be proper in order that the *claim* and the *recovery* may be made to correspond without unnecessary delay. Cf. Deyo v. Morss, 144 N. Y., 216, 218 ((1894); Smith v. Savin, 141 N. Y., 316 (1894). For the positive nature of the limitation see Heath v. N. Y. Banking Co., 146 N. Y., 260, 263 (1895).

justice. Both seek to give effect to the principle that courts exist not for the sake of discipline, but for the sake of deciding matters in controversy.[1] And the express enactments on this point of both the American and English codes accord so closely in spirit and in letter, that English decisions on the general policy of amendments are hardly less valuable to the Americn practitioner than the decisions of different code states of the Union, while the enactments themselves, when compared, serve to bring out more clearly what is essential in both codes.

Their fundamental enactments compared.

Sec. 308. The fundamental enactment of the American system on this point is found in the following "most righteous provisions," which reappear, in ipsissismis verbis, or with immaterial changes, in all but two or three of the codes: "The court *may*, at any time, in furtherance of justice, and on such terms as may be proper, amend any pleading or proceeding, by adding or striking out the name of any party, or a mistake in any other respect, or by inserting other allegations material to the case, or by conforming the pleading or proceeding to the facts proved, whenever the amendment shall not change substantially the cause of action or defense." . . . "The court *shall*, in every stage of an action, disregard any error or defect in the pleadings or proceedings, which shall not affect the substantial rights of the adverse party; and no judgment shall be reversed or affected by reason of such error or defect."[2]

[1] Cropper v. Smith (C. A.), 26 Ch. D., 700, 710 (1884); Becker v. Walworth, 45 O. S., 169, 175 (1887); Bohlen v. Metropolitan Ry., 121 N. Y., 546, 551 (1890); Cook v. Croisan, 25 Ore., 475 (1894).

[2] New York Code of 1848, §§ 149, 151.

Amendments by leave of court.

Sec. 309. The fundamental provisions of the English rules on this point declare, with some iteration, that "the Court or a judge *may*, at any stage of the proceedings, allow either party to alter or amend his endorsement, or pleadings, in such manner and on such terms as may be just, and all such amendments *shall* be made as may be necessary for the purpose of determining the real questions in controversy between the parties";[1] that in all cases not provided for by the rules, "application for leave to amend may be made by either party to the Court or a judge, or to the judge at the trial of the action, and such amendment may be allowed upon such terms as to costs or otherwise as may be just";[2] that "the Court or a judge may, at any time, and on such terms as to costs or otherwise as the Court or judge may think just, amend any defect or error in any proceedings, and all necessary amendments shall be made for the purpose of determining the real question or issue raised by or depending on the proceedings".[3]

These enactments, it will be observed, are less explicit than those of our codes in requiring that the amendment shall not change substantially the claim or defense. Apparently the English rules of 1883 go even further than the code of 1848 in "creating a perfectly irresponsible despotism in the court," and in giving judges the authority "of the Autocrat of Russia".[4]

Amendments without leave.

Sec. 310. The similarity of the two systems appears also in their provisions as to amendments without leave of court. Under most of our codes, a pleading may be once

[1] Order XXVIII, r. 1.
[2] Order XXVIII, r. 6.
[3] Order XXVIII, r. 12.
[4] Ante, § 304.

amended by the party, of course, without costs and without prejudice to the proceedings already had, at any time before the period for answering it expires, or it can be amended at any time within certain days after the service of the answer or demurrer to such pleading. The corresponding rule under the judicature act provides that "the plaintiff may, without any leave, amend his statement of claim, whether endorsed on the writ or not, once at any time before the expiration of the time limited for reply and before replying, or, where no defense is delivered, at any time before the expiration of four weeks from the appearance of the defendant who shall have last appeared";[1] and that "a defendant who has set up any counterclaim or setoff may, without any leave, amend such counterclaim or setoff at any time before the expiration of the time allowed him for answering the reply, and before such answer, or in case there be no reply, then at any time before the expiration of twenty-eight days from defense."[2]

Explicitness of the English rules.

Sec. 311. Such amendments may be made "as of course"; but the right thus conferred is not absolute in either system. Here, however, the judicature rules are more explicit and perhaps give the court a wider power of supervision. Our courts, reasoning from general principles, have declared that an amendment "as of course" must be made in good faith and not for the purpose of delay, and that it must not amount to a *substitution* of an entirely new case of action. If an amendment comes under the ban of these decisions, the court on motion may strike it out. The English rules provide expressly that "where any party has amended his pleading under either of the last two preceding rules, the opposite party may, within eight days

[1] Order XXVIII, r. 2.
[2] Order XXVIII, r. 3.

after the delivery to him of the amended pleading, apply to the Court or a judge to disallow the amendment, or any part thereof, and the Court or judge may, if satisfied that the justice of the case requires it, disallow the same, or allow it subject to such terms as to costs or otherwise as may be just".[1]

Construction illustrating the principles of both systems.

Sec. 312. How liberally these very liberal enactments of the English code have been construed may be profitably illustrated by an extract or two from decisions in the Court of Appeal. "My practice," said Bramwell, L. J., in 1878,[2] "has always been to give leave to amend unless I have been satisfied that the party applying was acting *mala fide*, or that, by his blunder, he had done some injury to his opponent which could not be compensated for by costs or otherwise." "Pleadings and particulars," remarked Bowen, L. J., in 1884,[3] "are wanted to enable you at the trial to decide the true rights ot the parties. That being so, suppose there is a slip or an error, it may be in omitting to take a step or adopt a line of conduct in the case, which the party can not abandon without difficulty, what is the principle on which such a slip is to be set right? That is to be done *whenever you can put the parties in the same position, for the purpose of justice, that they were in at the time when the slip was made.* Sometimes to correct the error would lead to injustice which could not be cured, as when a witness who could give evidence can not be got at, or the solvency of one party is doubtful. The question must be whether, if the slip is set right so as to enable the

[1] Order XXVIII, r. 4. The "last two preceding rules" are the last two preceding in the text.

[2] Tildesley v. Harper, 10 Ch. D., 393, 397 (1878), considering rules which are similar to those of 1883.

[3] Clarapede v. Commercial Union Association, 32 W. R., 263 (1884).

right question to go to trial, the parties will be put into the position they were in before the slip was made; for if so, that should be done. In most cases, it is a question of costs." So Kekewich, J., remarked in 1889:[1] "The rule which I have laid down in many cases has been always to allow any amendment in accordance with the facts at the trial, subject to this, that the Court should see that justice is done between the parties, that is to say, if anyone is taken by way of surprise, then the amendment must be made upon proper terms, so that the party against whom the amendment is to be made should be protected."

A rule of conduct.

Sec. 313. In short, the reformed procedure is held to prescribe a rule of conduct rather than of rigid law. It may be departed from when the circumstances of a particular case are very exceptional. But as a rule of conduct, if the proposed amendment can be made without injustice to the other side, the amendment should be allowed, however late it may be, or however negligent or careless may have been the first omission.[2]

This wide discretion, however, is affected in some cases by the operation of other principles of the judicature acts and rules, as by the principle that an allegation of fact not denied in the pleadings of the opposite party shall be taken to be admitted.[3] And in general the English

[1] Lowther v. Heaver, 41 Ch. D. (C. A.), 248, 254 (1889).

[2] Clarapede v. Commercial Union Association, 32 W. R. (C. A.), 263 (1884); Steward v. North Metropolitan Tramways Co., 16 Q. B. D., 556, 558 (1886); Laird v. Briggs, L. R., 19 Ch. D. (C. A.), 22 (1879). But a court should deal more favorably with amendments which are sought before trial. Per Baggallay, L. J., in Clarapede v. Commercial Union Association.

[3] Lowther v. Heaver, 41 Ch. D. (C. A.), 248, 255 (1889): "Here I have some facts distinctly proved, which are inconsistent with the case as I find it upon the pleadings, and my disposition would be, as far as possible, to do that which would enable me to decide according to the real

courts apparently incline to refuse an amendment by which a party seeks at the trial to set up an entirely new case.[1]

Section II. Other codes in the British Empire.—General character of the English reform movement in the provinces.

Sec. 314. The movement which brought on the codes of civil procedure in the United States and the judicature acts in England was not confined to these countries. Wherever English law prevailed, the need of a more simple and direct relaton between the substantive law and the law of procedure came to be regarded as an urgent and practical matter. Once fairly started by definite enactments in America and England, the reform spread so rapidly through the wide limits of the British Empire that "code pleading," despite the radical nature of its changes and the ultra conservatism of practitioners, made the circuit of the earth in less than fifty years. The statutory changes in the British colonies commonly followed those of the

facts, but I think upon the general balance of convenience in the administration of justice that I should adhere to the rule which has just been laid down ['an allegation of fact not denied in the pleadings of the opposite party shall be taken to be admitted'], and that notwithstanding this evidence ought not to disregard it, and to fall back upon the admission and hold the defendant to it."

[1] James V. Smith (1891), 1 Ch., 384, 389: "By Order XIX, r. 15, the defendant is bound to plead the Statute of Frauds if he intends to rely upon it, but the rule does not oblige him to plead the particular section. Here the defendant has pleaded the fourth section; and it is admitted now that on the fourth section he must fail, and that he must rely on the seventh section. Then I am asked, at the last moment, to allow an amendment to be made, so that his defense may read that he will rely on the seventh section. I have said frequently, and I repeat it, that there is no judge on the bench who is more willing to allow amendments, even at the last moment, than I, provided there is no surprise; but I think I should be going too far if I were to allow it in this action, and it would be introducing a laxity which I ought not to introduce." Per Kekewich, J.

mother country, both in time and in their general character; but in some instances they ran ahead of the actual legislation for England.

Indian code of civil procedure.

Sec. 315. This was especially true of British India, so long the great experimental field of English codification.[1] As early as 1854 a body of commissioners in England, appointed under a statute of the previous year,[2] addressed themselves to the task of preparing a simple and uniform code of pleading and practice for India.[3] The result of their labors was an elaborate act, passed in 1859, and known as a "Code of Civil Procedure". Greatly amended and revised, it now contains many provisions copied from the judicature acts; but it still keeps its name, code of civil procedure. Some of its provisions appear to come at first hand from the New York code; the differences, however, are many and suggestive.

Influence of the English judicature acts and rules.

Sec. 316. At a later day, the influence of the judicature acts and rules brought on similar legislation in widely separated commonwealths of the British Empire—in Ireland, in North America, in Australia, and elsewhere.[4]

[1] The codification of English law, both substantive and adjective, began in India as far back as 1829. It has resulted in several codes of great value to American and English students of the law, enactments which are now accessible in "The Anglo-Indian Codes," edited by Mr. Whitely Stokes.

[2] 16 & 17 Vict., c. 95, s. 28.

[3] A "Code of Civil Procedure of the Courts of East India Company" had been drafted, eo nomine, in 1853 and 1854, but was not enacted.

[4] A paper prepared in June, 1893, for the Columbian Exposition at Chicago, by Mr. David Dudley Field, gives the following as the list of the English colonies which at that date had followed the Judicature Act of 1873: "Victoria, Queensland, South Australia, Western Australia, Tasmania, New Zealand, Jamaica, St. Vincent, the Leeward Islands,

The general result has been the rise within the British Empire, and for the most part since the year 1880, of an influential group of codes, similar in spirit, and often in the letter, to the great family of codes within the United States.

Characteristic examples of these British codes.

Sec. 317. It is unnecessary to treat of all these British codes or to go far into the details of any. In essentials they appear to follow closely the provisions of the parent code—the English judicature acts of 1873 and 1875 with their rules of court. The family likeness between them is quite as strong as that between the different codes in the United States, stronger in most instances. And this, it should be observed, is the more noteworthy since the conditions of life, occupation, and commerce which these widely separated codes were designed to meet run to greater extremes than do the conditions which confront the codes in the United States.

The progress of the change may, however, be illustrated by a word or two concerning the judicature acts of Ireland, Ontario, New Zealand, Victoria, and Nova Scotia, representing as they do the whole family of the British codes, and suggesting the diverse conditions which surround them. And in this connection it will be worth our while to notice another thing—the unanimity with which these codes, despite their diverse surroundings, have followed the English act in guarding against a fossilization of the new procedure, by permitting the *courts* to change the rules of pleading without a resort to direct legislation.

British Honduras, Cambia, Grenada, Nova Scotia, Newfoundland, Ontario, and British Columbia." This list is quoted in the form given above by Mr. Dillon (Laws and Jurisprudence, page 260 (1894),), and by Judge Phillips (Code Pleading, § 166 (1896),). I do not attempt to verify it, although it is apparently open to modification in some particulars. See also 1 Juridical Review, 22 (1889); 25 Am. Law Rev., 524, 525 (1891).

The Irish judicature act and rules, 1877.

Sec. 318. Two years after it had passed the English judicature act of 1875, parliament carried the same reform into Ireland. The statute is known as the "Supreme Court of Judicature Act (Ireland), 1877".[1] It was accompanied with a Schedule of Rules, which parliament declared should be read and taken as part of the act, and which were framed very closely upon the lines of the rules of court drawn up under the English acts. These rules constitute the bulk of the Irish code and, as the reader will remember, correspond closely in purpose and effect to the rules which make up the bulk of our codes of civil procedure.

To keep the code of Ireland in touch with current needs —to prevent its fossilization—authority to annul, alter, amend, or add to its rules at any time is given the Lord Lieutenant of Ireland, acting with the concurrence of a majority of the judges present at any meeting called for the purpose. But it is expressly provided that in making these changes regard must be had to the rules of court in force for the time being under the English judicature acts, in order that "the pleading, practice, and procedure" of the Irish Court may "*be the same* as the pleading, practice, and procedure" of the English Court, "so far as may be practicable and convenient, having regard to the difference of the laws and circumstances of the two countries". The act was amended, but not to any great extent, in 1882, 1887, and 1888.[2]

[1] 40 & 41 Vict., c. 57.

[2] 45 & 46 Vict., c. 70; 50 & 51 Vict., c. 6; 51 & 52 Vict., c. 27.

The Ontario judicature act and rules, 1881.

Sec. 319. In 1881 a judicature act was passed by the legislature of the Province of Ontario.[1] Like the English and the Irish code, it disinguishes between a body of cardinal provisions declared directly by the legislature, and a more numerous body of rules relating to pleading and practice, which while given the authority of the legislature, are the direct work of certain judges and subject to modification by them as occasion may require. As a whole, then, this code of Ontario has two divisions, (1) the statute proper, consisting of ninety-one sections, and (2) a schedule of Rules of Court, published with the act, and comprising sixty-two Orders, with from one to twenty or more rules in each, and appendices of forms, one hundred and eighty-four in number. The bulk of the code, one hundred and seventy-one of its two hundred and six pages, including most of the principal rules of pleading and its details of procedure, comes within this second division, and therefore within the special keeping of the court.

Both the act and the rules were revised in 1887.[2] A further revision, accompanied with a consolidation of certain statutes, was made in 1895 in a statute designated as "The Judicature Act, 1895".[3] This new statute, apart from its rules of court, runs to one hunded and ninety-two sections.

Significance of the revision of 1895.

Sec. 320. It is noteworthy that the revision continues, and no less positively than before, the policy of leaving the rules of pleading to the fostering care of the judges who

[1] 44 Vict., c. 5. "An act to consolidate the Superior Courts; establish a uniform system of pleading and practice; and make further provision for the due administration of justice.

[2] Ontario Rev. Stats., 1887, c. 44.

[3] Stats. of Ontario, 58 Vict., c. 12.

have to administer them. After fourteen years of experience in the matter, the legislature has deemed it wise to enact again (1) that the court may "at any time, with the concurrence of a majority of the judges thereof present at any meeting held for that purpose, alter and annul any *rules of court* for the time being in force, and may make any further or additional rules of court for carrying this act into effect";[1] and (2) that "where any provisions in respect of the practice or procedure of any courts, the jurisdiction of which is vested by this act in the High Court, are contained *in any statute*, rules of court may be made for modifying such provisions to any extent that may be deemed necessary for adapting the same to the High Court, unless, in the case of any act hereafter passed, this power shall be expressly excluded".[2]

In line with this same purpose, to keep the rules of pleading and practice in touch with current needs, are two other provisions of the act of 1881 which are repeated in the revision of 1895 as worthy of preservation. (1) The Lieutenant-Governor in Council may from time to time authorize the Chief Justice of Ontario, the Chief Justice of the Queen's Bench, the Chancellor, the Chief Justice of the Common Pleas, and any one or more of the other Justices of the Supreme Court to make rules of court, with the scope which the act gives the rules of court, "and the judges so appointed, or any three of them, may make such rules, and the same shall have the same effect as if made by all the judges".[3] (2) A council of the judges of the court must assemble once at least in every year for the purpose of considering the operation of this Ontario code, "and of inquiring and examining into any defects which

[1] Ontario Judicature Act, 1895, § 132 (1).

[2] Ontario Judicature Act, 1895, § 132 (2). Ib., Ontario Judicature Act, 1881, § 55 (6).

[3] Ontario Judicature Act, 1895, § 135.

may appear to exist in the system of procedure or the administration of the law in the High Court of Justice or the Court of Appeal, or any other court, or by any other authority; and they shall report annually to the Lieutenant-Governor what (if any) amendments or alterations it would, in their judgment, be expedient to make in this act, or otherwise relating to the administration of justice, and what other provisions (if any) which can not be carried into effect without legislative authority it would be expedient to make for the better administration of justice''.[1]

New Zealand supreme court act and code of civil procedure.

Sec. 321. In the year following the adoption of the first Ontario judicature act, a similar reform was inaugurated by the colonial legislature of New Zealand, in ''the Supreme Court Act of 1882''.[2].

The statute proper consists of forty-one short sections, but it includes as a ''schedule'' an elaborate ''code of civil procedure,'' enacted under that name as a distinctive appellation.[3]

[1] Ontario Judicature Act, 1895, § 137. Cf. Ontario Rev. Stats., 1887, c. 44, § 110; Ontario Judicature Act, 1881, § 56.

[2] New Zealand Statutes, 1842–1892, Badger's ed., vol. 1, p. 648. This act is to be distinguished from the "Court of Appeal Act of 1882." Cf. Ib., p. 142. The "Supreme Court" of New Zealand, it may be said, is a tribunal with the widest original jurisdiction. It is declared to have "all judicial jurisdiction which may be necessary to administer the laws of the colony," § 16.

[3] "Subject to the power of revocation and alteration hereinafter contained (see § 321, infra), the practice and procedure of the court, in all causes and matters within the jurisdiction of the court, shall be regulated by the rules contained in the *Code of Civil Procedure*, printed as the second schedule to this act, except only in those matters as to which the practice or procedure of any of the Superior Courts of England is by the said code expressly retained." Supreme Court Act, 1882, § 30.

Power of the judges to modify the code.

Sec. 322. The latter division consists of clear and succinct statements of the rules of pleading and runs to five hundred and seventy sections, arranged under nine heads. It includes also a considerable number of precedents in pleading. Like the rules of court under other judicature acts, this "code of civil procedure" is expressly made subject to modification by judges; but the New Zealand attempt thus to give elasticity to a statutory system of pleading goes very far. "It shall be lawful," declares the statute, "for the Governor in Council with the concurrence of the judges of the said Court or any two of them from time to time by other rules to be made for the purpose to alter or revoke the rules contained in the said code or any of them or any other rules of the Court which may hereafter be in force and also from time to time to make such additional rules touching the practice and procedure of the Court in all causes and matters within the jurisdiction of the Court as may be deemed advisable and all rules so made or altered shall have the same force and effect as if they had been inserted in the second schedule of this Act," that is, in the Code of Civil Procedure.[1]

Victorian judicature act, 1883.

Sec. 323. In 1883, the legislature of the colony of Victoria passed an elaborate act "to improve the jurisdiction and procedure of the Supreme Court and for other purposes connected therewith".[2] This was in the line of the other "judicature acts," and is commonly referred to as such; in the following year the customary "Rules of the Supreme Court" were framed to complete the code.

[1] Supreme Court Act, § 31; the second schedule is the Code of Civil Procedure; the first schedule is a brief list of acts repealed.

[2] 47 Vict., 761.

The civil pleading of Victoria, therefore, was based upon the provisions of the "Judicature Act of 1883" and "the Rules of Supreme Court of 1884". The act proper has seen some revision, and now appears as the "Supreme Court Act of 1890".[1]

Its rules are subject to the provision that "the Court may at any time, with the concurrence of a majority of the judges thereof present at any meeting for that purpose held, alter and annul any Rules of Court for the time being in force in its various jurisdictions, and make any further or additional Rules of Court for carrying this act into effect".[2] These rules include the provisions which correspond to the enactments of our codes regulating the pleading, practice, and procedure of the court, and the initiating of actions and proceedings therein. But this great power of the judges has a limitation, like that found in the English system.

All the Rules of Court thus drawn up must be laid before the legislature within a certain number of days, "and if an address is presented to the Governor by either House of Parliament within the next subsequent forty days on which the said House shall have sat, praying that any such rule may be annulled, the Governor shall thereupon by order in Council annul the same; and the rule so annulled shall thenceforth become void and of no effect, but without prejudice to the validity of any proceedings which may in the meantime have been taken under the same".[3]

[1] Vict. Stats., 1890, vol. 4, p. 3165.

[2] Supreme Court Act of 1890, § 23.

[3] Supreme Court Act, 1890, § 24.

The Nova Scotia judicature act and rules, 1884.

Sec. 324. In 1884, the province of Nova Scotia also established code pleading, enacting a Judicature Act and Rules of Court.[1] The Act proper runs to but forty-seven sections, and is embraced within twenty-one of the three hundred and forty-five pages of the entire code. Most of the Rules, which are grouped into seventy Orders and occupy one hundred and fifty-eight pages of the entire code, are transcribed or adapted from the English judicature rules of 1883 or from the Ontario judicature rules of 1881. And like these rules, they may be annulled, altered, amended, or added to at any time, by the court or a majority of the judges present at a meeting for the purpose.[2] But all rules so made must be laid before the legislature of the province within a certain number of days, and may be annulled by an address presented to the Lieutenant-Governor within twenty days thereafter.[3]

Value of the British codes to American code pleaders and the cause of reform.

Sec. 325. Further than this it seems unnecessary to go. Our interest in the codes of the British Empire is indirect—for purposes of illustration; and the examples already given will suffice.

But it may be said again, and in conclusion, that although indirect, the American practitioner's interest in these codes is very considerable. They are later efforts towards the same end which is sought by code pleading in the American Union. They occupy a very wide field; they meet many diverse conditions. They have been framed in the light of our own experience, and themselves throw no little

[1] Nova Scotia Rev. Stats., Fifth Series, 1884, c. 104, pp. 799-1144.
[2] Nova Scotia Judicature Act, 1884, § 34.
[3] Nova Scotia Judicature Act, 1884, § 42.

light upon the essentials of code pleading, and upon the path of development which the codes of the United States will naturally follow. For it is still true that the purpose declared in our earliest code, the code of 1848—"to simplify and abridge the practice, pleadings, and proceedings of the courts"—has been realized as yet in part only. Nor has the movement which brought on the code of 1848 and its successors in this country come to a perpetual end.

Our seven and twenty codes, even at the end of a half century, are a beginning, essentially bold and progressive, yet only a beginning, and as such often crude and imperfect. Certainly a final code was not to be expected as the direct result of this first movement in 1848 and its succeeding years.[1] Sooner or later the movement to simplify our procedure will begin again. Already there are signs of the discontent which precedes organized efforts for reform. And it is possible, at least, that the present generation may see considerable progress towards the greater American code, which, while preserving the essentials of the existing system, will be at once more simple, elastic, and durable.

[1] "I do not claim finality for Mr. Field's code, or any other form of words. To adopt the perfect code at the first or second movement is to expect impossibilities. Moreover it is not certain that the absolutely perfect code can be framed until the book of the experience of society has been closed, and our civilization entered upon its decadence. It was so in Rome, and may be so with us. For, as new emergencies arise, and new wants appear, any code of human origin will require repairs, amendment, enlargement. The codes of civil procedure have not yet had their final touches. What I hope and claim is that before many years a code of rights as well as remedies, the same in substance, though very likely differing in detail, will be in force in every American state, and within the limits of its powers be adopted by federal legislation." Hon. George Hoadly, in an address before the Yale Law School in 1884, 12 W. Law Bulletin, 106, 127.

INDEX.

INDEX.